Regulating the Platform Economy

This book analyses novel and important issues relating to the emergence of new forms of work resulting from the introduction of disruptive technologies in the enterprises and the labour market, especially platform work.

The first part of the book examines the platform economy and labour market, to address the more general challenges that the recent labour platforms pose for employment and the labour market, while the second part of the book considers the implications of the rise of different ways of work in the enterprises due to the incorporation of technology in a global context. Providing a rich analysis and evaluation of the numerous theoretical and practical regulatory problems arising from constantly developing technology, this book makes important and informed suggestions on how to solve the numerous problems which have arisen. The collection of chapters in this volume are varied and are dealt with from different disciplinary angles, and from a diverse range of countries and legal systems to create an interesting and unique global picture on the topics studied therein.

With an international perspective, the book will be of interest to students and scholars of economy and technology law.

Lourdes Mella Méndez is Professor of Labour Law and Social Security at the University of Santiago de Compostela, Spain.

Alicia Villalba Sánchez is Assistant Professor of Labour Law and Social Security at the University of Santiago de Compostela, Spain.

Regulating the Platform Economy

International Perspectives on New Forms of Work

Edited by
Lourdes Mella Méndez

Coordinated by
Alicia Villalba Sánchez

LONDON AND NEW YORK

First published 2020
by Routledge
2 Park Square, Milton Park, Abingdon, Oxon OX14 4RN

and by Routledge
605 Third Avenue, New York, NY 10017

Routledge is an imprint of the Taylor & Francis Group, an informa business

First issued in paperback 2021

© 2020 selection and editorial matter, Lourdes Mella Méndez; individual chapters, the contributors

The right of Lourdes Mella Méndez to be identified as the author of the editorial material, and of the authors for their individual chapters, has been asserted in accordance with sections 77 and 78 of the Copyright, Designs and Patents Act 1988.

All rights reserved. No part of this book may be reprinted or reproduced or utilised in any form or by any electronic, mechanical, or other means, now known or hereafter invented, including photocopying and recording, or in any information storage or retrieval system, without permission in writing from the publishers.

Trademark notice: Product or corporate names may be trademarks or registered trademarks, and are used only for identification and explanation without intent to infringe.

Publisher's Note
The publisher has gone to great lengths to ensure the quality of this reprint but points out that some imperfections in the original copies may be apparent.

British Library Cataloguing-in-Publication Data
A catalogue record for this book is available from the British Library

Library of Congress Cataloging-in-Publication Data
A catalog record has been requested for this book

ISBN 13: 978-0-367-46240-6 (hbk)
ISBN 13: 978-1-03-223798-5 (pbk)
ISBN 13: 978-1-003-03500-8 (ebk)

Typeset in Galliard
by codeMantra

This book is a result of the following Research Project:

MINISTERIO DE ECONOMÍA, INDUSTRIA Y COMPETITIVIDAD. UNIÓN EUROPEA. Proyecto de Investigación nacional del MINECO, titulado "Nuevas (novísimas) tecnologías de la información y comunicación y su impacto en el mercado de trabajo: aspectos emergentes en el ámbito nacional e internacional" (DER2016-75376-R).

MINISTERIO DE ECONOMÍA, INDUSTRIA Y COMPETITIVIDAD. ESPAÑA. Red de Excelencia: Red de estudio y difusión del impacto de las nuevas TICS en la empresa (DER2017-90700-REDT). Financiación de la Agencia Estatal de Investigación.

Contents

List of contributors ix
Foreword xi

An introduction about regulating the platform economy 1
LOURDES MELLA MÉNDEZ

PART ONE
The platform economy and the labour market:
some key issues 9

1 The platform economy: the main challenges for
   labour law 11
   MANFRED WEISS

2 Uber: regulatory and institutional experimentation
   in the taxi industry in Quebec 21
   URWANA COIQUAUD AND LUCIE MORISSETTE

3 Comparative study on Japanese employment-like
   working style: whether we are discussing the same
   phenomenon or not 39
   QI ZHONG

4 Identifying labour relationship in the sharing
   economy: judicial practice in China 48
   XIAOHUI BAN

5 Informality, neoliberalism and the gig economy in Chile 62
   DENISA MEIROSU

6 Regulating technology at work 70
   MARÍA MARTA TRAVIESO

PART TWO
Other new forms of work, new workforce and new skills 87

7 New forms of work and contractual execution: towards the "smart labour contract" 89
ALICIA VILLALBA SÁNCHEZ

8 Spanish telework and Italian "agile" work: a comparison 100
ANA MURCIA CLAVERÍA

9 Robotics and work: labour and tax regulatory framework 116
MARÍA YOLANDA SÁNCHEZ-URÁN AZAÑA AND MARÍA AMPARO GRAU RUIZ

10 Technology and jobs: has what was old become new? 132
MATTHEW W. FINKIN, ALBERT J. HARNO AND EDWARD W. CLEARY

11 Technologies and powers: marginal notes on the Amazon wristband 147
ROSA DI MEO

12 New forms of work and trade unions in the digital age 161
MARÍA LUZ RODRÍGUEZ FERNÁNDEZ

13 Emerging skills and occupations in the Fourth Industrial Revolution: how to respond to changing work demands 176
ANETA TYC

14 The resilience: the main skill for the Industrial Revolution 4.0 189
CHRISTIAN THOMSON VIVAS GARCÍA

Index 203

Contributors

Xiaohui Ban is Associate Research Fellow at Research Center for Labour and Social Security La at Law School of Wuhan University, China.

Ana Murcia Clavería is Associate Professor of Labour Law and Social Security at University of Valladolid, Spain.

Edward W. Cleary Chair in Law is Professor of Law at Center for Advanced Study Professor of Law, University of Illinois, USA.

Urwana Coiquaud is Professor of Labour Law at HEC Montréal, Quebec, Canada.

Rosa Di Meo is Researcher at Polytechnic University of Marche Region, Italy.

Matthew W. Finkin is Professor of Law at University of Illinois, USA.

María Amparo Grau Ruiz is Professor in Fiscal Law at Complutense University, Spain.

Albert J. Harno is Professor of Law at Center for Advanced Study **Professor of Law, University of Illinois, USA**

Denisa Meirosu is Researcher at SNSPA Bucharest (National School of Public Administration and Political Studies), Romania.

Lourdes Mella Méndez is Professor of Labour Law and Social Security at the University of Santiago de Compostela, Spain.

Lucie Morissette is Associate Professor of Labour Law at HEC Montréal, Quebec, Canada.

María Luz Rodríguez Fernández is Senior Lecturer of Labour Law and Social Security at University of Castile-La Mancha, Spain.

Alicia Villalba Sánchez is Assistant Professor of Labour Law and Social Security at University of Santiago de Compostela, Spain.

María Yolanda Sánchez-Urán Azaña is Professor in Labour and Social Security Law at Complutense University, Spain.

María Marta Travieso is Specialist at Future of Work Unit, at International Labour Organisation (ILO), Switzerland.

Aneta Tyc is Assistant Professor of Labour Law at the University of Łódź, Poland.

Christian Thomson Vivas García is Specialist in Labour Law and Specialist in the Exercise of Fiscal Action, Venezuela.

Manfred Weiss is Professor Emeritus of Labour Law at University of Goethe, Germany.

Qi Zhong is Researcher at the Japanese Institute for Labour Policy and Training, Japan.

Foreword

Law affects everyone. It determines what taxes people pay, how their children are educated and what they are prohibited from doing. Bad law can have disastrous consequences. It is important that legislators enact clear laws, drafted to deliver what is expected of them. Laws are subject to interpretation. Cruel and unusual punishment may be prohibited by law, but where is the dividing line between punishment that is cruel and unusual and that which is not? Drafting matters. To be prohibited, the punishment has to be cruel and unusual, not cruel or unusual.

It is thus important to know not only what the law says but also what it means. Explaining and interpreting law is core to making sense of how a nation is regulated. Works on law that complement the formal wording of legislation play an essential role in understanding and are of value not only to lawyers and parliamentarians but also to all those wishing to understand the significance of what has been enacted. Understanding the law empowers citizens.

I therefore warmly welcome the publication of this volume. Society cannot function without workers. The scope and nature of how labour is deployed has become more complex as nations have industrialised and become more specialised. Laws to protect workers have developed over time, though the nature of the development has varied from nation to nation. Labour law is now substantial and is often complex. There are changes in how people work, affected now by increasingly sophisticated technology. Adapting to changing economies, including the gig economy and the capacity to work from home in the digital age, pose challenges for the regulation of labour markets. How do individual nations legislate to meet their own needs in the context of changes in practice and media that do not necessarily recognise borders?

I thus welcome the publication of this broad-ranging and substantial volume, covering economic changes, working practices and technological developments in a dozen nations spanning Europe, Asia and the Americas. An impressive array of leading scholars has been marshalled to produce a rich collection of analyses. It is a major contribution to the literature, both in size and in the range of topics covered.

Philip Norton
[Lord Norton of Louth]

An introduction about regulating the platform economy

Lourdes Mella Méndez

It is a great honour for me to introduce a new collective book of international scope, with studies by prestigious scholars and experts from different countries and areas of knowledge. This book, ambitiously entitled "Regulating the platform economy: international perspectives on new forms of work" (Germany, Canada, Japan, China, Romania, Switzerland, Spain, USA, Italy, Poland, Venezuela), deals with new and important issues relating to the emergence of new forms of work resulting from the introduction of ICTs in the enterprises and the labour market, especially platform work from an international perspective. In order to maximise the analysis of this developing topic, the volume is divided into two major and complementary parts, namely "The platform economy and the labour market: some key issues" and "Other new forms of work, new workforce and new skills".

The first part, named "The platform economy and the labour market: some key issues", addresses the more general challenges that the recent labour platforms pose for employment and the labour market.

One of first challenges of the platform economy is its distinction from other new forms of work also related to new technologies as telework, ICT-based mobile work or even the broader phenomena called Industry 4.0, where smart robots communicate with each other and humans to perform complex and interconnected tasks. The platform economy is not a homogeneous phenomenon as there are many different types of platforms: internal, external, collaborative and labour platforms. Focusing on the latter, the labour services provided by digital labour platforms can be broadly distinguished as online services performed *digitally* (i.e. micro tasks or clerical and data entry) or physical services performed *on-location* (i.e. transport, delivery or housekeeping), that is, by means of a direct contact between the worker and the final client. According to the level of skills required by different services, we can distinguish between professional services (high skills) and non-professionals services (medium and low skills); both can be present in digital and on-location services, even though the latter are generally low skills services. Most platform workers provide more than one type of services, and are active on two or more platforms, often combining high- and low-skilled activities, suggesting that some platform workers may be reducing income risk (and possibly increasing variety in work). The most common labour service provided is online clerical and data entry.[1] The challenges of this new economy are both relevant and complex.

In Chapter One, Professor Manfred Weiss, from Goethe University (Germany), selects and analyses with wisdom the two main challenges which labour platforms pose for labour law, namely the impact that the platform economy has on the scope of the application of labour law protection. The author tackles the meaning of the traditional conceptual framework of the employment relationship and ponders on what manner the notions of employee and employer will have to be reconceptualised in this new labour environment. In relation to the protection of the worker, he asks where the protection limits are. Many lawsuits all over the world are dealing with the question on whether platform workers (i.e. UBER drivers, Globo and Deliveroo riders) are employees or self-employed persons according to the autonomy or dependency features they present when they perform their tasks. The main problem is those persons who, in view of the traditional categories, undoubtedly are self-employed but are in a similar position to employees. Among the online crowd workers, they are the majority. There are several alternatives to address this issue and to protect that type of worker: (a) to redefine the notion of employee to broaden significantly its scope and then grant those workers labour law rights; (b) to develop an intermediary category between an employee and a self-employed, that is, an economically dependent autonomous worker and provide a specific set of protections for such person which is already happening, as is already happening in some legal systems, such as Spain and Italy; (c) to simply extend the scope of application of labour law and of social security to self-employed persons up to a certain level; or (d) to develop specific and common legislation for platform workers irrespective of whether they are employees or self-employed. In connexion with the latter idea, it is important to point out that the recent ILO Report entitled "Work for a brighter future", published by the Global Commission on the Future of Work, recommend the establishment of a *Universal Labour Guarantee* for all the workforce, which includes: (a) the fundamental workers' rights: freedom of association and the effective recognition of the right to collective bargaining and freedom from forced labour, child labour and discrimination; and (b) a set of basic working conditions: (i) adequate living wage; (ii) limits on hours of work; and (iii) safe and healthy workplaces.

The second challenge addressed by Professor Weiss analyses the impact that the platform economy has on collective representation of the persons performing the work. He reflects upon the trend of individualisation in labour market and what mechanisms can be used to fight this trend, and then develop a consciousness of solidarity and thereby promote collectivisation for the whole workforce. It is necessary to develop collective structures among digital workers, especially in the context of platforms, for facilitating the workers' participation, be it by

---

1 Pesole, A., Urzí Brancati, M.C, Fernández-Macías, E., Biagi, F., González Vázquez, I., *Platform Workers in Europe*, evidence from the COLLEEM Survey, JRC Science for policy report (2018), pp. 21–27.

institutionalised schemes or by collective bargaining. Whether this goal can be achieved or whether it remains to be an illusion in the digital economy is still an open question. But there is, however, no doubt that the answer to it will decide the future development and the sustainability of digital work.

Chapter Two analyses the paradigmatic case of one of the main labour platforms in Canada. More specifically, Professors Coiquaud and Morissette, from HEC Montréal, aim to examine the arrival of Uber in Quebec and its impacts on the regulation of transportation by taxi. This is a special case inasmuch as it has involved a real process of regulatory experimentation leading to institutional hybridisation. Nothing comparable has been observed in the United States or in any European country; hence its high interest in our edited book. After a two-year latency period (2014–2016), the State reacted to put an end to the Uber activity outside the Quebec public policies, and a temporary regulatory mechanism called a "pilot project" was adopted, leading to the layering and coexistence of old and new rules in the city. This pilot project allowed Uber Canada to operate legally by negotiating with the Quebec government temporary rules which were distinct from those applying to traditional taxi drivers.

The authors respond to the following questions: Why and how has this compromise been reached? What pressures has this new regulatory framework placed upon the industry actors? And what lessons can be learned from this experiment? A critical look at this temporary regulation reveals that it enabled the Government to assess a complex situation requiring the collection of reliable data, and it may also have been used as a strategic tool to temper disputes in the traditional taxi sector with new actors. However, the final assessement will depend on the outcome of the various court actions regarding the legality of the pilot project as well as of the class actions instituted against Uber and the Government of Quebec. As some more interesting anwers will be found within the chapter, we recommend its reading to our readers,.

In the third chapter, researcher Qi Zhong, from the Japanese Institute for Labour Policy and Training, studies the phenomena of the platform economy in Japan, which has led to various new forms of work referred to as "employment-like working style". Although experts discuss the extension of traditional labour protection to these new forms of work, it is necessary in the first instance to clarify the reality of those new types of work and determine whether they are new or simply an extended form of traditional self-employment or of traditional subcontracting. In some instances, in Japan, it is possible to give sufficient legal protection to the workers with a new working form without fundamentally changing the current regulatory framework. The reason is related to the fact that in those new forms of work the means of communication from the telephone to the internet has simply been changed. However other new forms of work are totally new, using the internet platform to match the supply and demand of labour within a wider range without going through traditional companies. In these cases, a fundamental review is required for the principle of recognising the relationship of the parties according to the actual employment situation, and the basic concepts of worker and employer.

The situation in another Asiatic country, namely China, is examined by Professor Xiaohui Ban from the Law School of Wuhan University in Chapter Four. In China, the sharing economy has emerged strongly and has a significant role in solving the unemployment problem in the process of economic transformation. As is the case in numerous other countries, the identification of the status of the labour relationship has proved to be a difficult problem in practice. Besides, there is no legal concept for labour relationship or any explanation of subordination in the basic labour law of China. The Labour Dispute Settlement Authority has managed to explain subordination in the cases of the sharing economy, but still cannot unify the judgement criterion. In the crowdsource model, the judges find it hard to consider the subordination element of workers in accordance with the freedom to work clauses in the digital contract. In the outsource model, there are conflicting judgements on the issue of who is the real employer. To deal more effectively with such cases, contract performance should be considered in the first instance, and the identification criterion of subordination should be examined based on the character of the digital technology. In other words, this criterion can still be used to resolve the new forms of employment in the sharing economy but need to be flexibly explained and comprehensively considered based on the work characteristics of the platform enterprise.

Changing the continent, Chapter Five addresses the complex problem of the informal work on the digital economy of Latin America, more specifically in Chile. Researcher Denisa Meirosu, from the SNSPA Bucharest (National School of Public Administration and Political Studies), reflects on the reasons for the increase of such phenomenon. As trade on social platforms is not yet regulated, most of the entrepreneurial initiatives of independent workers are informal or fall under commercial contracts, which are usually non-enforceable. Informality in Chile is a constituent part of the current labour market as the characteristics of such a market have not changed significantly over the last decades. Different theories, for example, the structuralist school of thought, the voluntarist school of thought, the neoliberal theory and so on, have attempted to contribute to depict informal work, but most of them failed to capture its complexity. The author considers that one of the reasons is that theories presents the situation in terms of dichotomies (voluntary/involuntary), and they have missed one important characteristic of informal work: namely its chameleonic nature to the adaptation to a labour market, which, in its turn, follows faithfully the modes and means of production that the markets offer.

The elimination of informal work is seldom complete, and traditional forms of informality have always coexisted with their modern siblings, resulting in a multilayered phenomenon. This situation is well reflected by the gig economy, which starts to shape a parallel global market, regulated not by public policies but by the networks.

The sixth and the last chapter of this first part serves as a bridge to the second part as it analyses some important aspects of platform work and other new forms of work such as telework. Author Marta Travieso, a specialist at the ILO's Future of Work Unit (Switzerland), considers that technological innovation brings new dimensions and new possibilities, moving the frontiers of human capability much further than we could have ever imagined. These challenges have prompted reflections about the appropriateness of existing regulations and policies, and the consequences for the world of work. So, the new platform work is changing the way of doing business in many sectors; while it can constitute an entrance to the world of work for many, it might also be a low-quality job trap. The debate here focuses on a radical change in the way of working and in the emergence of autonomous work. The owner of the platform is presented as a non-traditional employer; he does not hire subordinate workers, but self-employed workers. The problem is the non-application of the employment law to these employees who are left without any labour guarantees. A unique solution can be difficult as the diversity of the models available in the labour market makes a one-size-fits-all approach almost impossible. On this topic, the author treats the particularities of Dutch and Spanish cases.

The second part of the book, entitled "Other new forms of work, new workforce and new skills", is related to the rise of different ways of work in the enterprises due to the incorporation of technology.

In Chapter Seven, Professor Villalba Sánchez, from the University of Santiago de Compostela (Spain), addresses the new way of working when parties enter into a smart labour contract, which is based on the blockchain technology. A smart contract is a computer protocol through which the elements of a legal relationship are formalised, with the purpose that their programmed terms are automatically demanded once a predefined condition has been fulfilled. So, blockchain technology is now being used to ensure the execution of standardised contracts built according to the employer's interest. This technology provides efficiency and legal security to the employer. However, blockchain implementation may increase the risk of imposing abusive conditions on the employee, a risk which is aggravated by guaranteed automatic execution. According to the author, it is necessary to review the applicable legal framework of the contract as well as the reinforcement of the information duty of the employer.

The chapter which follows, written by Professor Ana Murcia, from the University of Valladolid (Spain), deals with new forms of distant working, thanks to the development of new technology. Thus, the regulation on telework in Spain and the "agile work" in Italy are analysed in their respective contexts. A comparison is made between the purpose and legally defined concept in each of the legislations, the formal requirements of a telework agreement and the rights and responsibilities which make up their legal regime. The approach to the Regulations in each of the countries is criticised constructively and the author suggests conclusions which relate to the need for an "update" of existing Regulations, both international and European (the AMET of 2002 and the ILO Convention of 177), as well as national laws (article 13 of the Workers' Statute in Spain). Furthermore, collective bargaining is considered by the author as decisive when regulating telework, thus establishing a minimum framework within which this kind of work will be made compatible to individual workers and employers and complying with the working conditions regime established by law and the collective agreement.

In Chapter Nine, Professors Sánchez-Urán and Grau Ruiz, from the Madrid Complutense University, analyse the effects of new ways of working with robotics. The authors examine the possibility that a ("intelligent") robot can be considered as a worker and even enjoy a certain employment status, but they reject the idea of a robot being a salaried or self-employed worker. Labour law is based on human work and a robot, even one with a high dose of AI, cannot be considered as such.

As the robotisation of the labour market implies the replacement of human jobs by robots, the chapter contemplates the idea that ethics should be used as a starting point to reflect on the principles, scope and methods of regulatory intervention needed to protect human rights and human dignity. The legal framework cannot be designed as a barrier against robotic technological innovation but should rather be geared towards formulating measures to boost socially and legally responsible robotic innovation. To this end, based on the fundamental rights enshrined in the international law, it is necessary to promote legislation which balances the guarantee of entrepreneurial freedom with that of workers' rights.

Furthermore, the authors analyse the fiscal perspective and the imposition of a special tax for robots. In that case, the financial and tax regulation should always look for equilibrium between technological and social progress.

In Chapter Ten, Professor Matthew Finkin, from the Illinois University (USA), reflects upon the impact that the introduction of technology will have on the labour market, especially on employment rates. The author examines the theory that suggests that the automatisation of industries and the use of the new workforce – robots – in companies will replace human skills and so supplant human labour. Although the pace and sectors of displacement are not and are unlikely to be either in tandem or uniform, it seems clear that some jobs will be lost and others will be created. Anyway, the fear of persistent, long-term unemployment wrought by the replacement of humans by machines is a recurring motive in American history, as is very well explained in the chapter. According to Finkin, if history is instructive, the fear is without foundation as, in the previous industrial revolutions, it brought new opportunities for economic growth. Currently, on one hand, the agony of technology is the growing economic inequality, social marginalisation and political discord, the prospect of which is real. One solution for these negative effects could be the provision of a basic income for everyone. The idea has received some popular attention, political agitation and scholarly study, but it is generally acknowledged that providing for a basic income, at least in any meaningful amount, will be a reach. On the other hand, the ecstasy of technology is a life of universal comfort and leisure, the prospect of which is fictional, still.

In Chapter Eleven, Professor Di Meo, from the Polytechnic University of the Marche Region (Italy), analyses Amazon's electronic wristband as a new working instrument and its implications in relation to the employer's powers. The author suggests that the introduction of this electronic tool can be positive in the workplace as it is a good replacement of the dictatorial employer's powers;

however, it is necessary to take into account some possible risks or negative effects related to the employee's fundamental rights. More clearly, the electronic wristband is able to collect a large amount of information about the employee, even not related to the work performance, so it is crucial to have limits to the use of that data. The difficult task of the researcher is to identify what information could be legally utilised by the employer, without compromising the privacy and the dignity of the employee. According to the author, if the device is designed in order to collect additional information to what is necessary for the fulfilment of the contract, then the data collected by the company would not be usable against the worker because it was collected for a disproportionate and unnecessary purpose, and therefore becomes illicit.

Chapter Twelve, written by Professor Rodríguez Fernández, of the Castile-La Mancha University (Spain), analyses the new role of trade unions in the context of the appearance of new forms of work and digitalisation. Technological advances and their application to production processes and new business models also have an impact on the formulas for the organisation and defence of workers' interests. Indeed, faced with this emerging labour, social dialogue is – as pointed out in the chapter – one of the privileged and effective instruments that can be claimed in order to guarantee adequate protection of workers. Precisely, at this moment, the importance of the social dialogue in which governments and representative organisations of employers and workers must participate must be reclaimed, so that it can once again play a key role in the governance of work, accompanied by political and social consensus. In effect, the new legal regulation of the manifestations of this technological Revolution cannot be done outside the social partners. In this sense, it is relevant to bear in mind that trade unions will have to face the challenge of change, without forgetting that more traditional problems, such as unemployment, job insecurity and inequality, still exist and have even increased with the new forms of employment. To do this, they will have to bring up new contents to collective bargaining. Besides the use of technology by trade unions to create workers' networks and forms of collective action supported and boosted by social networks can reconstruct links and spaces for solidarity which technology itself has contributed to blur.

The next two chapters are related to the new skills that the digital workforce must attain to provide services through these new ways of working and avoid being excluded from the new labour market. The changes triggered by the Fourth Industrial Revolution, taking place at this very moment, are considered fundamental challenges to the future of work. Despite the growing debate, attention to new skills needed in the Industry 4.0 framework is currently lacking. As it is generally thought, many jobs that will be in demand in future years still do not currently exist. Universities, schools and other educational and skill entities are currently preparing students for jobs that do not exist yet in order to solve problems which we do not even know yet. Thus, Chapter Twelve by Aneta Tyc, of the University of Lodz (Poland), addresses the issue of responding to changing work demands. The author examines not only emerging skills and jobs, but also seeks to address ways to promote them. According to the author, we ought to begin difficult conversations on how to support development of new skills for new jobs and, in order to get us started on the right path, approach some of the proposals made in this area: for example, supporting life-long learning (*inter alia* by promoting MOOCs), upskilling and reskilling jobseekers and establishing bipartite training funds or standards-based educational reforms. Additionally, initiatives such as supporting mobility, targeting female talent, cross-industry and public-private collaboration are presented in the paper for debate in order to improve the future workforce planning.

In a similar manner, researcher and lawyer Vivas García, from Venezuela, points out the importance of resilience as one of the main skills for Industry 4.0. Resilience is present in each individual, whether that individual is developed or not, which helps in the productive processes and allows the individual to adapt to the new challenge based on her/his experience and knowledge, seeks stability in the employment and recognition of knowledge, and complements the new "how to do" with knowing how to do it better and well. This important capacity of being resilient must be cultivated both at an individual and organisational level. The changes experienced by companies are likely to be increasingly faster, so resilience will become essential for employees and organisations and give a sense of continuity to eventual changes. Besides, this factor will serve as a vehicle to acquire other skills and attitudes of the worker. For that reason, the employer should encourage it, as being one of the most important topics of the transformation of the work. According to the author, in order to combine the skills of the worker with the expectations of future work, it is necessary to initiate educational programmes for the worker in the company itself, adjusted to the expectations of the innovation. Work and education need to be a perfect binomial, which prepare the worker for any circumstances. That process of continuous and permanent education and training must be carried out in the company; it is the ideal place for knowledge to be present in the face of new technologies.

Within the pages of this book, the reader will find a rich analysis and evaluation of numerous problems combined with deep reflections on theoretical and practical problems arising from a constantly developing technology. Important and informed suggestions are made by experts on how to solve the numerous problems which have arisen. The collection of chapters in this volume is varied and is dealt with from different disciplinary angles. Moreover, the many nationalities of the authors, from diverse countries and continents, permit to bring up an interesting and unique global picture on the topics studied therein.

Finally, we wish to thank the authors of this volume for their professional collaboration and hope that the readers will find the content of this volume to be inspiring, scholarly and useful.

Santiago de Compostela, October 2019.

Part one

The platform economy and the labour market

Some key issues

1 The platform economy
The main challenges for labour law

Manfred Weiss

I Introduction

Digitalisation of working patterns has many faces – it is not to be conceived as a uniform or homogeneous phenomenon. Many details are still rather unclear. But undoubtedly it means a dramatic transformation of the world of work. Each of the different working patterns leads to different implications for labour law and industrial relations. Three types are most relevant in this context.

Already for several decades, communication technologies made it possible that work does not have to be performed in the premises of the employer but can be executed anywhere. The labels used for this type of work are "telework" or "mobile work".[1] The main problems arising with "telework" are in the area of working time and of data protection referring to privacy as well as to business secrets.

Another trend of this digital evolution is labelled "Industry 4.0", which stands for the fourth industrial revolution.[2] The label is somehow misleading because this type of work refers not only to manufacturing but also to services. Collaborative robots become intelligent, which means able to adapt, communicate and interact. Smart robots communicate with each other and with humans on interlinking tasks. These cyber-physical systems are quickly widening, including various functions in production, logistics or office management. There is no doubt that, at least to a certain extent, human beings will be replaced by robots, thereby losing their jobs. The challenge for labour law, however, will be to keep the number of these people as small as possible and to reskill those who are substituted in order to re-integrate them into the labour market. This implies a total reconsideration of training patterns. Since stress level in the context of Industry 4.0 will increase significantly a re-conceptualisation of health and safety towards prevention and cure of psycho-social diseases will be necessary.

---

1 For the problems arising in the context of telework, see the contributions in R. Blanpain (ed.), European Framework Agreements and Telework – Law and Practice, A European and Comparative Study, *Bulletin of Comparative Labour Relations*, 2007, 62, and in L. Mella Méndez (ed.) *Trabajo a Distancia y Teletrabajo*, Cazur Menor 2015.

2 F. Almada-Lobo, The Industry 4.0 Revolution and the Future of Manufacturing Execution Systems (MES), *Journal of Innovation Management*, 2016, 16–21.

It goes without saying that, of course, data protection also will play a big role in this context.

This sketchy article will neglect "telework" and Industry 4.0. It will focus exclusively on the third important trend: the increasing platform economy.[3] Here basically two types are to be distinguished: "internal platforms" to which only the workforce of a specific company has access and "external platforms" with open access for anybody meeting specific criteria. Among the "external platforms", again two types are to be distinguished: "work on demand via app", where the work is performed in a traditional way (transport, cleaning etc.), and "online crowd work", where work is performed by a crowd worker online. Again, there has to be a difference between platforms, where relatively simple tasks are performed by unskilled or low-skilled persons, and complex platforms, where highly skilled persons are confronted with complex tasks.

The challenge will be whether and how the work in view of digitalisation can be regulated in a way which will guarantee that the traditional goals of labour law are achieved: to protect the worker, to respect his or her dignity, in particular to guarantee his or her privacy as well as his or her physical, mental and psychic health.

How these challenges can be met is still rather uncertain. The purpose of this contribution is to briefly indicate the direction in which regulatory strategies in coping with the main challenges might be developed.[4]

II Selected perspectives of regulation

1 Reconsideration of the scope of labour law protection

1.1 Employment versus self-employment

Already, for quite a long time, it has become evident that the demarcation line between employment and self-employment is very difficult to draw.[5] To an increasing extent there are persons labelled as self-employed but, in reality, are employees. These bogus self-employed, of course, are to be included into the scope of application of labour law, even if it might often be very difficult to exactly identify their status. How difficult this is can best be demonstrated by the many law suits all over the world, dealing with the question on whether UBER drivers are employees or self-employed. Customers use an app on their smart-phones to request rides from a specific location. This information is instantly broadcast to

---

3 For different types of work in the platform economy, see V. De Stefano, Introduction: Crowdsourcing, the Gig-Economy and the Law, *Comparative Labor Law & Policy Journal*, 2016, 461–470.
4 For a good overview on this debate, see W. Liebman, The Gig Economy, Crowdwork and New Forms of Work, *Soziales Recht*, 2017, 221–238.
5 See for a comprehensive discussion of this problem, G. Davidov/B. Langille (eds.), *Boundaries and Frontiers of Labour Law*, Oxford / Portland 2006 and for an interesting proposal on how to overcome it M. Freedland/N. Kountouris, *The Legal Construction of Personal Work Relations*, Oxford 2011.

the drivers in the area. The driver who accepts is directed to the passenger and onwards to the required destination through the Uber app. Payment is taken automatically from the customer by the platform and, after the deduction of a commission, passed on to the driver. The drivers are rated afterwards by the customers.[6] The rating decides whether and how often the drivers are called again by the platform or whether they will no longer be used. Does the fact that drivers, at least theoretically, have the choice to decide whether they accept or refuse an order by the platform make them self-employed, even if they might be aware that they never will be called again by the platform if they don't accept an order? Or is the degree of control by the platform such that the drivers are to be categorised as being employees? This might be difficult to decide. Therefore, lots of litigation referring to the "workers" in the on-demand economy is going on.[7] But this is a problem which also for quite a time has been well known outside the context of the platform economy. Misclassification is nothing new. Long before the digital revolution, practices existed to hide employment relationships under the guise of false or bogus contractor situations. Also, the demarcation line between employees and independent contractors has been difficult to draw. In view of the difficulty to draw the demarcation line, it always has looked like a lottery in which box a person might end up, even if it is decisive for the inclusion not only into labour law protection but also – at least in most countries – into the social security system. This uncertainty, of course, is not a satisfying situation, but it is not new because of the platform economy. The platform economy, however, makes it even more evident than before.

The real problem is those persons which, in view of the traditional categories, are undoubtedly self-employed but in a similar position as employees. Among the online crowd workers, they are the majority. The question to be discussed is how to cope with them. There are several alternatives: (a) to redefine the notion of employee in a way to broaden significantly its scope; (b) to develop an intermediary category between employment and self-employment, and provide a specific set of protection; (c) to simply extend the scope of application of labour law and of social security to self-employed up to a certain level; or (d) to develop specific legislation for crowd workers irrespective of whether they are employees or self-employed.[8]

In most countries the classification as employee is not up to the denomination given to the contract by the contracting parties but depends on the actual features of the relationship. These features were steadily adapted over time. For example, in Germany it was originally characterised to be personal subordination,

---

6 For a very good illustration for such rating systems, see M. Silberman/L. Irani, Operating an Employer Reputation System: Lessons from Turkopticon 2008–2015, *Comparative Labor Law & Policy Journal*, 2016, 505–541.
7 See the list in M. A. Cherry, Beyond Misclassification: The Digital Transformation of Work, *Comparative Labor & Policy Journal*, 2016, 577–602 (584–585).
8 For the difficulty of categorisation of crowdworkers, see A. Aloisi, Commoditized Workers: Case Study Research on Labor Issues Arising from a Set of 'On Demand/Gig Economy' Platforms, *Comparative Labor Law & Policy Journal*, 2016, 653–690.

which meant that a person is not free in organising his or her work, or in determining his or her working time.[9] According to the latest amendment of the Civil Code in 1917 the classification as employee depends on the respective character of work. To find out whether there is an employment relationship, a comprehensive evaluation including all circumstances is necessary (section 611 a). This, of course, gives the judiciary an enormous leeway in assessing an employment relationship. Thereby compared to its origins, the notion of employee today is already much wider, including many more people who in earlier times would not have been considered to be employees. Nevertheless, it cannot be expected that mere widening of this notion resolves the problem. Otherwise the notion as such would become meaningless. There have to be limits in broadening the scope. An ongoing further widening of the notion might be detrimental by reason of legal certainty.

Therefore, in many countries already, long before the digital revolution, a hybrid third category between employment and self-employment has been established for the economically dependent self-employed. In Germany they are called "employee like persons".[10] The labels differ from country, be they "quasi subordinates" or "dependent contractors". They all have in common that it is not the whole protective scheme of labour law that is applied on them but only a limited set of rules, excluding, for example, the rules on minimum wage or on protection against unfair dismissals. Whether such an in-between hybrid category may be recommended as a solution for the problems arising in the platform economy is controversial. Very helpful in this context is the comparative study by Miriam Cherry and Antonio Aloisi,[11] which has analysed the advantages and disadvantages of this intermediate category in Canada, Italy and Spain, reflecting also the situation in the United States. In view of the experiences made with the third category in these countries, they are very sceptical whether this might be the solution for the platform economy.[12] According to them, "adding a third category would only increase the amount of arbitrage. Three categories create more room for mischief than two". They insist that "the kinds of rights and responsibilities that go along with the third category are just as important, if not more so, than the creation of the category itself".[13] They illustrate this arbitrary approach to the rights to be included by the exclusion of the rules on minimum wage. Since

> many platforms can measure precisely how much time and effort a worker spends on a task, down to the minutes spent waiting in traffic (in a case of a

---

9 See the explanation in M. Weiss/M. Schmidt, *Labour Law and Industrial Relations in Germany*, 4th ed., Kluwer Law International 2008, 45.
10 See B. Waas, Crowdwork in Germany, in B. Waas et al., *Crowdwork – A Comparative Law Perspective, Frankfurt* 2017, 142–186 (160–162).
11 M. Cherry/A. Aloisi, "Dependent Contractors" in the Gig Economy: A Comparative Approach, *American University Law Review*, 2017, 635–689.
12 Ibidem 675–682.
13 Ibidem 677.

ridesharing app) or the number of keystrokes in case of crowd-work)... one of the major concerns with platform work is not difficulty in tracing time, work and hours.[14]

Therefore, they insist that the inclusion for minimum wage would not raise any practical problems and also crowd workers should get it. No matter what rights might be included or excluded, the scepticism against an intermediate category as a magic tool sounds very convincing. Whether, however, the authors' proposal to rather shift to "changes regarding the default presumptions around employee and independent contractor status"[15] would be the way to follow may well be doubted. In my view it would be nothing else but widening the scope of the notion of employee, leading to the same problems already indicated there.

Of course, sticking to the two traditional categories – "employment" and "self-employment" – does not solve the problem yet. It would be necessary to build a protective roof for self-employed up to a certain level. The task to define the level up to which the self-employed are to be protected by labour law and social security remains. Again, it would be necessary to define the set of rights to be chosen for this category. Or to put it differently, the same problems as were identified in the context of an intermediate category would also arise with a mere extension of the scope of application of some labour rights to the part of self-employed who might be in need of such protection.

Special regulations only for platform workers would ignore the fact that the problem to be solved is not limited to this digital workforce. It is much broader, older and more general. Therefore, special regulation might not be the way forward.

These sketchy indications of the serious difficulties linked with all the different options may explain why, so far, no satisfying solution is in sight.

1.2 Who is the employer?

Even if it might be possible to elaborate a satisfying solution for the protection of platform workers within and beyond the traditional employment relationship, the question has to be answered: who is responsible for the obligations implied by these protective rules? Or, to put it differently, who is the employer; the platform operator; or, in case of crowd work, the crowdsourcer or both of them? Again, part of the problem may be illustrated by referring to Uber. This platform's terms and conditions require the customers to "acknowledge that Uber does not provide transportation or logistics services or function as a transportation carrier" and instead functions merely as an agent between driver and customer. Whether this is a correct assessment has become very controversial. The Court of Justice of the EU (CJEU) by judgement of 20 December 2017[16] rejected Uber's

---

14 Ibidem 678.
15 Ibidem 682.
16 CJEU judgement of 20 December 2015, Asociación Profesional Elite Taxi v. Uber Systems Spain, SL, Case C-434/15.

self-understanding and classified it as a transport company. Whether the court will confirm this position is to be seen. The example, however, shows that the categorisation cannot be left to the platforms themselves. Objective criteria are necessary to identify the employer. The Uber example, however, only shows the difficulty to correctly categorise the platforms' role. The problem is getting more complex if in a crowd work structure not the platform operator but the crowdsourcer as client of the platform is the user of the crowd workers' achievements. In this tripartite structure the employer's role might be split between platform and crowdsourcer or fulfilled by one of the two actors. Again, the problem of tripartite structures is not new; it is well known in the context of temporary agency work. However, it also has become more dramatic in view of the platform economy. Therefore, it is not surprising that efforts are taken to develop appropriate solutions to identify who is in such a constellation the employer and in what way.

The most promising suggestions in this context of multilateral relationships are offered by Jeremias Prassl and Martin Risak.[17] Traditionally in trying to identify the employer, the bilateral relationship between employer and employee was in the focus. The contract was the link between the two. Consequently, the employment contract was in the centre of scholarly attention. However, between crowdsourcer and crowd worker often a contractual relationship does not exist, this relationship only exits between platforms and crowdsourcer as well as between platforms and crowd workers. According to Prassl and Risak, it is necessary to not get lost in the analysis of separate bilateral contractual relationships but to understand the multilateral structure as a complex entity. In order to identify the employer, they suggest shifting the focus to the functions to be performed by an employer, and then look whether and in how far this fits to the platform and/or to the crowdsourcer. Thereby the platform might be identified to be the sole employer or there might be a multiplicity of employers sharing employers' functions. Their concept of employer is multi-functional comprising an ensemble of five functions: (a) Inception and termination of the employment relationship, (b) receiving labour and its fruits, (c) providing work and pay, (d) managing the enterprise's internal market and (e) managing the enterprise's external market.[18] Thereby they end up in a new definition of the concept of employer, which reads, "the entity, or combination of entities playing a decisive role in the exercise of relational employing functions and regulated or controlled as such in each particular domain of employment law".[19]

By referring to Prassl's and Risak's functional approach my intention is not to decide whether this is already the final solution of the problem on how to assess an employment relationship in the context of platform work. My interest rather

---

17 J. Prassl/M. Risak, Uber, Taskrabbit, and Co.: Platforms as Employers? Rethinking the Legal Analysis of Crowdwork, *Comparative Labor & Policy Journal*, 2016, 619–951, and J. Prassl/M. Risak, Working in the Gig Economy – Flexibility without Security?, in. R. Singer/T. Bazzani (eds.), *European Employment Policies: Current Challenges*, Berlin 2017, 67–95.
18 J. Prassl/M. Risak, *op.cit.*, *Comparative Labor & Policy Journal*, 2016, 636.
19 Ibidem 647.

is to show that the traditional concept of employer no longer serves the purpose of identifying the actor in these digital working structures who is responsible for the obligations linked to employer status.

2 Growing difficulties of collective representation

The traditional Fordist model was characterised by a relatively homogeneous workforce in a hierarchically structured factory or office. As indicated above, this model already fell apart by the segmentation and fragmentation of the workforce, divided in core groups and non-standard groups with significantly diverse interests. This trend is dramatically increased by the digitalisation of work. The example of the platform workers shows that there is no more link between the acting individuals, they don't know each other and work in splendid isolation.

Technological innovation cycles by digitalisation of work are growing faster and faster. The legislator will not be able to keep up with the changes and to adapt the rules to the respective needs. The legislator only can provide a relatively flexible framework. Solutions balancing the needs of the platforms and the workers are to be developed on a decentralised level, be it in the area of training, of working time, of health and safety or of data protection. These solutions cannot be left unilaterally to the employer but must be developed in cooperation with representative bodies of the workforce. In other words, the working conditions are to be shaped and monitored together with the employee's representatives, be it by way of information and consultation or even by co-determination. "Cooperative turn" has become the catchword for this approach.

The difficulties for workers' participation, of course, not only have grown due to digitalisation. Outsourcing and networking strategies have made it more and more difficult to identify the employer. However, these difficulties, as indicated above, have significantly grown in the platform economy.

The basic requirement for workers' participation, be it via institutionalised schemes or be it by collective bargaining, is the possibility to develop collective structures among digital workers, in particular in the context of platforms. Whether this goal can be achieved or whether it remains an illusion in the digital economy is still an open question. But there is no doubt that the answer to it will decide the future development and the sustainability of digital work.

The first step to be taken in this direction is to overcome the workers anonymity and isolation.[20] A group of trade unions from different countries have already started to devote themselves to this task; for example, representatives from trade unions from Austria, Denmark, Germany and the United States as well as from the Service Employees International Union met in Frankfurt (Germany) in April 2016, together with an international group of industrial relations experts to discuss possible strategies. This resulted in a joint declaration on platform-based

---

20 See the report on developments in the United States by W. Liebmann, Crowdworkers, the Law and the Future of Work: The U.S., in B. Waas et al., *op. cit.*, 24–141 (115–127).

work.[21] Therein they explained "the possibilities for a 'cooperative turn' in labour-management relations in the 'platform economy', in which workers, clients, platform operators, investors, policy makers, and worker organisations work together to improve outcomes for all stakeholders". And they identified platform providers as "appropriate negotiating partners for platform-based workers seeking to improve their conditions of work", even if in some cases "clients may also be appropriate negotiating partners". In particular, they insisted that "all workers on the platform regardless of whether they are employees or independent contractors" are to be included in "a platform's policies and information flows". As far as the "cooperative turn" is concerned, the declaration reads as follows:

> The 'traditional' conflictual processes of labour-management relations have secured crucial rights for workers over the years and will continue to be important. But insofar as platform operators understand that their long-term well-being, and that of society at large is bound up with the ability of workers – regardless of their status – to secure good work, future labour-management interactions may be organized around interests deeply shared by all parties. This possibility offers the hope of great gains for all parties.

This optimistic view was accompanied not only by a list of topics to be regulated (wages, social protection etc.) but in particular by a request for two strategies which might serve as a first step on this way to a "cooperative turn": establishment of transparency and of a mechanism of dispute resolution.

It is stated in detail that to a great extent the whole operation of platforms remains in the dark. This refers to processes for assigning tasks, the preconditions for account closure or computing worker reputation and other qualifications, to just mention some examples. Complaints refer to the fact that often the use of platforms is obscured by posting tasks under wrong names. The declaration states that "in short, the knowledge base required to make sound policy is missing". Therefore, transparency is understood to be the indispensable precondition to develop a strategy for the collective voice of platform workers.

As far as dispute resolution is concerned, the declaration proposes "that platform operators work – with workers, clients, researchers, worker organizations, and other actors as appropriate – to develop transparent, accountable methods for resolving disputes between clients and workers, and, as needed, between workers". In this context, it may be of interest that in November 2017 the German Metalworkers' Union "IG Metal", together with the German Crowdsourcing Association and eight important Crowd work platforms, has established an Ombudsman's Office,[22] composed of an equal number of platform

---

21 www.igmetall.de/docs_20161214_Frankfurt_Paper_on_Platform_Based_Work_EN_b939ef89f7e5f3a639cd6a1a930feffd8f55cecb.pdf.
22 www.igmetall.de/docs_2017_11_8_Presseinformation_OmbudsstelleCrowdworking_ef5ebcd3b52f834a38b64ec80377aee518d11009.pdf.

representatives on the one side and representatives of "IG Metal" and crowd workers on the other side, chaired by a judge of the Frankfurt labour court. It is supposed to mediate conflicts between crowd workers, platforms and clients, and to monitor the compliance with a code of conduct on which the participating platforms already in 2015 agreed as a form of voluntary self-regulation. The code was amended in 2017.[23]

This code of conduct contains 10 principles to be respected by the platforms: offering only lawful tasks, information of the crowd workers on the legal framework for their work, fair wages, user-friendly and motivating working conditions, respectful behaviour between platforms, clients and crowd workers, freedom of crowd workers to accept or refuse offers without fear of negative consequences, constructive feedback and open communication, transparent procedure of acceptance of work results by the platform and finally protection of personal data and privacy. All these details are further described and explained in order to make them workable tools.

At the same time, the "IG-Metal" has established a platform where crowd workers can communicate with each other and where the trade union can communicate with them. The idea is to, thereby, overcome the anonymity and isolation in order to create a collective consciousness, a basis for collective organisation and collective action. To promote this goal further, the "IG Metal" also conducts workshops with crowd workers and platform representatives at regular intervals.

Whether such initiatives will be successful in building up a collective structure remains to be seen. These are nothing more than first steps. But at least it shows that trade unions make efforts to promote such a development. Of course, such efforts cannot remain limited to national contexts since crowd workers of platforms may come from several countries. However, the already mentioned fact that trade unions in these efforts co-operate trans-nationally is a promising sign.

Whether most crowd workers may ever be able to develop collective power is to be doubted; such a large majority are low-skilled workers performing simple tasks. They can easily be substituted, which evidently has a negative impact on their bargaining power. Therefore, not too much should be expected. This, however, might be very different where complex tasks by highly skilled workers are performed. It might be quite difficult to substitute them, which increases their bargaining power. The problem there might be whether solidarity between them can be established since, within the platforms, they are competitors most of the time. In short and to make the point, there are first promising steps to overcome the isolation of crowd workers. The future will tell where they end up. It is a challenge for the international community of labour law to contribute to this development and, thereby, to make sure that crowd workers have a chance to work under decent working conditions.

---

23 www.igmetall.de/begruessenswerte-entwicklung-im-crowdsourcing-24652.htm.

III Conclusion

These sketchy remarks may leave us very frustrated. My intention merely has been to demonstrate that the platform economy cannot be conceived by our traditional set of concepts. So far it is an attack on the traditional understanding of labour law. But my intention also was to indicate that debates and activities are under way which provide reasons for optimism that these challenges can be met. It needs a joint effort of the international scholarly community of labour law and social security law to develop suitable regulatory patterns for this new phenomenon. Congresses like the one held at Santiago de Compostela are the ideal platform to discuss potential solutions and further develop them.

IV Bibliography

Almada-Lobo, F., The Industry 4.0 Revolution and the Future of Manufacturing Execution Systems (MES), *Journal of Innovation Management*, 2016, 16–21.

Aloisi, A., Commoditized Workers: Case Study Research on Labor Issues Arising from a Set of 'On Demand/Gig Economy' Platforms, *Comparative Labor Law & Policy Journal*, 2016, 653–690.

Blanpain, R. (ed.), European Framework Agreements and Telework – Law and Practice, A European and Comparative Study, *Bulletin of Comparative Labour Relations*, 2007, 62.

Cherry, M.A., Beyond Misclassification: The Digital Transformation of Work, *Comparative Labor & Policy Journal*, 2016, 577–602.

Cherry, M.A./Aloisi, A., "Dependent Contractors" in the Gig Economy: A Comparative Approach, *American University Law Review*, 2017, 635–689.

Davidov, G./Langille, B. (eds.), *Boundaries and Frontiers of Labour Law*, Oxford / Portland 2006.

De Stefano, V., Introduction: Crowdsourcing, the Gig-Economy and the Law, *Comparative Labor & Policy Journal*, 2016, 461–470.

Freedland, M./Kountouris, N., *The Legal Construction of Personal Work Relations*, Oxford 2011.

Liebman, W., The Gig Economy, Crowdwork and New Forms of Work, *Soziales Recht*, 2017, 221–238.

Mella Méndez, L. (ed.), *Trabajo a Distancia y Teletrabajo*, Cazur Menor 2015.

Prassl, J. / Risak, M., Uber, Taskrabbit, and Co., Platforms as Employers? Rethinking the Legal Analysis of Crowdwork, *Comparative Labor & Policy Journal*, 2016, 619–951.

Prassl, J./Risak, M., Working in the Gig Economy – Flexibility without Security?, in Singer, R./Bazzani, T. (eds.), *European Employment Policies: Current Challenges*, Berlin 2017, 67–95.

Silberman, M./Irani, L., Operating an Employer Reputation System: Lessons from Turkopticon 2008–2015, *Comparative Labor Law & Policy Journal*, 2016, 505–541.

Waas, B., Crowdwork in Germany, in Waas, B. et al., *Crowdwork – A Comparative Law Perspective*, Frankfurt 2017, 142–186.

Weiss, M./Schmidt, M., *Labour Law and Industrial Relations in Germany*, 4th ed., Kluwer Law International 2000.

2 Uber
Regulatory and institutional experimentation in the taxi industry in Quebec

Urwana Coiquaud and Lucie Morissette[*]

I Introduction

This chapter aims to examine the arrival of Uber in Quebec[1] and its impacts on the regulation of transportation by taxi. This is a special case inasmuch as it has involved a real process of regulatory experimentation leading to institutional hybridisation. Indeed, nothing comparable has been observed in the United States or in any European country[2]; hence its being of interest.

After a two-year latency period (2014–2016), during which decision-makers watched – with a mixture of dismay, concern and fascination – the arrival of Uber and its sprawling ability to deploy its services outside of Quebec public policies, the state reacted to put an end to this "gray market".[3] In fact, a temporary regulatory mechanism, called a "pilot project", was adopted, leading to the layering and coexistence of old and new rules. This pilot project allowed Uber to operate legally by negotiating, with the government, temporary rules which are distinct from those applying to traditional taxi drivers.

This coexistence of rules will be examined in this chapter. We will address the following questions: Why and how has this compromise been reached? What pressures has this new regulatory framework placed on industry actors? And what lessons can be learned from this experience? In fact, as several authors[4]

---

[*] At the time of writing, in 30 March 2019, a draft law on the deregulation of the taxi industry has been submitted to the Quebec Parliament. Discussions on now occur in the National Assembly.
1 In broad terms, Quebec occupies a special place in the Canadian Confederation due to its history (French, then British colonization), language (French) and a civil law system which prevails in a common law country.
2 Kathleen Thelen, "Regulating Uber: The Politics of the Platform Economy in Europe and the United States," *Perspectives on Politics* 16, No. 4 (2018): 938–953.
3 Thelen, "Regulating Uber," 938.
4 See, in particular, Daniel Rauch and David Schleicher, "Like Uber, But for Local Governmental Policy: The Future of Local Regulation of the 'Sharing Economy'," *George Mason Law & Economics Research Paper* No. 15-01(2015): 1–61, access 20 February 2019, http://dx.doi.org/10.2139/ssrn.2549919; Derek McKee, Finn Makela and Teresa Scassa (eds.), *Law and the "Sharing Economy"* (Ottawa: Les Presses de l'Université d'Ottawa, 2018), 1–452.; Ruth Berins Collier, Veena Dubal and Christopher Carter, "Disrupting Regulation, Regulating Disruption: The Politics of Uber in the United States," *Perspectives on Politics* 16, no 4 (2018): 919–937.

have pointed out, governments are still looking for the best normative experimentation to deal with digital platforms, and Uber's arrival provided a fitting laboratory for advancing public policy thinking in this respect.[5]

This study will examine the case of Quebec, which has put forward a singular response to Uber's arrival, thus adding to the diversity of regulatory responses to platform economies.

To understand fully the case of Uber in Quebec, we will rely on the legal and neo-institutional literature. The legal literature notes that the concept of experimental legislation provides a means for governments to try out new regulations, first on a small scale and for a limited period before enacting permanent, general and better laws.[6] Traditionally, consultations, expert advice and impact assessments are part of their tools. Indeed, experimental regulation makes it possible to collect information to address social, legal or economic issues in an uncertain, changing or complex context. It is a means of improving the regulation in force, obtaining a consensus or espousing the specific characteristics of certain environments and decentralising the regulatory power.[7]

The neo-institutional literature,[8] for its part, is used to grasp the role of actors (governments, pressure groups, Uber) in the adoption of new rules, able to transform the institutional landscape. According to Mahoney and Thelen,[9] institutions are expected to change gradually, for example, when new rules are attached to existing ones; this process is referred to in the literature as layering. Therefore, gradual re-regulation can be seen, with the effect of modifying the logic behind the existing institutional framework.[10] This phenomenon occurs when actors seek to maintain the original vocation of an institution (in this case, the regulatory framework of the taxi industry before Uber's arrival) but have little power to impose the veto, except for a few means of recourse, such as resorting to the courts.

This "bricolage" undertaken by the actors[11] illustrates through an object – regulation – a very clear manifestation of the institutional changes at work in the taxi industry in Quebec. A well-established regulatory system, to which tra-

---

5 Peter Gourévitch, "Étude comparative des réactions des Grandes Puissances face à la crise économique de 1873 à 1896," *Études internationales* 6, no 2 (1975): 188; Thelen, "Regulating Uber," 938; 949.
6 Rob Van Gestel and Gijs van Dijck, "Better Regulation through Experimental Legislation," *European Public Law* 17, no 3 (2011): 541–542; Gabriel, Domenech-Pascual, "Sharing Economy and Regulatory Strategies towards Legal Change," *European Journal of Risk Regulation*, 7, no 4 (2016): 724–725.
7 Ittai Bar-Siman-Tov, "Temporary Legislation, Better Regulation, and Experimentalist Governance: An Empirical Study," *Regulation & Governance*, 12 (2018): 193–195.
8 James Mahoney, and Kathleen Thelen, "A Theory of Gradual Institutional Change," in *Explaining Institutional Change*, ed. James Mahoney and Kathleen Thelen (New York: Cambridge University Press, 2009), 1–37. Colin, Crouch, *Capitalist Diversity and Change: Recombinant Governance and Institutional Entrepreneurs* (Oxford: OUP, 2005).
9 Mahoney and Thelen, "A theory," 1.
10 Martino Maggetti, "The Role of Independent Regulatory Agencies in Policy-Making: A Comparative Analysis," *Journal of European Public Policy* 16, no 3 (2009): 450–451.
11 Crouch, Recombinant governance, 71.

ditional drivers are subject, is confronted with a patch of novel regulatory law, via a pilot project, designed to accommodate Uber by freeing it from the current regulation on transportation by taxi.

However, this regulation is grounded in both theory and practice. In theory, there is a consensus in the literature regarding the importance of regulating the taxi industry, given the low cost of entry into this market, the difficulty for consumers of assessing the quality of service before taking a trip and the high volatility of prices due to the instability of supply and demand.[12] In practice, regulatory authorities have historically relied on a three-part regulatory framework to ensure control of quality, quantity and fare setting. The literature refers to this as the "QQE Framework" (Quality, Quantity and Economic controls).[13] Harding et al.[14] (2016) explain it as follows:

1   Quality Control: Several requirements are set for the driver (criminal record, holder of a specific permit and training) and the vehicle (vehicle age, appearance and disability requirements, all enforced by testing and inspections).
2   Quantity Control: Controls on the number of taxis (permit issuance) in a particular jurisdiction modified according to analyses of demand and projections of future demand.
3   Economic Controls: Fare setting based on regular analyses of operator costs and revenues with the aim of providing fair compensation for operators and stable prices for passengers.

Although the taxi industry in Quebec became institutionalised around these three "QQE" pillars (I), its questioning following the arrival of Uber has provoked resistance from local actors, leading the state to seek a compromise through regulatory experimentation in the form of a pilot project (II).

II The industry of transportation by taxi before Uber: a history of necessary interventionism

It took several decades for the taxi industry to acquire a regulatory and institutional framework (1), whose characteristics are based on the three major pillars recognised in the literature (2).

1 History of the industry's regulatory and institutional construction

The taxi industry in Quebec emerged in the early twentieth century. Municipalities soon sought to regulate it but with little success, given the predominance

---

12 Simon Harding, Milind Kandlikar and Sumeet Gulati, "Taxi Apps, Regulation, and the Market for Taxi Journeys," *Transportation Research Part A* 88 (2016): 18–20.
13 James Cooper, Ray Mundy and John Nelson, *Taxi! Urban Economics and the Social & Transport Impacts of the Taxicab* (Farnham, United Kingdom: Ashgate, 2010), 15.
14 Harding, Kandlikar and Gulati, "Taxi apps, regulation," 17–18.

of laissez-faire economics. It was not until the *Transport Act* (via the *Regulation respecting transport by taxicab*) adopted in 1973 that a control of pricing and the number of permits was instituted.

During this period, regulation was transferred from the municipal to the state level. The *Commission des transports du Québec* (Quebec Transportation Commission, CTQ) was created. The CTQ determines agglomerations, safety and customer service rules and sets fares for trips. The Act also imposes new representative bodies to respond to the desire of the industry's actors to collectively defend their interests: taxi leagues brought together owners and service associations in the municipalities of Montreal.[15] However, these institutions were soon embroiled in vigorous internal quarrels, leading to their dissolution.[16] As regards the drivers, as of 1974, they sought to unionise, but without success. This urge to unionise re-emerged in 1980, but suffered the same fate, because in the same year the Supreme Court of Canada denied the status of employee to taxi drivers in Alberta.[17] A new attempt to unionise drivers was undertaken in 1989[18] in Quebec, but it also failed.[19]

A decade later, when the *Act respecting transportation by taxi*[20] was adopted in 1983, the government sought to open up new markets for the industry in the area of adapted and medical transportation and proposed a new division of responsibilities through a decentralisation of powers to the municipalities.[21] However, the industry was reluctant to develop these new market niches. Rather, it was concerned that the number of permits in circulation was too high and was hurting the drivers' incomes. A voluntary buyout programme entirely funded by the permit holders was set up, thus removing 20% of permits in the Montreal agglomeration.[22]

In 2000, the State intervened again, this time to redefine the territory. This reasoning was not trivial, as it determined the potential profit zone for drivers. The Act also proposed an overhaul of the industry's representative institutions, but thisdid not produce the expected results.

In 2005, the Després Report[23] provided an assessment of this new regulatory framework. The first observation involved the failure of the representative

---

15 Quebec's largest city.
16 Martine D'Amours, "Histoire du taxi à Montréal. Plus ça change plus c'est pareil, " *Vie Ouvrière* 157 (1981): 13.
17 Yellow Cab Ltd. v. Board of Industrial Relations, [1980] 2 S.C.R. 772.
18 Union des chauffeurs de taxis, Métallurgistes unis d'Amérique, local 9217 v. Taxi Cartier inc., D.T.E. 89T937 (C.T.).
19 Martine D'Amour, "Des tentatives de s'en sortir" *Vie ouvrière*, 157 (1981): 46–48. Urwana Coiquaud, "Le difficile encadrement juridique des travailleurs autonomes en situation précaire: Le cas des chauffeurs locataires de taxi, " *Relations industrielles* 64, no.1 (2009): 98.
20 Act respecting transportation by taxi, RSQ c. T-11.1.
21 Michel Després, *Rapport sur la Loi concernant les services de transport par taxi* (Québec: Gouvernement du Québec, Bibliothèque nationale, 2005), 5.
22 Michel Trudel, L'offre et la demande dans l'industrie du taxi au Québec. Évaluation du plan de rachat de permis de taxi dans l'agglomération de Montréal (Québec: Gouvernement du Québec, Ministère des Transports, 1988), 1.
23 Després, *Rapport*, 9–10.

institutions established by regulation. It thus recommended the official recognition of other organisations stemming from emerging solidarities, namely the *Regroupement des travailleurs autonomes Métallos* (United Steelworkers' independent workers' association, RTAM[24]) created in 2002 and the *Association haïtienne des travailleurs du taxi* (Haitian taxi drivers' association, AHTT) founded in 1982.[25] The second observation concerned the quality of service. It revealed the uneven quality of the training provided to drivers from one territory to another. It called for the training contents to be updated and standardised. It also called for vehicle modernisation. In this respect, the service intermediaries reiterated their request to have a GPS or on-board computer installed inside the vehicles. The Report also returned to the subject of opening up the market to adapted transportation. It noted the industry's difficulty taking advantage of this opportunity. Last, as regards determining permit quotas for owners and agglomerations, the Report suggested that this responsibility be transferred to the CTQ.

Several of this Report's recommendations were taken up when the legislation was revised in 2009, including a tightening of the rules around illegal taxi transportation and the conditions for becoming a permit holder. Several observations emerged from this brief historical review, which will be explained in the following section.

2 Lessons from history: the need for regulation

Several observations can be brought out regarding the period discussed above. First, with encouragement from the State, the taxi industry emerged from an unstable regulatory period and entered a phase of institutionalisation. Early on, the State actor was crucial in structuring the taxi industry, since the local actors (municipalities, owners, drivers etc.) were unable to form a federation to realise their aspirations. To ensure consumer protection, the State initially took upon itself to centralise and unify the industry. Other actions were then aimed at modernising it by proposing representative institutions. Although the State coordinated these changes, it also sought to co-construct them with its main interlocutors. It thus opened the door to decentralised regulation and encouraged the development of new markets. The numerous reforms undertaken since the 1970s reflect this desire, but also the actors' difficulty grasping this opportunity.

During this pre-Uber period, the state thus acted as an institutional entrepreneur.[26] The adopted regulatory framework aimed to provide quality services. Prerequisites for exercising the occupation of taxi driver were henceforth required and controlled by government or municipal agencies (driver training, vehicle inspection etc.). Supply management was ensured through conditions of entry into the occupation and by controlling the number of permits. When the

---

24 Affiliated with the FTQ, a major Quebec federation of labour.
25 Its mission involves defending its members' civil rights.
26 Crouch, Capitalist diversity and change, 3–4.

number of permits issued generated a surplus of supply resulting in meagre incomes for drivers, mechanisms such as permit buyout or non-renewal of expired permits were put in place. The government also exercised economic controls by setting fares for taxi services. Fares were set with a dual concern for fairness, that is, for both consumers and drivers. It can therefore be concluded that the "QQE framework" was enshrined in the Quebec regulatory framework.

As regards collective organisation on the part of the actors, even though they experienced failures, they managed to gain experience in collective action which would prove very useful when it came to preparing an offensive against Uber. Because, although the regulatory framework was imperfect, the actors were attached to it, especially to the system of permits, whose value gave economic security to their holders. Last, as regards opening up to new markets, this did not materialise due to the lack of conditions for success, such as entrepreneurship, group cohesion, leadership and marketing capabilities.[27] Uber, which better meets these criteria, would partly disrupt the taxi industry in Montreal.

III The advent of Uber: a reconfiguration of regulatory and institutional frameworks

In the fall of 2014, Uber began operating in Quebec. Through its platform, the multinational company allowed individuals, without a taxi driver's or taxi owner's permit, to provide transportation services for a fee. For a while, it was able to evade the applicable regulations, claiming that it was simply a "tech firm" in the service of the "sharing" economy. However, these claims were undermined by the courts.[28] In fact, Revenu Québec was able to successfully claim that Uber Canada was helping its drivers avoid paying sales taxes by using a subterfuge that described its services as a citizen carpooling service, whereas its activities actually constituted remunerated transportation services covered by a regulatory framework (1). However, the real denouement took place on the legislative scene. In 2016, a novel regulatory mechanism was put in place to allow Uber to operate under a regime that was distinct from the traditional framework. This experimental phase can be described as layering when new rules are attached to old rules, which, in all likelihood, should lead to a re-regulation of the regulatory framework (2).

1 From dismay to first actions

When Uber entered the Quebec market, some actors, including the Mayor of Montreal, declared this activity illegal. Faced with the government's inaction,

---

27 Michel Trudel, "The Fundamentals of Taxi Regulation and the Quebec Experience" (presentation at the 7th Congress of the European Taxi Confederation, Donostia-San Sebastian, Spain, 20 February 1995).

28 "One cannot claim that one's business is beyond the reach of the law on the basis that one is operating in violation of the clear and unambiguous terms of the law" (trans.) in *Uber Canada inc.* c. *Agence du revenu du Québec*, 2016 QCCS 2158 (CanLII), paragraph 204 (leave to appeal refused, 2016 QCCA 1303 (CanLII).

taxi drivers, taxi owners, the RTAM, the regulatory authorities and other actors joined forces and coordinated several collective actions in 2014, which involved demonstrating, strengthening the fight against illegal transportation, seizing 400 vehicles, demanding that the Minister of Transport suspend the permits of illegal drivers and resorting to the courts.

During this time, in 2015, and with little opposition, a new provision[29] of the *Act respecting transportation services by taxi* (ARTST) was adopted under section 89.1. Through its wording, the Minister of Transport may authorise any person or body which is a holder of a permit to establish temporary pilot projects designed to experiment or innovate in the industry, in compliance with standards and rules that this person or body will have negotiated and that differ from those set out in this Act and the regulations. In other words, the Minister may authorise a third party to penetrate into this industry for a purpose determined and assessed by the government without being bound by the full constraints of the regulatory framework governing it. This legislative addition marked a first step in the legalisation of Uber's operations.

A new step was taken with the announcement, in February 2016, of the holding of a parliamentary committee on remunerated passenger transportation by automobile. In search of a compromise, the Minister announced that technological innovation cannot be avoided and that supply management may have come to an end. He aspired to review the regulatory framework to preserve a "fair, competitive and innovative business environment and eliminate tax evasion"[30] (trans.). Four issues were to be discussed: (1) the maintaining of state responsibilities to ensure the safety of users; (2) the quality of customer services; (3) the creation of a fair business environment; and (4) the emergence of new business models facilitated by new technologies. A bill was tabled in May 2016. In the meantime, the traditional industry's actors demonstrated in favour of maintaining the *status quo* of the regulatory framework and expressed openness to respond better to customers' needs.[31] Finally, the legislation was adopted in June 2016 – a gag order, essentially to allow the government to recover Uber's unpaid sales and income taxes.[32] Moreover, "The final version […] provides for the launch, within three months, of a pilot project with Uber – a last-minute addition, which made some drivers fear the introduction of a two-tier system

---

29 An Act to amend various legislative provisions mainly concerning shared transportation, SQ 2015, c 16, section 11. www.assnat.qc.ca/fr/travaux-parlementaires/commissions/cte-41-1/journal-debats/CTE-150604.html#_Toc443379166.
30 Ministère des transports et de la Mobilité Durable et de l'Electrification des transports, *Document d'information sur le transport rémunéré de personnes par automobile* (Québec: Gouvernement du Québec, 2016) 2, accessed 20 February 2019, www.transports.gouv.qc.ca/fr/ministere/acces-information-renseignements-personnels/documents-reglement-diffusion/demande-acces/Documents/2016/05/lai-2016-2017-018-document-information-transport.pdf.
31 Association Haïtienne des Travailleurs du Taxi (AHTT), *Mémoire, Consultations particulières sur le transport rémunéré de personnes par automobile* (Montréal: AHTT, 2016), 4–5.
32 Radio Canada, "Le projet de loi sur l'industrie du taxi adopté sous le bâillon." Accessed 20 February 2019, https://ici.radio-canada.ca/nouvelle/786828/taxi-uber-loi-baillon-couillard-khadir-chauffeurs.

of which Uber would come out the winner"[33] (trans.). Some organisations, including the RTAM, saw this legislation as a reversal by the government and were disappointed and angry when it was passed.

What did this reform provide for? Several provisions accommodated Uber. They broadened the definition of in-service intermediary to include requests for taxi transportation services using a digital platform, as was the case with Uber. Moreover, while the CTQ retained the prerogative to issue permits, it lost to the government the prerogative to establish the maximum number of taxi owner's permits and determine the agglomerations. To sum up, this legislation unlocked a number of regulatory obstacles to Uber's arrival by centralising supply management within the government and liberalising the definition of taxi transportation service intermediary. At the same time, it punished illegal taxi transportation services more severely by substantially increasing fines while clearly defining voluntary transportation and carpooling.

On September 30, 2016, a ministerial order presented the terms and conditions of the pilot project[34] created via the Agreement-in-Principle negotiated between the Government of Quebec and Uber.[35] To meet the requirements of the pilot project, Uber had to obtain the status of taxi transportation service intermediary,[36] a status that allowed it to fulfil a role prescribed by the Act, and thus legitimised its place in the industry.[37] The government facilitated Uber's task[38] by amending the *Regulation respecting transportation services by taxi*, removing certain conditions to be respected and suspending the public hearing on Uber's application for an intermediary's permit. Thus, on 21 October 2016, the CTQ had no choice but to issue an intermediary's permit to Uber.[39] The traditional actors brought the matter before the CTQ,[40] complaining that they had been prevented from presenting their observations and formulating their objection to this application for a permit. However, this action was in vain.

33 Radio Canada, "Des chauffeurs de taxi abasourdis par l'adoption du projet de loi 100." Accessed 20 February 2019, https://ici.radio-canada.ca/nouvelle/786914/uber-loi-baillon-taxi-chauffeurs-industrie-reactions.
34 *Order number 2016-16 of the Minister of Transport, Sustainable Mobility and Transport Electrification dated 30 September 2016*, (2016) 148 Gazette officielle du Québec, II, No. 39A, 5247A, accessed 20 February 2019, www.ctq.gouv.qc.ca/fileadmin/documents/publications/Arrete_Ministeriel_UBER.pdf. www.ctq.gouv.qc.ca/taxi/projets_pilotes_dans_le_secteur_du_transport_par_taxi.html.
35 Agreement signed between the Ministère du Transport and the General Manager of Uber Canada Inc. on 9 September 2016.
36 "Entente," ministre des Transports, de la Mobilité durable et de l'Électrification des transports, accessed 20 February 2019, www.transports.gouv.qc.ca/fr/salle-de-presse/nouvelles/Documents/2016-09-09/entente-uber.pdf
37 www.pes.ctq.gouv.qc.ca/pes/faces/dossierclient/voirdecision.html?decision=81832.
38 O.C. *919-2016* (2016) 148 Gazette officielle du Québec, II, n. 42A, 5637A, accessed 20 February 2019, www2.publicationsduquebec.gouv.qc.ca/dynamicSearch/telecharge.php?type=1&file=65646.pdf.
39 Section 7, paragraph 2, *Taxi Transportation Regulation*, RSQR c S-6.01, r 3.
40 Comité provincial de concertation et de développement de l'industrie du taxi et Uber Canada inc., 2017 QCCTQ 224 (CanLII).

Although the government forced Uber into line by imposing on it a role as a service intermediary, it did not enforce the rules underlying this role in Uber's case. These regulatory amendments thus allowed Uber to emerge from illegality and operate under tailor-made rules. These substantive provisions can be found in the pilot project examined in the next section.

2 The pact between Uber and the government and institutional and regulatory changes: a tailor-made pilot project

While it took many decades for the taxi industry to acquire a regulatory and institutional framework, it took only one player to deconstruct this framework. We will first review the context and framework principles of the pilot project (2.1.), then examine in depth its content (2.2.) and end with a discussion of the effects of this regulatory experimentation (2.3.).

2.1 The Uber Pilot Project: context, principles and government justification

Since 2015, the government has authorised the implementation of pilot projects in the taxi transportation industry. The pilot project devoted to Uber,[41] based on a prior Agreement negotiated between the two protagonists, includes a statement of principles reproduced here for subsequent discussion:

> WHEREAS the principles that guide government decisions on pilot project authorization: fair competition; absence of major impacts on the stability of the value of permits; improvement of user services; integration of new technologies; transparency in fare setting; measures ensuring the safety of users; maintaining the notion of a single regime of remunerated passenger transportation; [emphasis added] (trans.).

This pilot project was established for a maximum period of two years, with a possible extension of up to one year. In 2017,[42] the date of its renewal, changes were made to it. Then, in 2018, the project was extended until 14 October 2019 by government order[43] without amendment. However, an element in this order

---

41 "Pilot project concerning remunerated passenger transportation services requested exclusively using a mobile application (Uber).". Accessed 20 February 2019, www.ctq.gouv.qc.ca/taxi/projets_pilotes_dans_le_secteur_du_transport_par_taxi.html.
42 Accessed 20 February 2019, www.ctq.gouv.qc.ca/fileadmin/documents/secteurs/taxi/Arrete_Projet_pilote_taxi_-_29_septembre_2017.pdf;www.transports.gouv.qc.ca/fr/entreprises-partenaires/entreprises-taxi/Pages/projets-pilotes-taxi.aspx; www2.publicationsduquebec.gouv.qc.ca/dynamicSearch/telecharge.php?type=1&file=69546.pdf.
43 *Order number 2018-23 of the Minister of Transport, Sustainable Mobility and Transport Electrification dated 10 October 2018*, (2018) 150 Gazette officielle du Québec, No. 41A, II, 5027A, accessed 20 February 2019, www2.publicationsduquebec.gouv.qc.ca/dynamicSearch/telecharge.php?type=1&file=69546.pdf.

should be underscored: namely, the justification for a further extension of the project Agreement. It is important to note that this occurred in the context of a change of government and thus prefigured the new government's policies. This Agreement, in part, reads as follows:

> CONSIDERING that, in the opinion of the Minister, the urgency due to the following circumstances justifies the coming into force on 14 October 2018:
> — it is expedient to maintain the Pilot project in force to collect and analyze additional information on the services offered by Uber Canada inc., in particular in respect of the safety and quality of the services, and to continue the study of the impact on the transportation services by taxi in order to define the standards that will apply to that area;
> Uber Canada inc. is the sole holder of a transportation service intermediary's permit for the purposes of the Pilot project and has seen a constant increase of its activities, in particular in the regions of Montréal and Québec [City]. The end or the interruption of the services of Uber Canada inc. in Quebec would have a definite impact on the quality and availability of the remunerated passenger transportation services, that would be jeopardized given the reduction of the provision of service, which would have immediate consequences on the mobility of persons; [emphasis added].[44]

Through these words, Uber gained political and economic legitimacy. Indeed, a return to the traditional model as desired by the industry's actors would now be difficult. Moreover, these actors' reaction was quick: "… everyone was talking about fairness, even the elected Premier […]. And people have been crying out for two years that this pilot project is not fair"[45] (trans.). Let us now examine this pilot project.

2.2 The content of the pilot project: creating a "temporary" experimental two-tier regime

Despite the government's statement of principles in both the Agreement and the content of the pilot project, the temporary regime creates a separate class of drivers for Uber. It allows the latter to operate according to new conditions for permit issuance by applying a pricing policy that is distinct from that which applies to traditional drivers and by adopting less stringent standards of entry into the occupation. A two-tier regime was thus created, legitimising the iniquity between traditional drivers and Uber.

---

44 Id.
45 Lia Lévesque, "Le projet-pilote d'Uber prolongé, les chauffeurs de taxi déçus," *La Presse.ca*, 12 October 2018, accessed 20 February 2019, www.lapresse.ca/affaires/economie/transports /201810/12/01-5200000-le-projet-pilote-duber-prolonge-les-chauffeurs-de-taxi-decus.php.

First, the government revisited the way supply is considered by introducing new drivers into the market, not just by adding new available permits, but by reinterpreting these permits in terms of a number of shareable hours, thus allowing the multinational company to distribute this number of hours among "partners-drivers" who no longer need to obtain a taxi driver's permit.

Second, the fares applied by Uber do not fully comply with the regulatory framework imposed on the traditional industry's actors, as shown in Table 2.1.

Thus, Uber enjoys threefold flexibility in its pricing system, offering a range of services, adding fees charged to the customer and varying prices depending on demand (surging price), the parameters of which it alone determines through algorithms. In many respects, this pricing system violates the government's statement of principle regarding respect for fair competition.

Besides unfair competition due to the fact that taxi drivers do not operate under the same regulatory framework, there is also a lack of transparency in pricing. Indeed, stories of customers being caught unawares by Uber's fares[46] have been the subject of news articles, revealing that control over costs has weakened to

Table 2.1 Comparison of fares for a traditional taxi and Uber in 2016 and 2019

	Traditional taxi	*Uber*			
2016					
Base fare	$3.45	$3.45/$2.50 Uber X			
		Booking fee: $1.30			
Per Km	$1.70	$0.85/$0.79 Uber X			
Waiting time/min	$0.63	$0.20/$0.19 Uber X			
		(9% of trip for operating expenses in Quebec)			
		UberX	*Uber XL*	*Uber Select*	*Taxi*[a]
2019					
Base fare	$3.50	1.90	4.30	4.30	3.45
Per Km	$1.75	0.79	1.33	1.75	1.70
Waiting time/min	$0.65	0.19	0.22	0.27	0.63
Minimum fare	X	6.80	8.80	8.80	3.45
Booking fee	X	2.10	2.10	2.10	X
Cancellation fee	X	5.00	5.00	5.00	5.00

a The Uber site consulted in January 2019 did not post the increase in fares already decided by the CTQ and in force since 1 June 2018, following representations made by the traditional industry during a public consultation ordered by the CTQ (fares had not been increased since 2012) and approved in Decision 2018 QCCTQ 0740 www.ctq.gouv.qc.ca/fileadmin/documents/Decision/2018QCCTQ0740.pdf.

46 Marie-Christine Noël, "Jour de l'An très coûteux pour des clients d'Uber," *Le Journal de Montréal*, 4 January 2016, accessed 20 February 2019, www.journaldemontreal.com/2016/01/04/jour-de-lan-tres-couteux-pour-des-clients-duber; Améli Pineda, "Juripop exige qu'Uber rembourse ses clients," *Le journal de Montréal*, 8 January 2016, accessed 20 February 2019, www.journaldemontreal.com/2016/01/08/juripop-exige-quuber-rembourse-ses-clients.

the detriment of consumers and that one of the regulatory pillars – economic controls – has been abandoned:

> ... the industry cannot operate with open access for supply as it would lead to lower efficiencies, falling wages and unacceptable externalities; and that the market for taxi trips is a thin one, which means that incumbents should receive regulatory protection in exchange for providing acceptable services at slim margins.
>
> (Harding et al. 2018:18)

Third, when the pilot project was extended in 2017, while some changes were made to increase passenger safety under Uber, the stricter requirements for traditional drivers remained in place. Thus, the new version of the pilot project provides for an increase of 15 hours of training (for a total of 35 hours) for new Uber partners-drivers. As shown in Table 2.2, although the rule was tightened, this requirement is still well below that imposed on traditional drivers.

Fourth, the new version of the pilot project has, however, tightened the security requirements. Thus, Uber now has to check the criminal records of its drivers in a database operated by the Ministère de la Justice. Previously, Uber could call on a private security firm to do this. The multinational company now has to comply with the requirements of the traditional industry. The same goes for mechanical inspections.

The coexistence of these two regulatory frameworks has allowed the government to make adjustments (strengthening standards in one case while relaxing them in the other), while also allowing the two protagonists to get to know one another, enabling a smoother cohabitation. Let us now examine the concrete effects of the pilot project.

Table 2.2 Comparison of training requirements for traditional drivers and Uber drivers in 2017

Traditional taxi drivers	Uber partners-drivers
Training (provided by certified establishments) 120 hours (90 hours on toponymy and geography; 53 hours of basic training; 7 hours on transportation of persons with disabilities) Cost: $1,200 On 21 September 2017, the government adopted a new pilot project that reduces the number of training hours to 35 and privatises the process, with service intermediaries or permit owners now being permitted to deliver the training themselves and assess the knowledge acquired.[47]	Training: 20 hours before 2017 and 35 hours as of 2017; Uber itself provides training to its partners-drivers and validates the knowledge acquired

47 Arrêté numéro 2017-08 du ministre des Transports, de la Mobilité durable et de l'Électrification des transports en date du 24 août 2017, (2017) 149 Gazette officielle du Québec, II, No. 36, 4008, accessed February 20, 2019, www.ctq.gouv.qc.ca/fileadmin/documents/secteurs/taxi/Arrete_Ministeriel_20170907.pdf.

2.3 Effects of the pilot project: institutional and regulatory disruption, and the courts' response

To date, the regulatory experimentation generated by the pilot project has led to an institutional change, as demonstrated in the following section. Although Uber's arrival, assisted by the government, has undermined the regulatory regime in place, we cannot speak of deregulation, since the regulation for traditional drivers has remained intact. Nevertheless, the pilot project is a clear attack on the existing regime in the taxi industry and its basis, that is, the "QQE Framework" aimed at ensuring the safety of users, and the predictability of fares and wages through a control of supply and fare setting. To sum up, the two regimes coexist and the more recent one, the pilot project, appears to have altered the virtues and validity of the pre-existing regime. While traditional taxi drivers have not found support from the government or the legislator, it appears that their salvation might come from court action.

TEMPORARY EXPERIMENTATION: BUT WHAT EXPERIMENTATION?

The pilot project will have lasted three years in all. The Minister justified its last extension based on "the urgency due to the circumstances", declaring that it was "expedient to maintain the Pilot project in force" for two reasons. The first one, to collect and analyse additional information on the services offered by Uber, in particular in respect of the safety and quality of services; to continue the study of the impact on the transportation services by taxi in order to define the standards which will apply to that area. However, no government data has filtered through to date, although the negative effects on traditional drivers are obvious.

The second reason put forward by the government was the importance of Uber on the Quebec scene, asserting that "the end or the interruption of the services of Uber Canada inc. in Quebec would have a definite impact on the quality and availability of the remunerated passenger transportation services [and] immediate consequences on the mobility of persons". These alarmist and peremptory remarks are puzzling, when the figures examined reveal the disastrous impact of Uber's arrival on the value of permits and the supply of services. Whereas nine bankruptcies were noted between 2011 and 2014, this number increased to 27 between 2015 and 2017.[48] On the Island of Montreal, a 38.6% decrease in the value of taxi owners' permits was observed between January 2014 and June 2017, from $192,694 to $118,375, respectively.[49] Based on these facts, several applications for authorisation to institute class actions were filed.[50] Since

---

[48] Matthieu Payen, "Les faillites de chauffeurs de taxi ont triplé depuis Uber," TVA Nouvelles, 23 March 2018, accessed 20 February 2019, www.tvanouvelles.ca/2018/03/23/les-faillites-de-chauffeurs-de-taxi-ont-triple-depuis-uber.
[49] Accessed 20 February 2019, www.transports.gouv.qc.ca/fr/entreprises-partenaires/entreprises-taxi/Documents/rapport-ministre.pdf.
[50] Infra.

then, the government has paid taxi owners compensation for the drop in the value of their permits, up to 56% of the loss estimated by the agglomerations.[51] According to some industry spokespersons,[52] the compensation offered by the government at taxpayers' expense is a way to legitimise or subsidise Uber, but especially to consider Uber's arrival as an opportunity to transform a taxi industry that was having a hard time renewing itself.

WILL THIS REGULATORY EXPERIMENTATION DISRUPT THE POSITION OF TRADITIONAL ACTORS? IT APPEARS SO

The proposals made by the traditional actors to introduce a pilot project that was more respectful of the regulatory framework were not considered by the government, thus undermining their position in the industry. In addition, the procedures for connecting people via the Uber platform do not refer to the traditional industry actors. The platform ousts the latter by becoming, with the State's complicity, an intermediary of services, thus avoiding dealing with the existing institutional structures and the actors associated with them.[53] It creates a circular system for connecting customers with drivers. It thus gets rid of the existing regulatory constraints and can grow through the support of a clientele that was conquered very early on, by illegally competing with the industry in place.

As for the traditional industry actors, their power is atomised because of their status as self-employed workers, their lack of solidarity and their methods of service provision, which offer them little space for exchange. Therefore, it is as if the facts of the debate, which nevertheless relate to an industry that is more than 100 years old, dismiss the traditional institutions and the actors involved, leaving only the State and Uber to decide on the regulation they are free to adopt.

This freedom of action, acquired through regulatory experimentation, has served as a transformational vector to carve out a place for the multinational company and induce the taxi industry to become more flexible and modernise. It took real political will to undertake these changes. Indeed, although this intention appeared to be vague at the beginning, it soon clearly emerged. The new legislation proposed a centralisation of powers to the government's advantage. In the midst of this crisis, the traditional actors organised and united to defend their interests in the streets and before the courts. And although their influence did not prevent deregulation, it undoubtedly softened it. However, one unknown remains, namely the outcome of the court actions initiated by the various industry stakeholders dissatisfied with the government's favoured treatment of Uber.

---

51 Stéphanie Marin, "Jusqu'à 46 700$ d'indemnité par permis de taxi, " *Le Devoir*, 18 August 2018, accessed 20 February 2019, www.ledevoir.com/politique/quebec/534775/quebec-octroie-une-aide-de-250-millions-a-l-industrie-du-taxi.
52 Patrick Bellerose, "Québec va compenser l'industrie du taxi, " *Le Journal de Québec*, 22 September 2017, accessed 20 February 2019, www.journaldequebec.com/2017/09/22/uber-le-projet-pilote-prolonge-dun-an.
53 Infra.

Court action: a path to salvation?

Although for a long time there was little solidarity among the traditional actors, this situation changed following Uber's arrival. In fact, faced with the government's inaction and disengagement from them, the traditional taxi drivers and owners energetically mobilised before the courts, both individually and collectively (mainly the "Common Front", including organisations such as the RTAM and the AHTT).

While some actions were unsuccessful,[54] others were successful, in particular the applications for authorisation to institute a class action against Uber,[55] the Attorney General of Quebec (AGQ) and the Government of Quebec.[56] In the first decision, the Superior Court authorised the plaintiff to represent all natural or legal persons holding a taxi owner's permit or taxi driver's permit since 28 October 2014, in a class action for damages to compensate for the taxi owners' and drivers' loss of income and the loss of value of the taxi owners' permits. In the second decision, the Court authorised a class action against the AGQ and the Government in the course of a civil liability action. The plaintiff will have to show among other things that Uber and its drivers were operating in violation of the regulation, and that the AGQ and the Government have allowed and tolerated a situation whereby Uber and its drivers unfairly compete with the traditional actors, giving rise to their civil liability. At this stage, the Court must determine whether it authorises the action. It will thus assess the application on its merits, in particular by examining whether the alleged facts are held to be true. This therefore represents a first victory.

Second, in 2017, the RTAM, AHTT and other groups sought to have the Agreement-in-Principle and the pilot project cancelled. These applications were rejected by the Superior Court, but the decisions were appealed.[57] Thus, the Court of Appeal will have to rule on the legality of the pilot project.[58] In the meantime, the authorisation to institute a class action against the AGQ and the Government of Quebec is suspended.[59]

---

54 *Regroupement des travailleurs autonomes Métallos, section locale 9840* c. *Québec (Procureure générale)*, 2016 QCCS 4491 (the Superior Court rejects the application for a provisional injunction seeking to suspend the application of the Agreement on the Pilot Project); *Regroupement des travailleurs autonomes Métallos, section locale 9840* c. *Uber Technologies inc.*, 2016 QCCS 4626 (the Superior Court rejects the application for an interlocutory provisional injunction ordering the Minister to suspend the implementation of the Agreement with Uber Canada Inc.).
55 Jean-Paul c. Uber Technologies inc., 2017 QCCS 164, par. 48.
56 Metellus c. Procureure générale du Québec, 2018 QCCS 4626.
57 Regroupement des travailleurs autonomes Métallos, section locale 9840 c. Uber Technologies Inc., Regroupement des travailleurs autonomes Métallos, section locale 9840 c. Procureur générale du Québec, 2017 QCCS 4447 (CanLII); The de bene esse application for authorization to appeal is deferred to the panel of the Court that will hear the appeal, 2017 QCCA 2056.
58 *Id.*
59 Metellus c. Procureure générale du Québec, 2018 QCCS 4626, paragraph 172.

IV Conclusions

We will conclude this chapter by going back to the three questions raised at the beginning. First, why has a temporary regulation, parallel to that which exists in the taxi industry, been introduced in Quebec to accommodate Uber? This can be explained by the involvement of the actors, the foremost of which has been the State. Moreover, is the State not the very same actor that has for decades been compensating for the industry's deficiencies? However, this actor is not neutral in its intervention. It has a right of veto that allows it to impose its vision. Over the years, its concerns have evolved. Before Uber's arrival, these concerns were structured around safety, fare setting and supply management (QQE Framework) while encouraging the industry's actors to become independent and develop a vision and collective action. With Uber, the State paid less attention to the taxi industry stakeholders. Yet, the latter were willing to modernise their industry without abandoning the institutional framework that gave them a degree of security in an already precarious environment. The State favoured technological innovation and competition, probably attracted by the offer of the multinational company Uber and sensitive to its pressures, in particular the threat that it might leave the province. Faced with little support from the State and having limited power of influence, the traditional actors were able to avoid the worst – deregulation – at least during the pilot project through their collective and court actions. Recent government policies, however, suggest that a more substantial transformation of these institutions is in the pipeline.

The second finding is that this regulatory experimentation has nevertheless led to a strengthening of solidarities among the traditional industry actors and a more effective organisation of their actions. In the face of adversity, it was easier to get them to join forces. Still, the pilot project has weakened the traditional taxi drivers. The value of their permits, their "pension funds" as they refer to them, has significantly decreased. Moreover, despite a discourse on the need to preserve equity in both regimes, the reality has been quite different. Even though it was said that there would be "no major impacts on the stability of the value of permits" or "fair competition", the traditional actors have been abandoned by a State that, it must be said, imposed on them a regime of permits, fare setting and training obligations – requirements with which they have complied. Thus, the iniquity goes far beyond the simple content of the pilot project. It extends to the very value which the State attaches to these actors compared to the importance accorded to a US multinational company.

What lessons can be learned from this experience? A critical look at this regulation reveals that, while it effectively enables the government to assess a complex situation requiring the collection of reliable data, it may also have been used as a strategic tool to temper disputes. It may also have long-term structuring effects through a layering of regulatory frameworks, inducing a process of re-regulation which could lead to less abrupt, slower deregulation but would be more difficult to oppose. However, this conclusion will need to be qualified based on the outcome of the various court actions regarding the legality of the Agreement and the pilot project as well as the class actions instituted against Uber, the Attorney General of Quebec and the Government of Quebec.

V Bibliography

Association Haïtienne des Travailleurs du Taxi (AHTT). *Mémoire, Consultations particulières sur le transport rémunéré de personnes par automobile.* Montréal: AHTT, 2016.

Bar-Siman-Tov, Ittai. "Temporary legislation, better regulation, and experimentalist governance: An empirical study." *Regulation & Governance*, 12 (2018): 192–219.

Bellerose, Patrick. "Québec va compenser l'industrie du taxi." *Le Journal de Québec*, September 22, 2017. Accessed February 20, 2019, www.journaldequebec.com/2017/09/22/uber-le-projet-pilote-prolonge-dun-an.

Coiquaud, Urwana. "Le difficile encadrement juridique des travailleurs autonomes en situation précaire: Le cas des chauffeurs locataires de taxi." *Relations industrielles*, 64, no 1 (2009): 95–111.

Collier, Ruth B., Veena Dubal, and Christopher L. Carter. "Disrupting Regulation, Regulating Disruption: The Politics of Uber in the United States." *Perspectives on Politics* 16 (2018): 919–937.

Cooper James, Ray Mundy, and John Nelson. *Taxi! Urban Economics and the Social & Transport Impacts of the Taxicab.* Farnham, United Kingdom: Ashgate, 2010.

Crouch, Colin. *Capitalist Diversity and Change: Recombinant Governance and Institutional Entrepreneurs.* New York: Oxford, 2005.

D'Amour, Martine. "Histoire du taxi à Montréal. Plus ça change plus c'est pareil." *Vie ouvrière* 31 (nov. 1981): 7–13.

D'Amour, Martine. "Des tentatives de s'en sortir." *Vie ouvrière* 31 (Nov. 1981): 46–48.

Derek McKee, Finn Makela and Teresa Scassa, eds. *Law and the "Sharing Economy".* Ottawa: Les Presses de l'Université d'Ottawa, 2018.

Després, Michel. *Rapport sur la Loi concernant les services de transport par taxi.* Québec: Gouvernement du Québec, Bibliothèque nationale, 2005.

Domenech-Pascual, Gabriel. "Sharing Economy and Regulatory Strategies towards Legal Change." *European Journal of Risk Regulation* 7, no 4 (2016): 717–727.

Gourévitch, Peter. "Étude comparative des réactions des Grandes Puissances face à la crise économique de 1873 à 1896." *Études internationales* 6, no 2 (1975): 188–219.

Harding, Simon, Milind Kandlikar, and Sumeet Gulati. "Taxi Apps, Regulation, and the Market for Taxi Journeys." *Transportation Research Part A* 88 (2016): 15–25.

Lévesque, Lia. "Le projet-pilote d'Uber prolongé, les chauffeurs de taxi déçus." *La Presse.ca*, October 12, 2018. Accessed February 20, 2019. www.lapresse.ca/affaires/economie/transports/201810/12/01-5200000-le-projet-pilote-duber-prolonge-les-chauffeurs-de-taxi-decus.php.

Maggetti, Martino. "The Role of Independent Regulatory Agencies in Policy-Making: A Comparative Analysis." *Journal of European Public Policy* 16, no 3 (2009): 450–470.

Mahoney, James, and Kathleen Thelen. *Explaining Institutional Change.* New York: Cambridge University Press, 2009.

Marin, Stéphanie. "Jusqu'à 46 700$ d'indemnité par permis de taxi." *Le Devoir*, August 18, 2018. Accessed February 20, 2019, www.ledevoir.com/politique/quebec/534775/quebec-octroie-une-aide-de-250-millions-a-l-industrie-du-taxi.

Ministère des transports et de la Mobilité Durable et de l'Electrification des transports. *Document d'information sur le transport rémunéré de personnes par automobile.* Québec : Gouvernement du Québec, 2016. Accessed February 20, 2019, www.transports. gouv.qc.ca/fr/ministere/acces-information-renseignements-personnels/documents-reglement-diffusion/demande-acces/Documents/2016/05/lai-2016-2017-018-document-information-transport.pdf.

Ministère des transports et de la Mobilité Durable et de l'Electrification des transports. *Entente entre Le ministre des Transports, de la Mobilité durable et de l'Électrification des transports, monsieur Laurent Lessard, dûment autorisé en vertu de la Loi sur le ministère des Transports (chapitre M-28) et Uber Canada inc., ayant une place d'affaires au 1751 rue Richardson, bureau 7, Montréal H3K 1G6, représenté par monsieur Jean-Nicolas Guillemette, dûment autorisé, tel qu'il le déclaré.* Québec: Gouvernement du Québec, 2016, accessed February 20, 2019, www.transports.gouv.qc.ca/fr/salle-de-presse/nouvelles/Documents/2016-09-09/entente-uber.pdf.

Noël, Marie-Christine. "Jour de l'An très coûteux pour des clients d'Uber." *Le Journal de Montréal*, January 4, 2016. Accessed February 20, 2019. www.journaldemontreal.com/2016/01/04/jour-de-lan-tres-couteux-pour-des-clients-duber.

Payen, Matthieu. "Les faillites de chauffeurs de taxi ont triplé depuis Uber." *TVA Nouvelles*, March 23, 2018. Accessed February 20, 2019. www.tvanouvelles.ca/2018/03/23/les-faillites-de-chauffeurs-de-taxi-ont-triple-depuis-uber.

Pineda, Améli. "Juripop exige qu'Uber rembourse ses clients." *Le Journal de Montréal*, January 8, 2016. Accessed February 20, 2019. www.journaldemontreal.com/2016/01/08/juripop-exige-quuber-rembourse-ses-clients.

Rauch, Daniel E., and David Schleicher. "Like Uber, but for Local Governmental Policy: The Future of Local Regulation of the 'Sharing Economy'." *George Mason Law & Economics Research Paper* 15, no 1 (2015): 1–61. Accessed February 20, 2019. doi:10.2139/25499919.

Thelen, Kathleen. "Regulating Uber: The Politics of the Platform Economy in Europe and the United States." *Perspectives on Politics* 16, no 4 (2018): 938–953.

Trudel, Michel. *L'offre et la demande dans l'industrie du taxi au Québec. Évaluation du plan de rachat de permis de taxi dans l'agglomération de Montréal.* Québec: Gouvernement du Québec, Ministère des Transports, 1988.

Trudel, Michel. "The Fundamentals of Taxi Regulation and the Quebec Experience." Paper presented at the 7th Congress of the European Taxi Confederation, Donostia-San Sebastian, Spain, February 1995.

Van Gestel, Rob, and Gijs van Dijck. "Better Regulation through Experimental Legislation." *European Public Law* 17, no 3 (2011): 539–553.

3 Comparative study on Japanese employment-like working style

Whether we are discussing the same phenomenon or not

Qi Zhong

I Introduction

In recent years, due to advancements in science technology and more detailed work manuals, it has become possible to guarantee the quality of the labour benefit outcome to some extent without directly supervising the process of the labour benefits of workers. Therefore, as a social phenomenon, many new forms of work have occurred, that is, received "labour outcome" instead of receiving "labour" itself, letting a third party receive labour instead of directly receiving it, entering the parties of workers and employers as an intermediary in receiving labour and receiving a brokerage commission, and so on. Traditional labour regulations, which are based on the idea that "employers pay a certain amount of compensation in return for the receipt of work", are under pressure, making it necessary to undertake a drastic review.

Nevertheless, this social phenomenon does not necessarily occur in all countries of the world, and even in countries where this phenomenon has already appeared, there are substantial differences in the specific form and its spreading speed. Traditional labour policy research mainly deals with one-to-one relationships between worker and employer, but new forms of work are not only limited to bilateral relationships[1] but encompass also multilateral relationships,[2] especially tripartite relationships.[3]

Studies on new forms of work being carried out in various countries do not necessarily capture this issue from the same viewpoint, which is evidenced also by the various names given to this social phenomenon.[4]

While foreign countries are actively developing discussions on new forms of work, Japan regarded this phenomenon as a form of working style reform and named it "Employment-like Working Style". Since October 2017, the Employment

---

1 For example, to change labour relationships to contracting or delegating relationships.
2 Multilayered contracting, supply chain and more.
3 For example, to separately establish a contractual employer or to participate as a mediator.
4 Fissured workplace, fragmentation, crowdwork, gig economy, sharing economy, platform economy and so on.

Environment and Equalisation Bureau of the Ministry of Health, Labour and Welfare has established the "Study Group on Employment-like Working Style" and released a report on 30 March 2018.[5]

In the report, the concept of workers in Japan and the regulations applied to them are compiled, the scope and extension examples of the workers' concepts in other countries are introduced, the current situation of employment-like working style in Japan is analysed and several opinions on specific protection methods are cited. It has been pointed out that, in view of the diversity of workers and other service providers, it is necessary to grasp and analyse the detailed situation of employment-like working style in Japan and to investigate the details and operations of various foreign systems.

However, as can be seen from the difference in naming, research on "Employment-like Working Style" does not necessarily set concern and scope of study to be the same with other countries. In Japan, many forms of work such as multi-layered contracting in the building industry, subcontracting in the manufacturing industry and so on have been used for a long time. However, whether these types of work, which traditionally were classified as self-employment, should be regarded as part of "Employment-like Working Style" has become subject to controversial discussions.

There are two ways of thinking about this point: developing countries such as China will focus only on the platform working style that matches the supply and demand of labour on the internet platform under the name "platform economy" or "sharing economy". It is reasonable that China focused on the platform economy, because labour regulation is still incomplete and there is still little accumulation of laws and theories covering the differences between employment and self-employment. The labour force, which worked originally under self-employment, was absorbed into working style via internet platform as a result of the increase in the sharing economy. Currently, there are only very limited possibilities to pursue an employment-like working style without the use of internet platforms in China.

Meanwhile, as many forms of work recognised as "new" in other countries have been used for a long time; legislation on these forms of work has already been well developed in Japan. In some cases, the difference between those work forms and the one via internet platform is only the medium that matches supply and demand for labour. For example, dispatch in Japan is classified into registered type and regular type dispatch. In case of registered type, the employment period of dispatched workers is linked to the dispatch period, which is decided by the client. When a request for dispatch comes to the labour dispatch agency via telephone or e-mail from the client, the dispatch agency calls or sends an e-mail to the registered worker and concludes an employment contract with the work applicant with the contract period for the dispatch period. In regulating the way of employment-like working style that matches the supply and demand

---

5 "Study Group on Employment-like Working Style Report". www.mhlw.go.jp/file/05-Shingikai-11909500-Koyoukankyoukintoukyoku-Soumuka/0000201113.pdf.

for labour through the internet platform, it is sufficient to refer to regulations on registered dispatch with regard to the question of who should bear the employers' responsibilities.

Therefore, Japan is studying broadly traditional employment and self-employment without limiting the scope of research. For the employment-like working style, Japan tends to respond by modifying the framework of existing legislation.

II Concept of "workers" and concept of "employers", and their extension

1 Judgement criteria of worker and its extension

The definition of worker in the Labour Standards Act constitutes a fundamental concept relevant for the whole individual labour regulations. According to article 9 of the Labour Standards Act, a worker is "someone who is employed at an enterprise or office (hereinafter referred to as 'enterprise') and receives wages from the enterprise, without regard to the kind of occupation".

However, as this definition is abstract, the report of the Labour Standards Act Study Group on 19 December 1985, established certain criteria to determine whether someone is a worker within the scope of the worker definition under the Labour Standards Act. According to this criterion, substantial judgement should be made regardless of the contract form concluded by the parties in judging labour quality. Then, as a general judgement criterion for judging whether a person is a worker under the Labour Standards Act,[6] the criteria with judgement factors of "presence of usage dependency"[7] are established. That is, (1) labour under the supervision of the employer and (2) receiving remuneration as reward for labour.

The concept of economic dependency is often argued as characteristic against usage dependency (human dependency). Economic dependency is based on the idea of unequal negotiating strength resulting, for example, from the non-possession of labour instruments, subordination to the unilateral decision of contract contents. The common opinion in Japan is that economic dependency does not endorse worker nature under Labour Standards Act. In response to this opinion, in order to extend the protection of individual labour relations, it is argued that economically dependent people should also be included even if their usage dependency is low. There is a discussion that certain protection should be exercised with those who have economic dependencies as "quasi-workers".[8] However, since the concept of economic dependency differs depending on the

---

6 "The Report of the Labour Standards Act Study Group." https://jsite.mhlw.go.jp/osaka-roudoukyoku/library/osaka-roudoukyoku/H23/23kantoku/roudousyasei.pdf.

7 Or it can be translated as "subordination" in order to emphasise the meaning of submission and subordination to the employer's command and supervision.

8 "The Report of the Future Way of Labour Contract Legislation Study Group." www.mhlw.go.jp/shingi/2005/09/dl/s0915-4d.pdf.

argument, discussion is still in a state of confusion. Meanwhile, economic dependency is considered as an important factor to determine whether someone is a worker under the Labour Union Act.

2 Approval of worker nature of individual contractors under the Labour Union Act

For those who are nominally under subcontracting contract only for the purpose of providing "deliverables", it is often a problem whether those who provide labour exclusively for the specified companies are "workers". Thus far, none of the "worker nature" under the Labour Standards Act was accepted by the Supreme Court. Meanwhile, technicians repairing the household sink,[9] express couriers delivering documents by bicycle or motorbike[10] and technicians performing on-site musical instrument repair[11] and so forth have been recognised as workers under the Labour Union Act.

3 Employer concept and extension of employers' responsibility beyond juridical personality

The most basic concept of the "employer" under individual labour regulations is that of the employer who has entered into an employment contract with his employee. Article 2 (2) of the Labour Contract Act defines the employer as "a person who pays wages to the workers he/she employs". Usually, the company which the employee joined or the business owner who hired the employee is clearly the counterparty who signed the employment contract; but there are several types of employment in which a plurality of companies is involved on the employer side of employment contract relationship. In these cases, it becomes difficult to determine the employer. In the following, it is proposed to introduce how to decide the employers' responsibility in these cases.

One way to extend employers' responsibility can be the doctrine of "Denying the Legal Entity of the Direct Employer".[12] According to this doctrine, if the juridical personality of a company is becoming mischievous or is abused, its juridical personality can be denied. In a parent-subsidiary relationship, the management of the subsidiary's business and the conduct of work at the level of the subsidiary are sometimes controlled by the parent company. In that case, the subsidiary can be recognised as part of the corporate organisation of the parent company. As a result, the employee of the subsidiary company can argue – based on the doctrine of denying the legal entity of the subsidiary company vis-à-vis

---

9 The Nation and Central Labour Relations Commission (INAX Maintenance) case, the Supreme Court (the Third Petty Bench), 12 April 2011, Rodo Hanrei, no. 1026, p. 27.
10 The Sokuhai case, the Tokyo District Court, 28 April 2010, Rodo Hanrei, no. 1010, p. 25.
11 The Nation and Central Labour Relations Commission (VICTOR) case, the Supreme Court (the Third Petty Bench), 21 February 2012, Minshu, Vol. 66, no. 3, p. 955.
12 The Supreme Court (the First Petty Bench), 27 February 1969, Minshu, Vol. 23, no. 2, p. 511.

the parent company – in favour of the existence of an employment relationship with the parent company.

Another theory to extend employers' responsibility is the "Theory of the Implied Employment Contract". According to Japanese case law,[13] even if there is no explicit contract relationship between a company and a worker, if the worker provides labour to such company and such company has compensated the worker in return, the establishment of an implied employment contract may be approved. However, for such purpose, it is not enough for a worker to only provide labour under the direction and supervision of a company. Moreover, the worker must prove that the company directs and supervises the labour provision of the worker and the company pays wages as compensation for the labour.

The "Theory of the Implied Employment Contract" also applies to other tripartite labour relationships such as worker dispatch relations.[14] Therefore, there is certain likelihood that Japanese courts will apply this theory also to contractual relationships in new forms of work.

III Various phenomena that cannot be explained by traditional legal theory

However, considering new forms of work in foreign countries via internet platforms and regulations applicable to them, there are at least the three phenomena which cannot be explained by traditional Japanese labour law theory:

1 Under certain employment conditions, the parties shall be entitled to determine the contract type

In Japan, in order to establish an employment contract, it is necessary for one party to work for the other party and the other party to pay for such work. As the conduct of work and the payment are clearly defined, whether the contract relationship between the parties falls under the "employment contract" definition or not is judged by the court in consideration of various factors. Even if a contract is titled as a "subcontracting contract", there is a possibility that the relationship between the parties will be recognised as a labour relationship in view of the facts of the case.

Meanwhile, in China, on 14 July 2016, the Ministry of Transportation announced the "Internet reservation taxi management service administrative

---

13 The Daiei image and more case, the Tokyo High Court, 22 December 1993, Rodo Hanrei, no. 664, p. 8.
14 The High Court ruling approved the establishment of an implied employment contract between dispatched worker and client on the ground that they are in disguise contracting or illegal dispatching relationships (the Panasonic Plasma Display (Pasco) case, the Osaka High Court, 25 April 2008, Rodo Hanrei, no. 960, p. 5), but the Supreme Court overruled the judgement (the Panasonic Plasma Display (Pasco) case, the Supreme Court (the Second Petty Bench), 18 December 2009, Minshu, Vol. 63, no. 10, p. 2754).

provisional method" to regulate taxi dispatch services (like Uber). Article 18 thereof provides the following:

> The internet dispatch service platform company guarantees that the driver, who provides the service, has legal employment qualifications, and according to the relevant laws and regulations, depending on characteristics such as working hours, service frequency, etc., in a variety of ways with the driver to conclude a work contract to clarify the rights and obligations of both parties [...].

In China, depending on the intention of the driver and the platform service provider, it is possible to select and conclude either an employment contract or a subcontracting contract. Regardless of the actual situation of work, the choice of the parties becomes legally binding and the court must respect that choice.

Such a concept, which respects the intention of the parties without judging the legal relationship between them based on the factual situation, does not exist in the Japanese labour law.

2 It is not possible to distinguish between primary and secondary jobs, and it is not clear who should bear the employer's responsibility

Employment relationships are typically bilateral, that is, between workers and employers. In case of worker dispatch or multi-layered contracting, the dispatch agency or contractor may enter the relationship as a third party, but the subjects to whom employer's responsibility is imposed is either the dispatch agency/contractor or the person who receives the work result (namely the labour recipient).

However, in case of crowdsourcing, a crowd worker may register on different internet service platforms and receive orders there. Even if the amount of business order from each internet service platform or individual customer is insignificant, when all these orders are combined, the amount of work might be large enough to cause overwork and stress, eventually leading to industrial accidents. In this case, there are multiple labour recipients, and it is not possible to identify whose task is liable for the accident because there is no distinction between primary and secondary jobs, and all operations are carried out simultaneously. How to distribute responsibility among multiple platformer service providers or customers is highly problematic.[15]

3 The perception of working hours has changed

One of the criteria to differentiate between employment and subcontracting contracts is whether remuneration is based on working hours or only on work results. In case of employment contracts, the object of compensation is the labour benefit process and remuneration is calculated by the number of working hours.

---

15 For example, if the driver injured in a traffic accident inadvertently when he is using two mobile phones and planning to be able to receive orders both from Uber and Lyft, who should bear the employer's responsibility?

In employment relationship, the traditional way of thinking is that more remuneration should be paid for more working hours, not directly for more deliverables. The higher the quality of the deliverables, the more the number of deliverables delivered and more working hours are assumed to have been spent. Therefore, even when the amount of compensation in employment relationship varies depending on the quality and the number of deliverables delivered, the remuneration is still paid for the working hours. Meanwhile, in the case of subcontracting relationships, remuneration is not paid for working hours spent to produce deliverables but is paid for the deliverables themselves.

However, in case of crowdsourcing, complicated projects are divided into small tasks. The shorter the time until the crowd worker completes a task, the higher the evaluation the worker receives and the higher the remuneration for each task. In this case, when trying to certify such a work form as employment relationship, the discrepancy between the fewer working hours, the higher remuneration as an actual situation and the traditional way of thinking about "employment relationship", according to which remuneration is paid for the number of working hours, should be resolved first.

IV Relevant Japanese laws and regulations

In the following part, the Japanese laws and regulations relevant for the employment-like working style shall be summarised.

1 Application of the Subcontract Act

Under the Subcontract Act, the primary contractor shall submit a document stating the details of the benefits of the subcontractor, the amount of subcontracting fee, payment due date, payment method and so on. The primary contractor has an obligation to determine the payment date of the subcontract payment within 60 days counting from the date of receipt of benefits. In addition, the primary contractor is, amongst others, not allowed to refuse the receipt, to delay the payment of subcontracting fees, to reduce subcontracting fees and to return the results of accurate work.

However, the Subcontract Act regulates only subcontract relationships. It is not applicable to employment relationships. As a condition for applying the Subcontract Act, it is necessary for the primary contractor and the subcontractor to have a certain disparity in capital. Also, even when the Subcontract Act is not applied because it does not meet the requirement of disparity in capital, it may become a problem under the Antimonopoly Act from the viewpoint of abusing the superior position of the primary contractor.[16]

---

16 Abusing the superior position of the orderer is recognised when the service provider is forced to accept the orderer's disadvantageous request in order to avoid discontinuation of the contract with the orderer, which will cause immense financial loss for the service provider. Supra note 6, at 10.

2 Utilisation of the labour protection concept under the Home Work Act

As a recent legislative trend, there are arguments that the Home Work Act should be revised so that it can deal with new forms of work. In the Home Work Act, a "home worker" is a worker who manufactures, processes or sells goods, or who engages in these businesses or conducts similar acts. A homeworker is a person engaged in the manufacture or processing of goods and so forth, primarily receiving consignment in order to obtain remuneration for his/her labour. There is no supervision of the consignor over the manufacturing process. In these respects, workers involved in sharing economy closely resemble homeworkers. Under the regulations of the Home Work Act, notebooks indicating the content of consignment work, the amount of remuneration, the due date of payment and so on are issued to homeworkers, and minimum wages and safety and sanitation measures to be taken by the consignor are stipulated to guarantee basic rights of homeworkers.

3 Guidelines for the proper implementation of self-employed telework[17]

Although it is not a mandatory regulation, this guideline shows the following matters to be complied with by clients and intermediaries (internet platform companies) when using crowdsourcing:

1 The client or intermediary has a legal obligation to indicate clearly the content of the work, the scheduled delivery date, the scheduled remuneration amount and so forth in documents, e-mails or on websites.
2 After consulting with the self-employed teleworker, the client must issue (or clearly indicate by e-mail etc.) a document clarifying the contractual terms such as the name and the address of the client, the content of the work and the remuneration amount, and keep a record of such document for 3 years.
3 The client or intermediary should be made aware of the following matters:

"Contents of work" indicated in contract terms should be clearly specified. The amount of remuneration should be decided so as to be able to secure appropriate profits of self-employed teleworkers by taking into consideration the remuneration for other self-employed teleworkers with identical or similar work, the degree of difficulty of work, the length of the delivery date, the ability of the individual and so on.

The delivery date needs to be set so that the working time is not too long and that the health of teleworkers remains unharmed. The upper limit (8 hours) of the regular working hours per day of regular workers should be used as a reference for the upper limit.

17 www.mhlw.go.jp/file/06-Seisakujouhou-11900000-Koyoukintoujidoukateikyoku/0000198641_1.pdf.

Before making any changes to the terms of the contract, it is important to ensure their declaration in advance. The client should not compel the change which would be detrimental to the self-employed teleworker.

V Conclusions

As mentioned above, in Japan, various new forms of work, which make use of internet platform services, are studied as "Employment-like Working Style" in the context of traditional subcontracting and self-employment relationships. In other words, it is considered possible to give sufficient legal protection to the workers with a new working form without fundamentally changing the current regulatory framework. In this author's opinion, there are many new forms of work, some of which simply change the means of communication from the phone to the internet, while others are totally new ones using internet platform to match the supply and demand of labour within a wider range without going through traditional companies. Attempts to apply traditional labour protection regulations can make use of previous studies for similar problems. However, in some cases, there is a possibility that a fundamental review is required for the principle of recognising the relationship of the parties according to the actual working situation and the basic concepts such as working hours, worker/employer.

Regarding the new form of work created by adding a new medium called an internet platform, should we evaluate it as a completely new social phenomenon, as in China, or, as in Japan, should this be positioned as an extension of self-employment problems and considered as Employment-like Working Style? Before considering specific regulations, it may be necessary to look back on whether we are really studying the same social phenomenon and to unify the viewpoint.

VI Bibliography

Araki Takashi, *Labour and Employment Law* (3rd edition, Tokyo: Yuhikaku, 2016).
Qi Zhong, "The Fissured Workplace in Japan: A Legal Anatomy," *Comparative Labour Law & Policy Journal*, Vol. 37, No. 1 (2015): 181–208.
Qi Zhong, "Atypical Work Organizations as a Social Phenomenon Occurring throughout the Contemporary Labour World: Current Status of Research and Future Issues," *Japan Labour Issues*, Vol. 1, No. 3 (2017): 135–140. www.jil.go.jp/english/jli/documents/2017/003-17.pdf.
Tadashi Hanami, Fumito Komiya and Ryuichi Yamakawa, *Labour Law in Japan* (2nd edition., Wolters Kluwer, 2015).

4 Identifying labour relationship in the sharing economy
Judicial practice in China

Xiaohui Ban

I Introduction: the explosive sharing economy and judicial challenge in China

The Chinese government has been promoting supply-side structural reform since 2015. The readjustment of the industrial structure further exacerbates the problem of structural unemployment.[1] With this background, the rise of the sharing economy has been taken as one of the most important impetus for the economy development and employment growth by the government. The Guideline on Promoting the Development Sharing Economy states that the government should actively play the role of the sharing economy in promoting employment, improve the contribution model of social insurance for flexible employment and protect the rights of workers.[2]

The annual report of the National Information Center of the Sharing Economy and Sharing Economic Work Committee of the National Internet Society revealed that the number of people involved in providing services was about 70 million in 2017, an increase of 10 million over the past year. The number of workers hired by the platform enterprise of sharing economy was about 7.16 million, an increase of 1.31 million over the previous year, accounting for 9.7% of the number of new jobs in the city (135.44 million).[3] The sharing economy has played a significant role in solving the unemployment problem in the process of China's economic transformation. The DIDI company, which is the largest ride-hailing platform in China, has provided 3.931 million workers from the de-capacity industry (coal, steel, cement, chemical, non-ferrous metals etc.) and 1.78 million military veterans with job opportunities. It also helped 1.33 million unemployed people and 1.37 million zero-employment families to achieve re-employment. By the end of 2017, the number of active riders of the Meituan

---

1 Liu Hanwei and Liu Jinxiang, "The Challenge and Opportunity of Labor Relationship in the Supply Side Structural Reform", *China Labor*, 3 (2017): 5.
2 Article 12, Guiding Opinions on Promoting the Development of Sharing Economy ([2017] No. 1245 of the National Development and Reform Commission).
3 The National Information Center of Sharing Economy, Sharing Economic Work Committee of the National Internet Society, Annual Report about China's Shared Economic Development, 2018, p. 9.

Platform, which is the world's largest online and on-demand delivery platform, has exceeded 500,000, of which 156,000 riders were formerly workers in traditional industries such as coal and steel, accounting for 31.2%.[4] Therefore, the Government adopts a more open and loose policy towards the sharing economy, and avoids excessive intervention which may hinder the development momentum of the sharing economy.

Meanwhile, relevant labour disputes have been gradually increasing on the issue of the status of the worker. The Chaoyang District Court of Beijing City issued the Trail White Paper concerning labour dispute of the platform enterprise. From 2015 to the first quarter of 2018, the Chaoyang District Court has accepted and heard 188 cases of labour disputes of the platform enterprise. The workers – around 61.2% of these cases – claimed that they were employees. One hundred and seven cases were settled by judgement, of which 37.1% confirmed that the platform enterprises had a labour relationship with the workers. A 55.2% of the cases held that the two parties did not establish labour relations and 7.6% of the cases were decided that the two parties established labour dispatch relations.[5] Therefore, classifying labour relationship in the sharing economy has been one of the most difficult cases for the court and a hot issue in the labour law field in China.

This article briefly explores the current judicial experience in dealing with relevant cases in China and concludes with a proposal for identifying labour relationship in the sharing economy. Part II examines the current identifying criterion of labour relationship and recent rules about identifying labour relationship in China. Part III explains the two main employment models in the sharing economy, namely crowdsource and outsource employment, and analyses the differences and trends in the current judgements; Part IV proposes some suggestions for improving the method of identifying labour relationship in the sharing economy.

II The identifying criterion of labour relationship in China

The concepts of "Employment Relationship" and "Labour Relationship" are different from the point of view of legal terminology in China.[6] The former always is used in the civil law system and the latter is adopted in the labour law system (e.g. labour law, labour contract law). A worker who provides labour for the employer only can be protected by labour law, when the labour relationship exists between the two parties. Therefore, in the background of binary protection, how to classify the status of the worker is very significant.

---

4 Ibid, pp. 9–10.
5 "Trail White Paper of Labor Dispute of Internet Platform by Chaoyang District Court", accessed 12 December 2018, http://bjgy.chinacourt.org/article/detail/2018/04/id/3261190.shtml.
6 Xie Zengyi, *Labor Law in China: Progress and Challenges* (Springer, 2015), 1.

1 Subordination: the core of the identifying criterion

The subordination is the core criterion of identifying the labour relationship. Normally, the subordination consists of personal subordination and economic subordination in theory. Some opinions add the organisation subordination as the third kind of subordination.[7] Personal subordination means that the work performance by the employee is subject to the control of the employer, for example, subject to the workplace rules, the work instruction, the work inspection and the work discipline of the employer. The organisation subordination is used for remedying the drawback of personal subordination in dealing with the work of high autonomy. It emphasises that the work of employee is an integral part of the employer's business, and the employee needs to obey the workplace rule of the employer. However, some points that the organisation subordination should not be taken as an independent subordination, and its indicators belong to the scope of personal subordination.[8] The economic subordination refers to the economic status of the employee, namely the fact that the employee is weaker than the employer, which makes the employee economically dependent on the employer. The employee has to depend on the equipment for performing the work and the wages paid by the employer for a living. The employer decides the working conditions and the employee does not undertake the enterprise risk or share the profit.[9] The other opinion is that the core of economic subordination emphasises that the employee performs the work is not for his own account, but for the interests of employer. The economic situation of the employee and employer is not related to the subordination.[10] The three kinds of subordination are always used by arbitrators and judges for classifying the labour relationship.

However, there is no legal concept for labour relationship or any explanation of subordination in the basic labour law in China. The present identification criterion only can be found in the rule of Ministry and judicial guidelines of local courts, which are relatively low in the legal hierarchy. In 2005, the former Ministry of Labour and Social Security, which was reorganised into the Ministry of Human Resources and Social Security (MOHRSS) in 2008, issued Notice (2005) No. 12.[11] According to the clause 1 of the Notice, despite the absence of a written labour contract, the employer shall be deemed to have entered into an labour relationship with an employee when all the following conditions are met: (1) the employer and the employee meet the legal qualification prescribed by law and regulation; (2) workplace rules stipulated by the employer according to law are applicable to the employee, while the employee performs paid work offered by the employer and is subject to the management of such employer; and (3) the

---

7 Huang Chengguan, *Labor Law* (Taibei: National Open University Press, 1996), 63.
8 Ibid, p. 65.
9 Wang Quanxing, *Labor Law* (Beijing: Law Press, 2017), 36.
10 Huang Yueqin, *New Theory on Labor Law* (Taibei: Hanlu Press, 2012), 125.
11 Notice of Certain issues on Identification of Employment Relationship (Notice [2005] No.12 of the Ministry of Labor and Social Security).

service provided by the employee constitutes a part of the employer's business. The Notice actually emphasises two kinds of subordination, namely the personal and organisation subordination.[12] However, the Notice has been criticised for the rigid identification criterion, which is fit for the traditional labour relationship but not for the gradually increasing flexible employment model.[13] Especially the requirement of all the three conditions having to be met constitutes an obstacle in respect to the new forms of workers.[14]

For improving the system of the identification criterion, some local judicial guidelines list more indicators for identifying the labour relationship. For example, article 6 of the Trial Guidelines on Labour Disputes, issued by the High People's Court of Tianjin City in 2017, prescribes the following eight indicators: (1) the contract of service that has been concluded between the parties; (2) the employee is subject to the management, command or supervision of the employer; (3) the payment of wages by the employer to the employee; (4) the work performed by the employee is integrated into the business organisation system of the employer and not the independent profession or business; (5) the employee has no right to subcontract his work; (6) the equipment for work normally is provided by employer; (7) the term of work provided by employee is continuous and not of short time duration; and (8) the employer pays the social insurance contribution for employee.[15] Compared with the notice of the Ministry, the guideline of Tianjin includes more indicators of subordination and especially emphasises that the court should "comprehensively consider" these indicators. However, how to evaluate the importance of different indicators in identifying employment relationship is still left to be decided by arbitrators and judges.

2 The relevant identifying rules about the sharing economy

In 2016, the Ministry of Transport, the Ministry of Industry and Information Technology and other departments jointly enacted Order (2016) No. 60 to regulate the online car-hailing service.[16] The order confirms the legality of the online car-hailing service but does not explain the legal relationship between the driver and the platform enterprise. According to article 18 of the Order, the platform enterprise would enter into different kinds of contract with the driver, which depends on the characteristics of work, including working hours, service frequency and so forth. Therefore, as to the issue of employment relationship, the government attitude is still ambiguous. The matter is left to arbitrators and courts to decide.

12 *Supra* note 10, p. 36.
13 Feng Yanjun and Zhang Yinghui, "Reflection and Reconstruction on the Identifying Criterions for Labor Relationship," *Contemporary Law Review* 6 (2010): 95.
14 Yu Yinjie and Wang Ling, "The Judicial Decision on the New Forms of Labor Relationship," *China Labor*, 10 (2018): 68.
15 See Trail Guideline Concerning Labor Dispute for Courts of Tianjin (High People's Court of Tianjing City, No. 246 [2017]).
16 Interim Measures for the Administration of Online Car Hailing Services (Order [2016] No. 60).

Faced with the ambiguity of legislation, some local labour dispute settlement departments enacted some guidelines for classifying the labour relationship in the sharing economy. In Jiangsu Province, the Labour dispute arbitration commissions issued the guideline for the difficult cases, which states that as regards classifying labour relationship involved in platform enterprise, the arbitration institution should pay attention to the balance of the relationship between protecting the labour rights of workers and promoting the flexibility of the labour market. The arbitrator should consider comprehensively the operation form of the platform enterprise, the working situation, the degree of management of the platform company and the way of income distribution, whether the worker bears independently the business risk and other factors. If the platform enterprise plays the role of intermediary for clients, provides service information and collects management or information fees through the network platform, the two parties should not be treated as being in an employment relationship.[17] The High People's Court of Guangdong Province held that the legal relationship of work should be identified according to the agreement in the delivery industry, but the courts should review the subordination criterion in the first instance.[18] Therefore, the department of labour dispute settlement insists on taking subordination as the identification core in the new employment.

III Judicial experience in identifying labour relationship in the sharing economy

In order to reduce labour costs, the platform enterprises always take "non-labour relationship" as the core of the employment management strategy. The workers of the platform enterprise face many difficulties in identifying labour relationship because of the flexible arrangement of contracts by use of internet technology. In practice, platform companies adopt multiple operational models. Taking the car-hailing industry as an example, some car-hailing platform companies operate with the asset-heavy model, which means that the ownership of cars is mainly owned by the companies, just like CAR Inc. Some platform companies operate with asset-light model, which means the serving cars are mainly provided by the individual drivers rather than the companies.[19] In the former model, the drivers are always hired by the platform companies or by labour dispatch companies. In the latter model, the status of drivers is always in dispute.[20] In practice, the latter normally has two main employment models, namely crowdsource and outsource.

---

17 Summary of the Symposium on the Difficult Cases of Labor and Personnel Disputes in Jiangsu Province (Labour and Personnel Arbitration Committee [2017] No. 1).
18 Article 2, Guideline on the Trial of Labor Disputes Case by High People's Court of Guangdong Province ([2017] No. 147).
19 Some people think that car-hailing companies with asset-heavy model are not real sharing economy; but the traditional rental car industry introduced the internet platform operate model, accessed 28 December 2018, http://money.163.com/16/0415/15/BKN2CTLI00253B0H.html.
20 Peng Qianwen and Cao Dayou, "Is the Labor Relations or the Service Relations? Analyze the Online Car Booking Platform's Nature of Employment Relations in China by the Example of Didi", *Human Resources Development of China*, 2 (2016): 95.

Judicial practice in China 53

1 Crowdsource model: free to accept or reject the task

The "crowdsource" is a typical employment model in the sharing economy. In order to effectively meet the temporary employment demand, the platform enterprises recruit unspecified workers to participate in the business by use of the App. When registering in the App, the workers need to provide some basic information with the platform enterprises and click the "agree button" of digital standard form of contract. After passing through the qualification examination, the workers can login into App and grab the order. In this employment model, the platform enterprises always expressly stipulate that there is no contract of service between the crowd worker and platform enterprise, and the platform normally has no specific requirements on the working time and load of crowd workers. The equipment (e.g. the electric motor for delivering food) for implementing service should be provided by the workers themselves. The workers are free to accept or reject the order sent by the platform. However, once they accept the order, they must obey the rules of platforms to complete the order.

In this model, it is very hard for workers to claim the employee status of the platform enterprise. In some *e-daijia* (an online designated driver company) cases, the courts found that the worker had autonomy in deciding the working time, had no fixed workplace, and did not receive the wage monthly, and held that the only evidence of work clothing and card could not be sufficient to qualify for the existence of a labour relationship.[21] Some points (*e-daijia* is a designated driver company, which connects the designated driver and the client [normally drunk] by using the APP) further analyse these cases and point out that the platform enterprise sends the demand information to the unspecific designated drivers, and the individual driver has the right to decide when he will open or close the App and whether to accept the order. Therefore, the behaviour of sending demanding information by the platform enterprise cannot be taken as a command. While driving, the designated driver can decide on the driving route to be followed, the driving speed and so forth, and receive payment from the customer according to the driving distance of every order, which is not the wage from the platform enterprise.[22]

However, some crowd workers successfully claimed the employee status. In the past two years, the two cases of Beijing have attracted much attention. One is the "Good Chef" platform case, which is known as the first labour dispute case of the sharing economy in Beijing,[23] and the other is the "FlashEx" platform

---

21 Zhuang Yansheng vs. Yixinyixing Company, Beijing First Intermediate People's Court (2014), Civil Case No. 6355; Sun Youliang vs. Yixinyixing Company, Beijing First Intermediate People's Court (2015), Civil Case No. 176; Wang Zheshuan vs. Yixinyixing Company, Beijing First Intermediate People's Court (2014), Civil Case No. 01359.
22 Wang Tianyu, "Classification of Employment Relationships in the Internet Platform: From the Perspective of E-Daijia Cases in Beijing, Shanghai and Guangzhou City," *Law Science*, 6 (2016): 51.
23 "The First Case about Work Hired by Internet Platform in Beijing has Hold a Court", accessed 12 December 2018, http://legal.people.com.cn/n1/2016/0810/c42510-28624665.html.

case. In both cases, the court denied the "cooperation agreement" between the platform enterprises and the workers, and found that there was a *de facto* labour relationship between the two parties.

1.1 "Good Chef" platform case

In this case,[24] the Good Chef platform was established by Lekuai Company for demanding information of chef services. The Cooperation Agreement between the two parties provided that they have established a cooperative relationship, and the Good Chef Platform (party A) provides the Chef (Party B) with online promotion of cooking service and provides customer reservation services for Party A. If the customer submits a home cooking appointment to the platform, Party B shall arrive at the service place designated by the customer at a certain time for cooking. Party A provides Party B with a set of professional cooking service tools and a set of tool timers. The cooperation agreement also emphasises that the agreement is a business cooperation agreement and Party B does not need to accept the management of Party A. There is no affiliation between the two parties. Party B accepts that the legal relationship between the two parties does not directly or indirectly constitute an employment relationship. Party A has the right to punish Party B if it fails to reach the service location requested by Party A on time or if the service cannot satisfy the customer. Party A has the right to terminate the cooperation relationship with Party B and request compensation. Party B cannot make an appointment to change the service price of the customer.

The court held that the legal relationship between the worker and the employer should not be subject to the "subjective understanding" of the parties. The court found that Lekuai Company only operated the chef business and the chef mainly provided chef skills, which means strong affiliation to the platform. During the execution process, the company actually had some management conducts, such as the dispatch order to the chef and rewards and punishment behaviour for the chef according to his/her working performance. The court also found that the payment of remuneration was fixed on a monthly basis. The company claimed that it was convenient for calculating the service fee monthly; the fee did not constitute wages for the employee, but the court believed that the employer failed to provide evidence. Based on the facts of this case, the court held that a labour relationship existed.

1.2 "FlashEx" platform case

The court went much further in this case.[25] The delivery man (Lixiang Guo) downloaded the FlashEx app on his mobile phone and engaged in grabbing

---

24 Zhang Qi vs. Lekuai Information Technology Company, 3rd Intermediate People's Court of Beijing (2017), Civil Case No. 11768.
25 Li Xiangguo vs. Tongchengbiying Technology Company, Haidian District Court of Beijing (2017), Civil Case No.53634.

the order and delivery work. The FlashEx platform claimed that the parties had intermediation contracts. The cooperation model was intermittent and accidental and had no continuity and subordination, which were the characteristics of employment relationship. When the worker selected the "listen" mode, the company would know the location of the worker. The customer sent the delivery request to the FlashEx platform. The FlashEx platform evaluated the cost according to the distance and weight; the customer can also float the fee on his own. The order information was sent to the worker surrounding the demanding customer. The worker had the right to decide whether to take or reject the order. After the worker had successfully accepted the order, he would pick up the package and deliver it to the recipient. The platform would randomly send the verification code to the recipient. After getting the verification code from the recipient, the flasher would input it into the platform, and then the delivery would be deemed successful. The court decided that there was the existence of a labour relationship based on the following reasons:

1. The court found that the two parties had no intermediation contracts. In view of such contract, the middleman only reports to the client about the opportunity to conclude the contract or provide intermediary service. The content of the contract was still determined by clients. However, in the FlashEx case, the company not only obtained the information of demand of the delivery service and sent it to many workers through the platform, but also stipulated the rights and obligations of the delivery contract, including service standards, charging standards and so forth.
2. Although the delivery worker would decide whether to take the order, once he accepted the order, he needed to complete the service according to the workflow specified by the company. In practice, the worker did not have much autonomy during working hours and workload in order to maintain his income level. In this case, the court found that Li Xiangguo worked about 10 hours per day.
3. The court held the opinion that the delivery vehicle was not the main means of production, the data information collected by the platform through Internet technology was the most important means of production. The worker had to depend on the technology information provided by the platform to complete the work. Moreover, the Court believed that during the working period, the remuneration from the FlashEx platform was the worker's main labour income. The company also explicitly required the worker not to provide service for other platforms at the same time. The worker obviously had economic dependence on the company.
4. The company mainly operated cargo transportation services. The delivery service provided by the worker is part of the business of the company.

In the above two cases, the courts adopted a more flexible explanation of legislation in determining the employment relations. On the one hand, the court emphasised that the facts of the contract performance took precedence over the content of the agreement, which is the electronic format clause adopted by the platform companies to avoid labour relations. On the other hand, the court did not rigidly apply Notice (2005) No.12. In the judgement of the personal subordination, the court focussed on the actual control indicator, such as dispatched order and reward or punishment policy and so on. In the second case – once taking the task, the worker had to follow the instructions of the platform enterprise – the court considered it as the indicator of personal subordination. Also, economic pressure would have given the worker no chance to refuse the order. In terms of economic dependence, the court considered the importance of information resources handed by the platform. On the issue of organisation subordination, the courts examined whether the business scope of the platform enterprise was specific and whether the services provided by the workers were consistent with the scope of the business.

2 Outsource model: who is the real employer?

For evading the responsibility of the employer, some platform enterprises have outsourced business to local agents, who are responsible for organising the recruitment of employees and forming a relatively fixed team. The platform enterprise takes on the identity as the information intermediary platform. The workers recruited by the local agents always perform the work depending on the APP of the platform enterprise, and in such circumstances, it is not very clear as to who is their real employer. In this model, the platform enterprise uses the subcontractor enterprise as the legal barrier for avoiding the status of employer.

2.1 The subcontractor is taken as the employer

The Liu YaYa case is a typical model.[26] In this case, Party A – Meituan platform (Sankuai Technology Company) – signed a commission contract of delivery cooperation with Party B – Veteran Running company, which stipulated that Party A authorised Party B to operate delivery service in Henan province, and the worker recruited by Party B had no labour contract or labour service contract with Party A.[27] In Practice, the worker Liu YaYa needed to wear the clothing, helmet and delivery box which have the logo of Meituan and was paid by Party B according to the number of orders in the APP. Party A paid the service fee to Party B. The Haidian District Court held that the worker was recruited, trained and paid by Party B, and the Meituan logo of the worker's equipment cannot lead to the conclusion of labour relationship. Therefore, the court ruled that the worker had no contract of service with Meituan platform. A similar situation

---

26 Sankuai Technology Company vs. Liu YaYa, Haidian District Court of Beijing (2016), Civil Case No. 40818.
27 In China, if an individual worker provides service for the employer without labour relationship, the contract between them always is called labour service contract and would be subject to the civil law.

happened in the Tang Tongyang case; the court held that: (1) the delivery service provided by the worker constituted a part of business of the local agent, who was in charge of the delivery business in the area agreed with Meituan; (2) the local agent inspected the wearing and sanitary condition of the worker, and evaluated his performance and deducted payment if the worker got a low score on the custom review; (3) as a full time delivery man, the worker depended on the wage received from the local agent for a living.[28] In the above two cases, the Meituan platform successfully avoided employer responsibility by using the local agent. However, the court failed to examine the real situation of outsourcing and the extent of "direct" in work by the platform enterprise.

2.2 The platform enterprise is taken as the employer

Not all courts accept the local agent as a shield. In the Shi Lei case, the court held that: (1) the recruitment by the local agent company in the name of the platform company (ELEME Inc.) should be taken as the civil behaviour of an agency; the food delivery man thought that he had worked for the platform company. Therefore, the platform company as an entrusted agent should take the responsibility of the recruitment. (2) There was subordination between the worker and the platform enterprise. The rules that the worker had to obey during delivery were in fact set by the platform enterprise. The wage of the worker was apparently paid by the local agent to the worker, but it was allotted to the local agent by the platform enterprise according to the order amount of the worker. The platform enterprise also paid accident injury insurance for the delivery worker. (3) The delivery service provided by the worker is an integral part of the platform enterprise's business. Therefore, the court decided the platform company had a contract of service with the worker.[29]

Comparing with the judgements above, the courts had different opinions on the relationship between the platform enterprise and local agent. The key point is who is the real employer of the workers? According to the article 94 of the Labour Contract Law of China, if the subcontractor is an individual, the outsourcer and subcontractor should take joint liability for the damaged rights of the worker recruited by the subcontractor. Therefore, if the subcontractor has the eligibility of employer, the outsourcer will have no liability for the worker of the subcontractor.[30] In the sharing economy, it is apparent that the local agent, as subcontractor of the platform enterprise, shared the management of the workers with the platform enterprise due to the use of the App. The work allocation, wage amount and service rules basically are decided by the platform enterprise, not the local agent. The workers wear the clothing and use the equipment with

---

28 Tang Tongyang vs. Kuaituitongcheng Company, Jiangsu 0804 (2017), Civil Case No. 1763.
29 Zhalashi Information Technology Company (Shanghai) vs. Shi Lei and Hanqun Technology Company (Wuhan), Hubei 0202 (2018), Civil Case No. 2068.
30 Wang Quanxing and Huang Kun, "The Circumvention Tendency of Outsourcing Labor and the Countermeasure of Labor Legislation," *Academic Journal of Zhongzhou*, 2 (2008): 86.

the logo of the platform enterprise and perform the task by using the App. It is even difficult for the customer to recognise which company the workers who are serving them belong to. Therefore, the current outsource of the platform enterprise should not be the absolute shield for employer responsibility, especially as some local agents also deny the labour relationship with the workers when the relevant disputes happen.

IV What is the future for identifying the labour relationship of the sharing economy in China?

Considering the advantages of human cost, evading establishing labour relationship with workers will still be the first choice of platform enterprises. Facing the continually increasing sharing economy and the employment pressure, it is not easy for the legislator to enact regulations to clarify the status of the workers in the sharing economy, especially as the management method of platform enterprises is still constantly changing with legal and judicial modification. The above cases can be taken as good examples to classify a labour relationship. However, since China is not a common law country and the judgements of labour disputes in China have strong regional characteristics, it is difficult for judicial cases discussed above to be deemed as the criterion for all such cases. Therefore, it is very significant to improve the identification criterion from national level for adapting to the new forms of employment. Based on the current judicial experience, the following suggestions could be considered.

1 Pay attention to the facts of contract implementation

The sharing economy further promotes the flexibility of the employment market and aggravates the issues of sham employment relationship. The digital standard form contract offers more spaces for the employer to set de-employment clauses. The workers, especially the unemployed workers from the traditional industry who want to participate in the sharing economy, have to use the intelligent and necessary digital tools. Therefore, they almost have no bargaining power with the platform enterprises in the digital contract. The situation would be worse with the enhancing tendency of monopoly in the sharing economy. The International Labour Organization in the Employment Relationship Recommendation (No. 198), in 2006, emphasised that "notwithstanding how the relationship is characterized in any contrary arrangement, contractual or otherwise, that may have been agreed between the parties", the facts relating to the performance of work should be primarily guided.[31] Therefore, the arbitrators and judges should identify the character of the relationship not only based on the digital contract between the platform enterprise and the worker or the agreement between the platform enterprise and the local agent, but also on the hidden truth of relationship between the enterprise and the worker when performing the contract.

---

31 Article 9, R198 – Employment Relationship Recommendation, 2006 (No. 198).

2 Flexibly explain the subordination in the platform enterprise

Is the current form of identifying criterion for labour relationship outdated? In truth, the subordination criterion still can be used for employment in the sharing economy. The difficulties in identifying labour relationship have existed since the development of flexible employment.[32] What needs to improve is the judgement of subordination initiators in China.[33] The judges should consider comprehensively the indicators based on the work character of the internet platform, and cannot deny the existence of labour relationship due to the lack of single indicator.

The indirect control conducts should be considered in examining personal subordination. With the flexible trend of the production and operation model, the management of business by the employer is towards automation and intelligence. In the sharing economy, the management between the workers and platform enterprises mostly is realised by the digital tool. Although it is free for workers to deal with the order according to some agreement, the platform enterprise can realise the aim of management by the technological tool and has no necessity to pay attention to the detail control of the worker. The judges should consider whether the following circumstances exist: the minimum order requirements for the worker with some punitive management; the service rules for the workers; the appraisal system for the work performance by the customer; the worker cannot subcontract his task; and so forth.

The organisation subordination should be emphasised as loose indicators for personal subordination in the new employment of the sharing economy. The judges should examine whether the provided service by the worker is an integral part of the business of the platform enterprise. The following aspects should be considered: the scope and category of the platform enterprise; the category of service provided by the worker; the frequency and continuity of the worker's work; and the service rules of the platform enterprise for the worker.

Furthermore, the court should evaluate the economic dependency of the worker on the platform enterprise. In the contract for intermediation, the intermediary normally has no right to intervene in the trade fees and rules, and its core function is providing information and promoting trade. Therefore, the judges should consider whether the worker has a right to negotiate the service fee and rules with the customer. If the worker receives the wage according to the order amount in the fixed price by the platform enterprises and has no bargaining right on the working conditions, this constitutes evidence that he works for the platform enterprise. However, the judges should not put the emphasis on who provides the equipment for service, as the most important equipment for realising work performance is the technological app provided by the platform enterprise.

---

32 Orly Lobel, "The Gig Economy and the Future of Employment and Labor Law", *U.S.F. L. Rev.* 51 (2017): 61.
33 Xie Zengyi, "Identifying Labor Relationship in the Internet Platform Enterprises", *Peking University Law Journal*, 6 (2018): 1557.

3 Enhance the joint employer responsibility for sham outsource

Article 91 of the Labour Contract Law requires the labour dispatching unit or the employing unit to take joint compensation responsibility for the damage caused by the employing unit. For purposes of fighting against the phenomenon of "sham labour outsources, but real labour dispatch", the article 27 of Temporary Regulation on the Labour Dispatch prescribes that if the employing unit uses the worker in the name of outsource, which in fact belongs to labour dispatch model, it should apply the labour dispatch rules. This would be a way for the worker to claim the joint employer liability in the sharing economy. However, some local judicial attitude for identifying the sham outsource is relatively loose. The trail guidelines of Shanghai points that in the labour outsourcing model, the outsourcer and subcontractor could share the rights of workplace management through the agreement. If the outsource agreement is not judged to be invalid, the controls on the worker of the subcontractor by the outsourcer exceed the authority of the agreement but do not definitively change the nature of legal relationship, the claim of the worker for establishing labour relationship with the outsourcer should not be supported.[34]

For combating the increase of sham outsourcing in the sharing economy, the legislator should further explain the identifying criterion of false outsource and clarify the joint employer responsibility. When the platform enterprise tries to adopt the outsource model and use the local agent as the shield of employer responsibility, the judges should examine the real situation of the workplace management: whether the rule which the worker obeys is stipulated by the platform enterprise; whether the amount and pay method of wages are decided by the platform enterprise; whether the platform has a punishment right on the worker; and so on. When considering the extent of intervention and the workplace management of the platform enterprise, the judges should not only focus on the "direct" intervention, the indirect or potential control also can lead to the joint employer responsibility.[35]

V Conclusion

Although labour laws in China are still in the initial stage, the country's employment forms have been changing rapidly. The encouraging environment of legislation and policy for the sharing economy further accelerates the flexible employment forms. The traditional identifying criterion still can be used to resolve the new forms of employment in the sharing economy, but it needs to be flexibly explained and comprehensively considered based on the work character in the platform enterprise.

---

34 Clause 11, meeting summary about the relevant issues on the law application of labour dispatch by the Bureau of Human Resources and Social Security and High People's Court of Shanghai City, 2015.
35 Charlotte Gardena and Joseph E. Slateraa, "Comments on Restatement of Employment Law (Third), Chapter 1," *Employee Rights and Employment Policy Journal* 21 (2017): 278.

The real challenge in the sharing economy for China's labour laws is how to combat the sham employment relationship and construct the multi-level protection system of labour laws in the future.

VI Bibliography

Charlotte Gardena and Joseph E. Slateraa, "Comments on Restatement of Employment Law" (Third), Chapter 1, *Employee Rights and Employment Policy Journal* 21 (2017): 265–305.

Feng Yanjun and Zhang Yinghui, "Reflection and Reconstruction on the Identifying Criterions for Labour Relationship," *Contemporary Law Review* 6 (2010): 92–98.

Huang Chengguan, *Labour Law* (Taibei: National Open University Press, 1996).

Huang Yueqin, *New Theory on Labour Law* (Taibei: Hanlu Press, 2012).

Liu Hanwei and Liu Jinxiang, "The Challenge and Opportunity of Labour Relationship in the Supply Side Structural Reform", *China Labour* 3 (2017):4–9.

Orly Lobel, "The Gig Economy and the Future of Employment and Labour Law," *U.S.F. L. Rev.* 51 (2017): 51–73.

Peng Qianwen and Cao Dayou, "Is the Labour Relations or the Service Relations? Analyze the Online Car Booking Platform's Nature of Employment Relations in China by the Example of Didi," *Human Resources Development of China* 2 (2016): 93–97.

Wang Quanxing, *Labour Law* (Beijing: Law Press, 2017).

Wang Quanxing and Huang Kun, "The Circumvention Tendency of Outsourcing Labour and the Countermeasure of Labour Legislation," *Academic Journal of Zhongzhou* 2 (2008): 86–92.

Wang Tianyu, "Classification of Employment Relationships in the Internet Platform: From the Perspective of E-Daijia Cases in Beijing, Shanghai and Guangzhou City," *Law Science* 6 (2016): 50–60.

Xie Zengyi, "Identifying Labour Relationship in the Internet Platform Enterprises," *Peking University Law Journal* 6 (2018): 1546–1569.

Xie Zengyi, *Labour Law in China: Progress and Challenges* (Springer, 2015).

Yu Yinjie and Wang Ling, "The Judicial Decision on the New Forms of Labour Relationship," *China Labour* 10 (2018):67–73.

5 Informality, neoliberalism and the gig economy in Chile

Denisa Meirosu

I Introduction

Technological advancements integrate regions at a fast pace, from developed to emerging worlds (it is estimated that 50 billion devices will be connected to the internet by 2020),[1] and experts suggest that this will lead to a profound renaissance of the global economy.

Latin America is not a leading force on the digital market: only 20% of its households were connected to internet in 2010. Investments in Information Technology (IT) infrastructure in the past decade increased connectivity considerably: 60% of households were using a broadband connection in 2015. The contrast between the countries of the continent is nevertheless sharp; in 2005, in some the penetration rate was below 5%, while in others it reached 60% – Chile, Costa Rica and Uruguay – increasing the inequality gap.[2] The IT infrastructure penetration has continued to expand since 2015. In 2018, 78% of the Chileans were connected to the internet,[3] and a significant growth was registered in e-banking services, mobile phones, e-tax and electronic marketing.

One of Chile's objectives is 95% connectivity in 2020.[4] The growth of the digital economy, which represented 3.5% of GDP in 2017, is expected to rise to 4.5% by 2020 as a direct effect of the IT infrastructure development.[5] As the free digital services that are self-produced, volunteer produced or produced by

---

1 *The Internet of Things: Evolution or Revolution?* Retrieved from www.biztositasiszemle.hu, last accessed on 9 June 2018.
2 *Estado de la banda ancha en América Latina y el Caribe*, 2016, retrieved from www.cepal.org/es/publicaciones/estado-la-banda-ancha-america-latina-caribe-2016, last accessed on 9 June 2018.
3 *Estudio de interacción digital*, "We are social", 2018, retrieved from https://digitalreport.wearesocial.com, last accessed on 9 June 2018.
4 *Centro de Estudios de la Economía Digital, Cámara de Comercio de Santiago*, 2016, *La economía digital en Chile*, retrieved from www.ccs.cl/html/economia_digital/docs/economia_digital_B.pdf, last accessed on 9 June 2018.
5 Ibidem 6.

platforms[6] are difficult to measure[7] it is believed that the contribution of the digital economy to the GDP is higher than what official figures report.

In Chile, the digital economy is represented by the turnover produced by sales in ICT infrastructure, software, services, telecommunications and e-commerce, which in 2015 amounted to USD 40 million, an increase of 11% from the previous year.[8] According to the same report, e-commerce was driving half of the total sales, and it was mainly represented not only by business to business, but also business to public institutions.

The study "*Estudio Índice País Digital*"[9] indicates that the highest rates of internet users are youths between 15 and 29 years of age, with 94% using internet at 15 years of age. The use of internet is widely spread amongst all levels of education, notably the secondary education (70%), reaching a 98% for users with postgraduate studies, while those with no formal education reach a 35% of total users. The figures show that levels of education are not necessarily an impediment in the use of information technology. Besides, 14 million Chileans use Facebook (approximately 78% of the internet users) and 6 million Instagram[10]; so the social media segment covers a potential huge market. Both Facebook and Instagram have dedicated places on their platforms where trading of used or new products and of services, within the local communities, are made simple.

Around 15% of the Facebook traffic globally is represented by users' engagement in the Facebook marketplace.[11] Statistics for this segment are not available for Chile; however, the total number of users of Facebook and Instagram in the country, by comparison with the rest of the platforms, is worth investigating.

II Entrepreneurship and informality

According to Mann, the expansion of internet has led to an upsurge of entrepreneurship, associated with self-employment and creation of new markets, innovation in strategies for production, marketing and sales for the established companies and a new way of interaction between businesses and consumers.[12]

---

6 IMF, *Measuring the digital economy*, 2018, retrieved from www.imf.org/en/Publications/Policy-Papers/Issues/2018/04/03/022818-measuring-the-digital-economy, last accessed on 9 June 2018.
7 *La Economía digital en el desarrollo económico*, 2015. An indirect measurement of those services carried out in the US show they represent at least 1% of the GDP (*The Attention Economy: Measuring the value of free digital services on the internet*, Erik Brynjolfsson, MIT and Center for Digital Business).
8 Ibidem 9.
9 *Fundación País Digital, Estudio Índice País Digital*, 2017, retrieved from www.indicepaisdigital.cl, last accessed on 9 June 2018.
10 Ibidem 11.
11 Facebook Marketplace: estos son los trucos para vender mejor en Facebook, http://pyme.emol.com/6033/facebook-marketplace-estos-los-trucos-vender-mejor-la-nueva-herramienta-facebook, last accessed on 9 June 2018.
12 Mann, C., 2001, *The Internet and the Global Economy*, retrieved from http://unpan1.un.org/intradoc/groups/public/documents/un/unpan000696.pdf, last accessed on 9 June 2018.

The revolutionary yet disruptive technological progress changed the conventional business model and gave birth to the gig economy, entailing a small-scale enterprise with a sole employee, whose national or global operations are facilitated by an infrastructure that is almost free of charge.

The attraction of the manpower to the gig sector is significant, as demand and offer can be connected by digital platforms at the press of the button anytime and anywhere. The comfortable entrepreneurial perspective, coupled with the failure of the markets to provide decent work opportunities, has led to a growing participation of independent workforce on the gig market. According to McKinsey,[13] there are 162 million independent workers in the United States and Europe and 15% of them are "people earning income by selling goods or services via e-commerce [...] and those who rent out assets (e.g. listing a spare room on Airbnb)".

The gig economy is often associated with the increase of the independent workforce, who "undertake small and discrete parcels of work through digital technologies that connect providers and customers".[14]

As trade on social platforms is not yet regulated, most of the so-called entrepreneurial initiatives of self-employed are informal.

Informality in Chile is a constituent part of the labour market today.[15] In August 2017, "Fundación Sol" reported 49.7% of informal[16] workers of the total Chilean workforce, that is, 4,107,527 persons.[17] The term "informal" is often employed to define the status of a person or enterprise whose activities are income

---

13 McKinsey & Company, 2016, Independent workforce: choice, necessity, and the gig economy, retrieved from www.mckinsey.com, last accessed on 9th June 2018.
14 Brinkley, I., 2016, *In search of the gig economy*, The Work Foundation, retrieved from www.theworkfoundation.com, last accessed on 9th June 2018.
15 Díaz, E. and Gálvez., T., 2015, *Informalidad laboral mas trabajadores productivos sin protección laboral*, retrieved from www.dt.gob.cl, last accessed on 9 June 2018.
16 From the perspective of "Fundación Sol", a new conceptualisation of informality to better capture the realities of the labour market in Chile is proposed; the informal segment is broken down in the following subcategories, displaying all or at least one of the vulnerabilities usually associated with informality: (1) subordinated service provider – mostly found in the public administration sector and who de facto carries out work for an employer in the same conditions as an employee; however, the relationship between the independent contractor and the employer is framed under a commercial contract, supply of services, and functions accordingly. It is the so-called disguised form of employment. (2) Self-employed – comprising those who are usually not in technical or professional professions and consider themselves informal. (3) Dependent independent – comprising the self-employed who are dependent on an employer who can be either formal or informal. (4) Unpaid family worker – comprising persons working in a family business without being remunerated for the work. (5) Informal employer – entrepreneurs in the informal sector, with less than six employees. (6) Sub-employee (contracted) – comprising employees of a company who are leased for specific tasks or amount of time to other companies; meaning that their dependency and subordination are related to the employer in terms of payment and to the company to which they are leased in terms of labour output. (7) Unprotected workers – usually referring to employees that do not benefit of protection: lack a labour contract, contributions to social security and more.
17 "Fundación Sol", Informe realizado por la Unidad Estadísticas del Trabajo, 2017.

generating, but who do not perform them under an established legal framework, and hence are prone to vulnerable labour conditions. The occupational categories which report a large share of informal workers are self-employed, excluding technicians or professionals, employers with less than five workers, employees in the public administration and the private sector whose work is unprotected, domestic workers and unpaid family workers.

In 2019, the occupational category with a major boost of informality was the self-employed, which augmented to 65.8%.[18] The economic sectors attracting most of the informal labour force is shown in Table 5.1.

More than 66% of the informal self-employed in Chile are active in commerce, agriculture and fisheries, construction and manufacturing industry. The remaining share pertains to the other subcategories of the informal sector.[19]

The statistics do not explicitly reflect a direct connection between the sectors where the share of informal labour force increased and the sectors where the digital platforms are active: passengers' transport, accommodation, delivery services and commerce. While for the former, this can be explained by the fact that due to the illegality of platforms such as Uber and Airbnb in Chile, statistics do not capture the whole workforce; for the latter, such as commerce, the effects are more obvious, even though social commerce facilitated by Facebook and Instagram marketplaces is not taken into account.

The self-employed trading goods or services on digital platforms in Chile come from all backgrounds, educational level, age and genders.

The arguments the individuals use to justify their presence on the digital market consist of either choice or necessity. Those who are genuine entrepreneurs and can exercise individualism in the construction of their lives are also those who join the independent market by choice.[20] It is still them that display an excessive tolerance towards the lack of protection, in particular social security, or other risks such as limited or no access to credit, the risk of not being paid for the

Table 5.1 Informality % per economic sector in Chile

Employers of domestic workers	55.9%
Other services[21]	49.4%
Agriculture and fishery	45.5%
Commerce	32.5%
Transport	30.1%
Accommodation and restaurants	34.1%
Public administration	10.4%
Education	11.3%
Professional activities	12.3%

Source: compiled data, *INE*, 2019.

18 INE, 2019, Estadísticas de informalidad laboral.
19 Ibidem.
20 Castel, R., 2009, *La montée des incertitudes. Travail, protections, statuts de l'individu*. Paris, Seuil.
21 In accordance with INE, other services include manufacturing.

work performed, licencing and regulatory compliance requirements difficult to comply with.[22] In Chile, a significant amount of the informal work corresponds to entry out of necessity. The level of earnings or the status on the labour market (unemployed, inactive) is key determinants in this respect. There is also an important share joining the digital platforms out of choice, to maximise profits, supplement their main income or to generate pocket money while in college.

The entry in informality is associated with a risk of limited social protection. While this creates growing anxiety for some (especially for those whose economic activity represent their main source of income), others appreciate more the flexibility and autonomy this type of work offers; however, this is especially encountered in the younger segments of the population 25–30 years old.

According to Kirsten Sehnbruch,[23] the Chilean self-employed chooses not to contribute to either a pension or a social insurance fund. Affiliation to the pension system of self-employed is voluntary, and evidence show that 85% of them do not contribute to the pension system. The independent workers contribute to the health insurance fund in Chile more significantly (45%) than to the pension insurance (15%). A similar situation is encountered with the self-employed on digital platforms. Social protection is an important aspect of their professional lives; however, the level of income as self-employed is too low or unstable, hence they cannot afford to pay expensive contributions for high standards private health and pension insurances. If they however contribute to the basic pension pillar and the health insurance in the public sector, which are more affordable, the quality of the services is lower and the coverage of the services is limited, which thus dilutes the interest in contributing constantly to the system.

III Informality – a neoliberal heritage?

In Latin America, informality was traditionally used to explain the level of poverty or of work precariousness. The premise was that informal work was performed to ensure subsistence and it was most of the times poorly paid, unprotected and insecure. As such, a simplistic perspective, negative, drawn upon the distinction formal – informal, positive – was used to inform political decisions on informality. Further expansion of the phenomenon and subsequent empirical evidence following studies carried out in the 1980s and the 1990s concluded that understanding the phenomenon of informality through dichotomies will prevent the understanding of its complexity and, most importantly, the relations with the formal economy.

Traditionally, Chile looked at informal work from a neoliberal perspective; informal work was the response to over regulation[24] that posed significant

---

22 McKinsey & Company, 2016, Independent workforce: choice, necessity, and the gig economy, retrieved from www.mckinsey.com, last accessed on 9 June 2018.
23 Sehnbruch, K., 2006, *The Chilean Labor Market – A Key to Understanding Latin American Labor Markets*.
24 De Soto, H., 1989, *The Other Path: The Invisible Revolution in the Third World*. New York: Harper and Row.

difficulties to micro-enterprises, which in an open market need to find solutions to be competitive (e.g. by reducing costs). In the legalists' point of view, the micro-enterprises consist of entrepreneurs who choose to exercise their own power through informality in relation to an over bureaucratic government.

The neoliberal military government of the 1970s introduced labour market reforms, which strongly deregulated the labour market so that it could face the competition of the open market: low dismissal costs, the prohibition of union activities and lower minimum wages were amongst the measures implemented by the new reform. The 1980s brought even more changes, with pensions and health insurance fully privatised, making Chile one of the least regulated labour market in Latin America. In Chile's case, the flexibilisation of the labour code however did not contribute to a decrease in informality as the legalists predicted, but rather contributed to the expansion of unprotected work. The neoliberal approach to support economic growth has thus contributed to a large extent to institutionalised informality. However, after the fall of the military government in 1990, the labour codes went through a slow come back to high levels of regulation that aimed to increase protection standards, including a significant increase in the minimum wage, higher costs of dismissal, broader coverage of union bargaining.

Today, the gig economy in Chile displays an informality that can no longer be attributed exclusively to the neoliberal system due to the progress with the labour code over the past 40 years; neither can it be attributed to the modernisation thesis, arguing that, as economies advance, the transition from informal to formal work is a natural process. Therefore, the more the economy advances, the less informality exists.[25] This theory stems from the premise that informality is connected to obsolete informal entrepreneurship that will be in decline while the country progresses.

Moreover, the neoliberal theory argues that the informality is a consequence of the market over regulation, public sector corruption and high taxes. Small and informal entrepreneurship is seen as a brave and voluntary resistance movement; despite the limited productivity potential they face as a consequence of informality and the lack of recognition of the property rights impeding them to transform their assets into real capital, they continue to choose to work informally.[26] This is no longer a valid explanation for Chile,[27] where there is little public corruption[28] and ranked by the World Bank at position 55 out of the total of 190[29] for the ease of doing business.

---

25 Williams, C., and Windebank, J., 1998, *Informal Employment in Advanced Economies: Implications for Work and Welfare.*
26 Maloney, W.F., 2004, *Informality Revisited. World Development.*
27 Albagli, Garcia and Restrepo, 2016, *Assessing the Flexibility of the Labour Market in Chile: An International Perspective*, last accessed on 9 June 2018.
28 Transparency International ranks it as the second least corrupt country in Latin America, www.transparency.org, last accessed on 9 June 2018.
29 World Bank, www.doingbusiness.org, last accessed on 9 June 2018.

The voluntarist school of thought sees informal work from a cost–benefit evaluation perspective of the formal employment; if the latter proves not worthy, people choose to be out of the formal employment as the services provided by the state in exchange for their contributions are of low quality.[30] From the analysis carried out, only a part of the workers active on the digital platforms are in this situation, in particular those who possess capital such as cars or apartments.

What we actually experience with the digital platforms is an informality connected to basic services such as transport, lodging, personal delivery. It is rather a continuation of the traditional labour market heterogeneity, which best fits the segmentation thesis that the informal market follows the same patterns and hierarchies of the formal one; as the analysis demonstrates, informal work is carried out not only by the unemployed, but also by those engaged in formal employment, who are interested to round up their incomes as well as by high skilled professionals who see informality as a means to maximise profits.

IV Conclusion

The above has tried to briefly depict informal work in digital platforms in Chile. The transformation of informal work is seldom complete, and traditional forms of informality have always coexisted with their modern siblings, resulting in a phenomenon that is both horizontally and vertically multi-layered and can never be treated outside the traditional labour market.

When it comes to the gig economy, informality is more visible, not new; its chameleonic nature and power of adaptation to a labour market that, in its turn, follows faithfully the modes and means of production that the markets offer is undisputable. The effects are unfair competition for the formal enterprises in avoiding taxes, other costs of production,[31] an increased number of informal workers and an even sharper segmentation of the informal labour market. In Chile's case this is a reflection of the domestic labour market's informal patterns.

V Bibliography

Albagli, Garcia and Restrepo, 2016, *Assessing the Flexibility of the Labour Market in Chile: An International Perspective*, last accessed on 9 June 2018.

Bracha, A., and Burke, M., 2014, *Informal Work Activity in the United States: Evidence from Survey Responses*, Current Policy Perspectives, no. 14-13.

Bracha, A., and Burke. M., 2016, *Who Counts as Employed? Informal Work, Employment Status, and Labour Market Slack*, Current Policy Perspectives, no. 16-29.

---

30 Williams, C. and Windebank, J., 1998, *Informal Employment in Advanced Economies: Implications for Work and Welfare*.

31 Chen, M.A., 2012, *The Informal Economy: Definitions, Theories and Policies.* WIEGO Working Paper, no. 1

Brinkley, I., 2016, *In Search of the Gig Economy*, The Work Foundation, retrieved from www.theworkfoundation.com/wp-content/uploads/2016/11/407_In-search-of-the-gig-economy_June2016.pdf, last accessed 9 June 2018.

Castel, R., 2009, *La montee des incertitudes. Travail, protections, status de l'individu.* Paris: Seuil.

Centro de Estudios de la Economía Digital, Cámara de Comercio de Santiago, 2016, *La economía digital en Chile*, retrieved from www.ccs.cl/html/economia_digital/docs/economia_digital_B.pdf, last accessed on 9 June 2018.

Chen, M.A., 2012, *The Informal Economy: Definitions, Theories and Policies*. WIEGO Working Paper, no. 1.

De Soto, H., 1989, *The Other Path: The Invisible Revolution in the Third World*. New York: Harper and Row.

Díaz, E., and Gálvez., T., 2015, *Informalidad laboral mas trabajadores productivos sin protección laboral*, retrieved from www.dt.gob.cl/portal/1629/articles-110457_recurso_1.pdf, last accessed 9 June 2018.

Estado de la banda ancha en América Latina y el Caribe, 2016, retrieved from www.cepal.org/es/publicaciones/estado-la-banda-ancha-america-latina-caribe-2016, last accessed on 9 June 2018.

Fundación País Digital, *Estudio Índice País Digital*, 2017, retrieved from www.indicepaisdigital.cl, last accessed 9 June 2018.

Global Digital Report, 2018, retrieved from https://digitalreport.wearesocial.com/, last accessed on 9 of June.

IMF, 2018, *Measuring the Digital Economy*, retrieved from www.imf.org/en/Publications/Policy-Papers/Issues/2018/04/03/022818-measuring-the-digital-economy, last accessed 9 June 2018.

Maloney, W.F., 2004, *Informality Revisited. World Development.*

Mann, C., 2001, *The internet and the global economy*, retrieved from http://unpan1.un.org/intradoc/groups/public/documents/un/unpan000696.pdf, last accessed 9 June 2018.

McKinsey & Company, 2016, *Independent workforce: choice, necessity, and the gig economy*, retrieved from www.mckinsey.com.

Sehnbruch, K., 2006, *The Chilean Labor Market – A Key to Understanding Latin American Labor Markets.*

The Internet of Things: Evolution or Revolution? Retrieved from www.biztositasiszemle.hu/files/201506/aig_white_paper_iot_english_tcm2538-677834.pdf, last accessed 9 June 2018.

Williams, C., and Windebank, J., 1998, *Informal Employment in Advanced Economies: Implications for Work and Welfare.*

Zaballos, A., and Rodríguez, E., 2017, *Economía digital en América Latina y el Caribe*, retrieved from https://publications.iadb.org/bitstream/handle/11319/8701/Economia-digital-en-America-Latina-y-el-Caribe-situacion-actual-y-recomendaciones.PDF, last accessed 9 June 2018.

6 Regulating technology at work

*María Marta Travieso**

I Introduction

Technological innovation brings new dimensions and new possibilities, moving the frontiers of human capability much further than we could have ever imagined. In the world of work, the impact of technology is manifold. The possible destruction and creation of jobs due to automation and robotisation has already triggered intense public debate on the "Future of Work". At the same time, working conditions have improved considerably in many sectors, and hazards have been reduced, thanks precisely to automation or robotisation. However, new challenges have emerged: new conditions of work, new forms of organising work and new requirements to perform work. In particular, technology has enabled new forms of work and new forms of organisation of work which are difficult to seize, where roles and responsibilities are not clear, where the limits between workers and employers are blurred or appear to be blurred, and where the time and space dimensions are diluted. Moreover, the irruption of big data and automated decisions in the world of work raises many questions from the point of view of workers' rights, transparency and accountability. These challenges have prompted reflections about the appropriateness of existing regulations and policies, and about the consequences for the world of work, for workers' rights and for business development. While the full impact of innovations on the world of work is difficult to seize, some facets are being closely examined to determine whether the existing regulatory frameworks are still fit for the purpose.

This short paper aims at providing an overview of three aspects of work where this examination could take place, acknowledging that it is in the nature of technological changes to disrupt the established order and routines, prompting society's reaction and the establishment of a new framework with a view to harnessing the potentialities and mitigating the negative effects of these seemingly tectonic shifts. Such a new framework takes shape through regulation, judicial decisions and policies.

---

* The author is a legal officer at the International Labour Organization. The usual disclaimer applies.

Before embarking on such analysis, there is a threshold question to be asked: Are these changes brought about by technology, a novel manifestation of previous trends or a radical departure from the past? The reply to this question is critical to determine whether existing regulatory, legal and institutional structures are still fit for purpose, albeit certainly with some adaptations, or whether we need to change them radically and adopt new models.

The paper is organised as follows. In the following section we will examine some aspects of platform work and in particular the special relation between the platform itself and those who perform work. The second section addresses how new technologies and the digitalisation of work have contributed to the elimination of the space and time dimensions and how this is affecting the organisation of work and production as well as workers' lives. In the last section, we will examine how big data could impact on the world of work and on workers and which could be the potential risks.

II New forms of work and the protection of workers

The classic standard employment relationship characterised by a full time permanent job, with fixed hours and social protection, is nowadays in crisis.[1] This crisis manifests itself in various forms, most notably through the increasing recourse to what the ILO calls "non-standard forms of employment" (NSFE) – an array of different situations in the labour market such as temporary employment, temporary agency work and other temporary arrangements involving multiple parties, ambiguous employment relationships and part-time employment. Some of them have always existed while others are the response to globalisation and technological innovations.[2]

One such NSFE is the so-called "Platform work", which is growing in importance throughout the world and is changing the way of doing business in many sectors – the so-called Uberisation of the economy. Platform work first appeared in very structured and rigid markets, like transport or accommodation, which used to be characterised by strict rules of entry, but it expanded afterwards onto other – more flexible – sectors, where any kind of service is provided.

This kind of work can take two forms: services delivered digitally (or crowd work) and services provided physically (work on demand via apps). In the former, once allocated to a specific worker, the task is provided by the worker through the internet (e.g. counselling, text editing, translation), and in the latter, the worker provides his/her work outside the platform (e.g. transport, cleaning,

---

1 Many consider that the standard employment relationship is not so standard and that it has always coexisted with other forms of employment. See, for example, Williams, S., *Introducing employment relations: a critical approach*, Oxford, 2014.
2 ILO, *Non-standard employment around the world, understanding challenges, shaping prospects*, International Labour Organisation, Geneva, 2016. See also, Drahokoupil, J., and Brian, F., *The platform economy and the disruption of the employment relationship*, ETUI Policy Brief No. 5/2016.

hosting). Although these two forms are different, they have many common features: they constitute a clear form of outsourcing of activities that were once performed by the company in-house; each of these categories is not homogeneous and differ from case to case. These features have obviously legal consequences regarding the type of contract, and the classification of workers' platform work is extremely flexible and, depending on the type of service concerned, may be a new entrance to the world of work for many workers that have difficulties accessing the labour market (e.g. young workers, old workers, workers with disabilities and workers with family responsibilities). Flexible access to work, flexible working time and autonomous organisation are some of the characteristics of this form of work. Some even argue that it overcomes some discriminatory practices existing in the open labour market, as platforms are colour- and gender-blind.[3] At the same time, this flexibility may lead to stress, long unpaid waiting hours as well as excessive or unsociable working hours. Workers are usually forced to work on diverse platforms to make a living. There is also a segmentation of jobs in menial tasks which facilitates the "commoditisation" of work. Workers do not enjoy work-related benefits such as holidays, health and accidents insurance, pension or maternity leave. A situation of informalisation and precarisation of work emerges, as in most NSFE, due to the shifting of responsibilities from the employer to the worker.[4]

Governments – and in many ways the society as a whole – are reflecting on the nature of platform work, the kind of relationships embedded in it and the correspondent parties' responsibilities.[5] Unions and workers associations have had a very active role in this regard. From the regulatory point of view, platform work presents many facets that have to be tackled simultaneously – workers classification, workers conditions of work, reputation, privacy rights, intellectual property and taxation, among others. For the purpose of this paper, I will focus mainly on the classification of workers and the relations among parties.

While the relationship between the client and the platform is generally "one of provision of services", the relationship between the platform and the persons that carry out the job or task requested is not so evident. There is no common understanding regarding the workers' status and consequently their rights. Indeed, the status of these individuals performing jobs within the platform will dictate the applicable law with regard to, inter alia, wages, working hours and collective bargaining. Three issues have to be determined: Is this work? Are the

---

3 See below the link to algorithm construction.
4 See Valerio Di Stefano, *The rise of the "just-in-time workforce": on-demand work, crowdwork and labour protection in the "gig-economy"*, International Labour Office, Geneva: ILO, 2016.
5 In the United Kingdom, for example, the 2016 Taylor Report prompted a series of consultations and reflections on issues relating to employment rights, agency work, transparency in the labour market and employment status. With respect to the latter, the issue consists in determining whether someone is an employee or not and providing all workers with adequate information about their contract ("written particulars") as well as a payslip for all workers, including zero hours. The issue of holidays was also considered.

persons performing it workers? What kind of relationship exists between the platform and these persons?

Different situations may arise. The first situation could be the isolated provision of a service, where the platform solely puts parties (provider and client) in contact. These parties establish the rules, and the service is provided following these rules, for example, the case of a gardener who advertises his or her services through a platform. This would be considered as autonomous work. As long as the person executing the work preserves his/her autonomy, it is legitimate to call this form of work "autonomous" and the worker "self-employed". The situation varies when the platform starts to provide more specific services to clients and put more stringent conditions on platform workers.

Platforms consider themselves as mere intermediaries or agents between the customer and what they call the "independent contractor" or the "service provider". This can be clearly seen in recent judicial and arbitral decisions in the United Kingdom. In these cases, the relevant platforms (i.e. Uber and Deliveroo) argued that they were agents serving as intermediaries between the drivers and passengers and between the riders and customers, respectively.[6] It is common that these enterprises insert clauses in the contracts with the person who performs the job that specifically define the relationship as self-employment.[7] Being a mere intermediary or agent, which was not recognised by the judicial decision, would enable platforms to avoid the costs and regulations associated with employment.

However, when platforms impose on these persons many requirements and obligations as regards working time, personal appearance, prices, conduct as well as stringent monitoring through customers reviews, they arguably go well beyond the role of intermediary or agent or that of the provision of services. Against this backdrop, relevant instances in many jurisdictions prefer to look at the real features of the relationship instead of focusing exclusively on the terms of the contract between platforms and individuals performing the relevant tasks.[8] For example, in Uber_B.V_ and others V Mr Y Aslam and Others (UKEAT

---

6 UK decisions: Central Arbitration Committee (CAC), Trade Union and Labour relations (consolidation) Act 1992, schedule A1. Collective bargaining: recognition decision on whether to accept the application: Independent Workers' Union of Great Britain (IWGB) and RooFoods Limited T/A Deliveroo, and Uber_B.V_ and others V Mr Y Aslam and Others UKeat 0056_17_ DA.

7 The nature of the company also matters. In that regard, platforms have also argued that they are only tech companies (an electronic intermediary serviced or an information society service) – an argument rebutted in a case before the US Supreme Court of California and more recently by the European Court of Justice that decided that Uber was a transportation service and had thus to abide by the law of the member state where it is established. The nature of the company has consequences concerning licencing agreements as well as labour legislation at national level.

8 In Uber_B.V_ and others V Mr Y Aslam and Others UKeat 0056_17_ DA, the Employment Tribunal rejected the label agency used in the contractual documentation. It found various examples of control being exercised by Uber (route to adopt, ratings by customers, average scores to have etc.) and decided to look at the reality of the obligations and of the situation. In Dewhurst v. Citisprint (Case No: 2202512/2Q1), the Employment Tribunal considered that the "Tender document does not, however, describe the reality of the situation".

0056_17_ DA), the employment tribunal noted that according to Uber, the driver was *an independent contractor* because she/he could work for other enterprises, including competitors, had to meet the expenses associated with running the vehicles, fund their own licences and treat themselves as self-employees for tax purposes. The tribunal considered however that the enterprise imposed too many conditions that curtailed the worker's freedom to choose whether or not to provide his/her work or even to work for different intermediaries.[9] Workers continued to have the possibility to accept or reject the job and to determine how much time they would spend on the job. However, as long as there is no real possibility to be substituted, tribunals in the United Kingdom have considered that they are "workers" entitled to some rights (concerning minimum wage, working time and holidays) in accordance with the relevant legislation which defines "worker" as an individual who undertakes to do or perform "personally" any work or services for another party to the contract who is not a professional client of his.[10] The fact that work could not be performed by a substitute was key to determine the worker status.

Tribunals in different jurisdictions have adopted other approaches to determine the worker status. Some of them have turned to the "control criteria", that is, the fact that the individual must follow specific instructions and that the platform bases the employment relationship or the control on customer ratings. In a decision adopted in 2015 in the United States, the Supreme Court of California argued that the "right of control need not extend to every possible detail of the work". Rather, the relevant question is whether the entity retains "all necessary control" over the worker's performance. The fact that a certain amount of freedom is allowed or is inherent in the nature of the work involved does not preclude a finding of employment status. "It is not a question of how much control a hirer exercises, but how much control the hirer retains the right to exercise".[11] This has also been the criteria adopted by the Employment Tribunal in the United Kingdom in *Dewhurst v. Citisprint*. In this decision, the employment tribunal also examined the "integration in the business organisation" to determine the "worker" status, the idea being that workers provide their work so that the enterprise, in turn, provides the service to the customer. These workers are key for the development of the business; without them there is no business. Another criterion is the bargaining powers of parties: while in a services model

---

9 The Court of Appeal, in its ruling of December 2018 ([2018] EWCA Civ 2748), upheld the Employment Tribunal Decision and dismissed Uber's appeal. It agreed on almost all the grounds considered by the Employment Tribunal, according to which "Uber runs a transportation business. The drivers provide the skilled labour through which the organisation delivers its services and earns its profits". The Court also agreed with the Employment Tribunal that "at the very latest the driver is 'working' for Uber from the moment he accepts any trip".
10 United Kingdom, Employment Tribunal in Dewhurst v. Citisprint (Case No: 2202512/2Q1).
11 US DOUGLAS O'CONNOR, et al. v. UBER TECHNOLOGIES, INC., et al. (No. C-13-3826 EMC ORDER DENYING DEFENDANT UBER TECHNOLOGIES, INC.'S MOTION FOR SUMMARY JUDGMENT (Docket No. 211), Northern District of California.

the contractor and the provider of the services have similar bargaining power, this is not the case between platforms and workers in the gig economy.

In June 2018, the Supreme Court, in a very much expected decision, upheld previous rulings concerning Pimlico Plumbers Ltd and recognised the worker condition of a plumber on the grounds that the enterprise exercised strict administrative control over him, including his pay, restricted his ability to work for competitors and had to perform the "work personally" rather than pass it on to a substitute contractor.

However, the situation is not always clear, as evidenced by a recent decision of the Central Arbitration Committee (CAC) in the United Kingdom concerning Deliveroo.[12] In this case, the CAC had to decide on a claim filed by the Independent Workers Union of Great Britain, who had applied for recognition for collective bargaining purposes under the Trade Union and Labour Relations (Consolidation) Act 1992. One of the requirements to grant this recognition is to prove representability of a certain percentage of workers. However, in November 2017, the CAC did not recognise the "worker" condition of Deliveroo drivers. The parties agreed that there was no "contract of employment", but did not agree whether under the contract the riders undertake to do or perform "personally" (as required by the law to be considered a worker) any work or services for Deliveroo. Two issues were at stake here: the obligation to perform work and the existence of personal service. According to Deliveroo, there was no legal obligation and no "personal" service obligation. Instead, there was a right to provide a substitute independently of the fact that the right had never been exercised. According to the CAC's finding, the fact that riders could be substituted and not required to perform the job personally, determined that they were not workers. For this reason, even if they could demonstrate representability, the fact that the riders were not workers implied that the Unions' claim for recognition to negotiate on pay, hours and holidays with Deliveroo could not be accepted. This decision was upheld by the High Court of Justice in December 2018.[13]

A similar decision, also concerning Deliveroo, was adopted by the Court of Appeal of Paris in November 2017.[14] The contract signed between the parties – a contract of provision of services – classifies workers as self-employed ("auto-entrepreneur" in French), even though the post had been advertised as a contract of employment. A contract of employment under French legislation requires that a person engages in work under the orders of another in return for remuneration. In its judgement, the court held that there was no employment contract because the plaintiff could not prove that the enterprise gave such directives or

---

12 United Kingdom, CAC, Trade Union and Labour relations (consolidation) Act 1992, schedule A1. Collective bargaining: recognition decision on whether to accept the application: Independent Workers' Union of Great Britain (IWGB) and RooFoods Limited T/A Deliveroo.
13 See, in this regard, United Kingdom, the High Court of Justice, Queen's Bench division administrative court [2018] EWHC 3342 (Admin) Case No: CO/810/2018.
14 France, CA Paris, Pôle 6-ch 2 9 novembre 2017, no. 16/12875. Lire en ligne: www.doctrine.fr/d/CA/Paris/2017/C125532D4DDC78DA11AE2.

itineraries. Moreover, the worker had full freedom to work or not to work and to determine when and how much to work. The worker concerned could not demonstrate the existence of a dependent relationship with the enterprise that would amount to an employment contract.

The situation is evolving rapidly. Judicial actions concerning the gig economy and the conditions of workers are pending all over the world. The decisions examined here have filled some gaps. With the exception of the cases of Deliveroo, these decisions have recognised that platform work is work, and that those performing the jobs are workers, ensuring that they will enjoy some labour rights. The decisions did not go as far as recognising the existence of an "employment relationship", which is much more difficult to prove, but which would have granted full labour protection to workers.

In this context, workers would be an intermediate category between full employment relationship and independent contractor or service provider. Other countries have also established a third category of worker (the "dependent contractors" in the United States or the "para-subordinate" in Italy), on the grounds that these types of workers can choose when to work, an option not available for the employee. That "choice", as already said, or that possibility to choose is not always real. It is unclear whether platform work brings new and different elements that would justify the establishment of this new category of workers. In fact, the conditions in which platform work is performed makes the proof of the employment relationship more difficult, but does not necessarily change the nature of the link between the platform and the worker. The establishment of a third category might actually push enterprises even more to use these structures to avoid responsibilities and costs, thereby curtailing workers' rights and increasing uncertainty. As explained by De Stefano, it is important to consider these jobs as work and address them within the wider labour market, so as to treat problems, shortcomings and difficulties holistically.

Measures are also being taken for the regulation of platform work at regional level. One such case is the resolution adopted by the European Parliament on 19 January 2017 to update the European Pillar of Social Rights. The resolution calls on EU Member States to work together to present a proposal for a framework directive on decent working conditions in all forms of employment, extending existing minimum standards to new kinds of employment relationships. It also calls for more effective and efficient implementation and control of existing labour standards in order to improve the enforceability of rights:

> for work intermediated by digital platforms and other instances of dependent self-employment, a clear distinction – for the purpose of EU law and without prejudice to national law – between those genuinely self-employed and those in an employment relationship, taking into account ILO Recommendation No 198, according to which the fulfilment of several indicators is sufficient to determine an employment relationship; the status and basic responsibilities of the platform, the client and the person performing the work should thus be clarified; minimum standards of collaboration rules

should also be introduced with full and comprehensive information to the service provider on their rights and obligations, entitlements, associated level of social protection and the identity of employer; those employed as well as those genuinely self-employed who are engaged through online platforms should have analogous rights as in the rest of the economy and be protected through participation in social security and health insurance schemes; Member States should ensure proper surveillance of the terms and conditions of the employment relationship or service contract, preventing abuses of dominant positions by the platforms.

There are other aspects concerning platform work that need to be addressed. Rules should be established concerning fundamental rights at work, but also concerning such other aspects as ratings and reputation. In the case of reputation management, currently clients may reject a provider on the basis of feedback from previous clients. Some consider that these reputations should also be portable.[15] While this could be beneficial if the reputation (rating) is good, it could also facilitate discrimination and black listing. Another issue to take into account is taxation. There are usually agreements between platforms and governments on tax policies. Countries like France and Estonia, for example, have taken concrete measures in this regard, considering workers performing tasks in the context of platforms as independent workers for the payment of taxes.

III Digitalisation and the time and space dimensions

One of the consequences of the latest wave of technological innovations, in particular Information and Communication Technologies (ICT), is the dilution of the time and space dimensions. It is now possible to work anytime anywhere.[16] This has obvious advantages: it provides increased flexibility, allowing the worker to conciliate work and family responsibilities, and it permits the conformation of teams with colleagues living all over the world. It can also permit the participation of workers with disabilities in the labour market.[17] Some also argue that this flexibility enables workers to be more productive, as some tasks are facilitated or even carried out by technological means, commuting time is reduced, autonomy is increased and workers are less prone to interruptions in case of teleworking.

---

15 See comments below concerning the General Data Protection regulation (GDPR).
16 See, in this respect, Messenger, J., Vargas Llave, O., Gschwind, L., Boehmer, S., Vermeylen, G., and Wilkens, M., *Working anytime, anywhere: The effects on the world of work*, ILO and Eurofound: Luxembourg, 2017. See also Rubery, J., Ward, K., Grimshaw, D. and Beynon, H., Working time, industrial relations and the employment relationship, *Time & Society*, Vol. 14, No. 1 (2005), pp. 89–1111.
17 In Case No. 12-2484, EEOC v. Ford Motor Company Originating Case No.: 5:11-cv-13742, the US Court of Appeal considered that telecommuting may be a form of reasonable accommodation in case of workers with disabilities.

Technology can be, however, a double-edge sword with negative impact on the quality of working life as well as on work-life balance. Work intensification, unpaid work, extended working hours (including during evenings and nights as well as during the weekends), blurring of boundaries between work and private life, family conflicts and increased stress and burnout are unwanted consequences of new ways of working facilitated by ICT. ICT may also facilitate an excess of control over employees. Therefore, while ICT helps streamline and accelerate processes, workers may end up having additional workloads.

This is contrary to what Keynes envisioned when he wrote about the reduction of working time and the increasing free time.[18] Some talk in this respect about the ICT paradox,[19] that is, the fact that while working hours have been considerably reduced throughout the twentieth century, and many developed countries are already taking measures for further reductions, individuals – this time as consumers – demand a 24-hour society where services and goods are available uninterruptedly throughout the day.

Telework, which is facilitated by ICT, is increasingly used by workers and employers throughout the world. Telework could be divided in two types: regular telework and overtime telework. The former is regularly carried out in places of office work – many enterprises have a percentage of their workforce which works under this form of telework, either teleworking 100% of their working time or sharing their working time between teleworking and working within the employers' premises – and the other form involves work done as telework, but on top of office work, as overtime work.

As a corollary of the blurring of lines between work and leisure due to the possibility of working anytime, anywhere, workers have come under increasing pressure to be permanently available. This is easily perceivable, for example, among professionals, managers and clerical workers rather than in manual work. There is an increased tendency to continue teleworking (in particular, replying to mails and being reachable) after working hours, at night and during weekends. This is one of the consequences of a changing work organisation and working culture. It is not necessarily requirements imposed on workers. However, there is a perception among management and workers of higher involvement and compromise with the enterprise when there is full-time availability. Moreover, with globalization, enterprises interact with clients from other countries with different working days and/or different time zones. As mentioned above, this has consequences on work-life balance and on health as it is the source of increased stress and burn out. This overtime work does not necessarily translate into increased pay, and goes many times unrecognised and uncontrolled.

These aspects or at least some of them have already been addressed by some countries, while others are currently envisaging the adoption of specific measures.

---

18 In 1930, in the essay "Economic Prospects for our Grandchildren", Keynes forecasted that in a century's time (that is around 2030), we would all be working 15 hours a week.
19 Messenger, op.cit. and Korunka, C., Hoonakker P., (ed) *The impact of ICT on quality of working life*, Springer editions, New York, 2014.

In France, for example, the labour law of 2016 established the "right to disconnect".[20] The new law makes it mandatory for enterprises with more than 50 employees to negotiate with social partners the modalities for the use of digital tools, with a view to ensuring that rest and leave periods as well as personal and family life are respected. This includes the possibility of not replying to emails after working hours. If no agreement is reached, the employer is required to draw up a charter after consultation with the works council or failing that with staff delegates, laying down the procedures for exercising the right to disconnect and providing for the implementation of training and awareness-raising activities on the reasonable use of digital tools for employees and management. The law does not provide for sanctions in case of non-respect, though. Similarly, in the United States, a bill presented to the New York City Council on 22 March 2018 provides for the prohibition for any private enterprise to require employees to check emails on non-working hours. Other countries like Chile and the Netherlands are also examining the adoption of such measures.

Similar measures have also been adopted at the firm level. For example, Daimler Benz has established limits to the possibility of checking emails outside normal working hours. In the same vein, BMW reached an agreement with the works council allowing employees to register time spent working outside the employer's premises.[21]

Working time regulations at national and international level are also being re-examined as they no longer respond to reality. Many of them date back decades and do not take into account how ICT have impacted the world of work.

Several other aspects have to be taken into account when examining telework: classification of workers, remuneration, access to training and promotion, supervision of working conditions, representation of workers and the role of collective bargaining as well as internal rules of the enterprise.

The place where the worker carries out his/her job should not affect his/her classification as an employee. There can be employees working outside the workplace and independent contractors working in the workplace. Two essential and substantive elements must be considered when examining telework: the kind of work performed by the worker and the degree of control the employer has on the worker.

The determination of remuneration has also been an object of debate. How to control working hours and determine productivity? Some suggest in this respect that remuneration of teleworkers should be based on objectives fulfilled, while others on time effectively worked which has been rendered possible by innovative software. In addition, teleworkers should be treated equally to those workers performing functions on the employer's premises – they should have access to equal remuneration for work of equal value as well as equal

---

20 Article 55 of the Labour Law.
21 See Messenger et al., op.cit.

opportunities in access to training and promotions. Another aspect to take into consideration is isolation. This has two concrete consequences. First, it is difficult to ensure adequate monitoring of working conditions, and second, it is difficult for workers to access trade unions and *vice versa*, including for collective bargaining purposes.

Several countries have already adopted regulation concerning telework.[22] Telework has also been addressed through collective bargaining. In Europe, for example, the European Trade Union Confederation (ETUC), the Union of Industrial and Employers' Confederations of Europe–the European Union of Crafts and Small and Medium-Sized Enterprises (UNICE–UEAPME) and the Centre of Enterprises with Public Participation (ECPE) adopted in 2002 a framework agreement on telework which establishes general rules concerning employment conditions. The framework guarantees that teleworkers will have the same overall level of protection as workers who carry out their activities at the employer's premises. With regard to working time, the agreement provides that, within the framework of the applicable legislation, under the collective agreements and the company rules: (1) the teleworker manages the organisation of his/her working time and (2) the workload and performance standards applicable to the teleworker should be equivalent to those of comparable workers at the employer's premises. Interestingly, the framework also addresses such issues of interest to teleworkers such as data protection, privacy, equipment, occupational health and safety, training and career development and collective rights.

IV Big data and algorithms at work

Never before have human beings had access to as much information as it is available today. Together with evolutions in ICT, data has increased exponentially and has become what we call nowadays big data. This data may be combined and analysed – through the use of algorithms – by powerful computing systems in order to determine trends and patterns. Artificial intelligence enables the adoption of automated decisions on the basis of ever-increasing amounts of data. Big data is characterised by its volume, its variety (variety of sources) and its velocity (to collect and analyse).

Big data includes the collection of large amounts of personal data, which comes from very diverse sources. This personal data may concern all aspects of a person's life, from gender to age, to civil status and address (the most common) through to personal characteristics (race, religion, health, minority status, disability status), studies, behaviour, lifestyle and political views. This information can be used with multiple objectives. It is widely used by business to predict

---

22 See, in this regard, Luque Parra, M., and Camargo, A., *Teleworking and labour conditions: conclusions.* IUS Labor 2/2017 and, International Labour Organisation, *Ensuring decent working time for the future*, General Survey concerning working-time instruments, International Labour Office, Geneva, 2018.

consumer behaviour,[23] and by governments in the framework of security policies and crime prevention. Enterprises increasingly use it for human resources management.[24]

There are several aspects to take into account when addressing big data from the perspective of work. First of all, big data provides the opportunity to adopt more adequate policies based on available information.

Big data is also changing many professions. Access to information on a big scale enables professionals to adopt better informed decisions. Medicine is a case in point: availability of information based on medical cases throughout the world allows better-founded diagnosis. The same happens with legal services, where the availability of jurisprudence and case law may support better advice to clients. Together with healthcare and the legal profession, the insurance and financial sectors are also particularly impacted. Big data is having a decisive influence in many work domains. It is legitimate therefore to enquire about the relationship between big data and work and, in particular, about the impact that big data – or the use of it – may have on the world of work.

Control and privacy are crucial elements to take into account when talking about personal data. Who controls the data? Who controls the use of private data? How to ensure that privacy is respected? Where is the boundary between privacy and public domain? How to ensure that consent is provided? Is it possible to use data for any purpose without the specific consent of the owner? Can all sources of information be valued equally? Rule of law and transparency as well as accountability should be taken into account in big data management, in particular when automated decisions are involved.

Let us focus, for example, on human resources management – hiring and promotion policies and practices, in particular. Many consider that the use of big data and the law of big numbers ensure objectivity as well as diversity and inclusion. The more employers use analytical tools for recruiting and hiring, the more the decisions will become objective and unbiased. Would that be the case at all times? Big data can be used to support diversity but, at the same time, the use of predictive analytics and technology-driven decisions could have adverse effects on some workers, particularly those who lack "a robust digital footprint". Moreover, some observers question the manner in which this data is analysed, and consider that it is highly likely that the algorithms used to discern patterns and trends arising from the data be biased or lead to biased and discriminatory decisions.[25] They can either be set to filter certain information discriminating, for example, on the grounds of race or colour or they can be set to learn from human decisions following their pattern for decision-making, which can, in

---

23 Recent events concerning *Cambridge Analytica* and its influence on US national elections are a clear example of how far it is possible to go with big data.
24 See, in this regard, Reinsch, R. and Goltz, S., Big data: Can the attempt to be more discriminating be more discriminatory instead, *Saint Louis University Law Journal*, Vol. 61, No. 35 (2016).
25 For example, the combination of domicile and consumer behaviour can contribute in some cases to racial or ethnic discrimination.

turn, be biased.[26] Others simply question the quality and nature of the data that is used for these technology-driven decisions. What is the quality of this information? Is the system using all the information available or is it making a selection? If the latter, on what basis? Are all sources of information equally valid and reliable?

The ownership of data has also been the subject of heated debate. Indeed, the collection of big data has been facilitated by the increased capacity to stock it in very powerful data centres that are owned mainly by the biggest multinationals. In that regard, many even refer to big data as the enterprises' new raw material or as a new commodity.[27] Can data be commoditised? What are the consequences of considering data as a simple commodity? Would it be possible for individuals to take back the control of their own data and even to get some income from it? On another note, much of the data that can be found in the internet is controlled by thousands of people throughout the world (mainly platform workers) that exercise some kind of content control (e.g. with respect to the use of aggressive language, display of pornography, political opinions, religious messages etc.). These persons eliminate supposedly "useless information", correct texts or even edit language. However, when carrying out these activities, these persons may be involuntarily incorporating some bias or a priori value judgements into the information. They may be, for instance, deleting some substantive information that would have enabled a different reading of a person's profile. Generally, these persons do not receive any specific training or awareness raising to prevent bias or stereotypes from contaminating the information.

Albeit with delays – regulation always lags behind technological innovation – governments around the world have started to review and adapt existing legislation to respond to the challenges posed by big data management and the rapid evolution of related technology.[28] In the European Union, the General Data Protection Regulation (GDPR) adopted in 2016, and which will enter into force on 25 May 2018, contains significant provisions from the perspective of work. The main improvements over the previous regulation – the 1995 Data Protection Directive – concern the increased territorial scope, the introduction of more stringent rules of consent, which can be withdrawn at any time, and the right of the individual to request information concerning his or her own data. It also establishes the principle of purpose limitation which means that data can be used solely with the purpose it was collected for. Importantly, the Regulation also provides for the right of the individual to be "forgotten" (i.e. the individual may get his/her personal data erased) and for data portability (i.e. the right for

---

26 Reinz et al., op.cit. p. 40. See also, Wagner, B., *Algorithmic regulation and the global default: Shifting norms in Internet technology*, Centre for Internet & Human Rights, European University Viadrina, ETIKK I PRAKSIS NR.1 2016, p. 5.
27 See, in this respect, Arrieta Ibarra, I., Goff, L., Jiménez Hernandez, D., Lanier, J., and Wyl, G., *Should we treat data as labor? Moving beyond "free"*, Data as Labour, May 2018.
28 For example, the US Equal Employment Opportunity Commission is examining the impact of big data and its challenges for the individual.

an individual to transmit that data to another controller), thus enhancing the individual's sovereignty over his/her own data.[29]

The question of consent has many interesting facets from the point of view of the employment relationship. According to the Regulation, this has to be "freely given". However, the proof of this is harder when power between parties in the relationship is unbalanced. This is one of the reasons that explains that the conditions of consent are stricter. In the GDPR, consent has to be distinguishable from other matters, easy to give and easy to withdraw and separate consent for separate activities might be sought.

The regulation defines "Profiling" as:

> any form of automated processing of personal data consisting of the use of personal data to evaluate certain personal aspects relating to an individual, in particular to analyse or predict aspects concerning that individual's performance at work, economic situation, health, personal preferences, interests, reliability, behaviour, location or movements.[30]

Aiming at ensuring objective and unbiased decision-making, the GDPR prohibits the processing of personal data revealing racial or ethnic origin, political opinions, religious or philosophical beliefs or trade union membership, and the processing of genetic data, biometric data for the purpose of uniquely identifying a natural person, data concerning health or data concerning a natural person's sex life or sexual orientation shall be prohibited. The exceptions to this provision are very limited. The Regulation also protects the right of the individual to refuse to be subject to a decision based solely on automated processing, including profiling, which produces legal effects concerning him or her without any human intervention. This includes the refusal of applications or e-recruiting. The Regulation also enables Member States, by law or by collective agreements, to adopt rules to ensure the protection of the rights and freedoms in respect of the processing of employees' personal data in the employment context, in particular for the purposes of the recruitment, the performance of the contract of employment, including discharge of obligations laid down by law or by collective agreements, management, planning and organisation of work, equality and diversity in the workplace, health and safety at work, protection of employer's or customer's property and for the purposes of the exercise and enjoyment, on an individual or collective basis, of rights and benefits related to employment and

---

29 It is still difficult to determine the manner in which this portability will be implemented. In this regard, it could be interesting to study more deeply how data protection and blockchains or other forms of distributed ledger technologies could interact to facilitate data portability. See, in this respect, Finck, M., *Blockchains and data protection in the European Union*, Max Planck Institute for Innovation and Competition Research Paper Series No. 18-01.
30 It also defines "Personal data breach" as any "breach of security leading to the accidental or unlawful destruction, loss, alteration, unauthorised disclosure of, or access to, personal data transmitted, stored or otherwise processed."

for the purpose of the termination of the employment relationship. Although not yet in force, this Regulation is a valuable response to the multifaceted challenges posed by big data, algorithms and automated decisions. Reality will tell if they are effective.

The European Union is not alone in this exercise. Other initiatives are being pursued by countries such as the United Kingdom and Spain. A bill concerning data protection is currently being examined in the United Kingdom and the General Courts of Spain are currently examining a Draft Organic Law on Data Protection.

China has also adopted relevant legislation in this respect that will also enter into effect in May 2018, the Information technology – Personal Information Security Specification (GB/T 35273-2017) and the 2016 China Cybersecurity law 2016. These include provisions concerning data processing activities, including the collection, retention, use, sharing and transfer of personal information. The regulation, which applies to any private or public organisation (similar to the data controller of the GDPR), regulates the processing of personal information and sensitive personal information. Data controllers are recommended to follow basic principles relating to the processing of personal data. The specification is only a guideline but will serve the authorities to evaluate corporate practices adopted to ensure data protection. It is yet to be seen whether these regulations have the same approach to privacy as the GDPR.

V Conclusions

The advent of new technologies brings increasing diversity both in the world of work (for workers and employers) and in the modes of consumption and production. At the same time, it is possible that new technologies concentrate the benefits of work in the hands of fewer people. While this diversity could be beneficial (e.g. new flexible ways of working and of combining family and professional responsibilities), it needs to be managed effectively in order to avoid an increase in precarious, low-quality or dangerous jobs as well as a rise in inequality.

This paper has addressed some of the main issues raised by technology, namely platform work, the elimination of the space and time dimensions and the impact of big data. As we have seen, technology poses significant challenges for the world of work. In a way, paradoxically, technology raises challenges but is also an indispensable tool to address them. Technology, and in particular data availability, can support an adequate weighing of the pros and cons of the developments brought about by technological change. In that regard, constructive dialogue between employers and workers is essential for the assessment of the risks imposed by technology and for the adoption, if needed, of appropriate mitigating measures.

Platform work and telework are only two among the many aspects of the world of work that are being impacted by technology. For some, the fact that workers may choose whether to work or not and when to work goes against the existence of an employment relationship. In the eyes of many, this would justify the introduction of a third category of workers or, at least, the establishment of rules that are specific to this kind of work, by nature more flexible. But the reality may be too complex to address it through a simple definitional exercise. Developments in the labour market may have rendered the tests used to determine the existence of the employment relationship inefficient. This does not mean that the employment relationship does not exist but that we may have to look for other means to prove its existence. Yet, the diversity of the models available in the labour market makes a one-size-fits-all approach almost impossible. Telework – a response to the requirements of contemporary society – also contributes to the dilution of boundaries between work and private life. The regulation of telework aims at avoiding abuse and ensuring that the boundaries do not get completely blurred.

A delicate balance needs to be stricken between the benefits that big data analytics bring, and the ethical and privacy risks it poses. Some regulatory approaches, for example, the European GDPR, try to address both aspects. Increased transparency on how algorithms are constructed is essential for the governance of the system. Regulators should have access to algorithms on which decisions are based to ensure that they are not biased. Capacity building and holistic approaches are needed to adopt adequate policies concerning big data management and the protection of the rights of individuals. At the same time, individuals are not without responsibility when posting their personal data without taking into account possible consequences – further awareness raising is needed in that regard. Finally, awareness raising – if not specific deontological rules – should be extended to all those in charge of the elaboration of algorithms in order to ensure transparency, neutrality and non-bias.

Change due to technology is nothing new. But this time, change is happening at a much faster pace than ever before, which is making the divide between technological change and regulation (that always comes later) even more important. This calls for increased flexibility not only from workers and employers but also from governments. Changes are so radical and fundamental that – in this author's view – an ethical debate becomes unavoidable. It is worth noting in this regard that the fact that something is feasible thanks to technology does not mean that the society is obliged to adopt it or cannot shape it with a view to ensuring high ethical standards. Society needs to establish some lights and beacons that do not constrain innovation but are aimed at ensuring that technology remains "humane". Changes are indeed significant, wide-ranging and extremely diverse. However, it is not yet possible to conclude whether they are so radical as to require a completely new approach to these issues or whether they are new manifestations – complex, certainly – of previous trends that could be addressed by adapting current structures. In any case, some kind of grievance mechanism should be considered to protect workers against the negative impact of technology.

VI Bibliography

Arrieta Ibarra, I., Goff, L., Jiménez Hernandez, D., Lanier, J., and Wyl, G., *Should we treat data as labor? Moving beyond "free"*, Data as Labour, May 2018.

Calvo Gallego, J., Nuevas tecnologías y nuevas formas de trabajo, 2016. http://grupo.us.es/iwpr/2016/09/05/nuevas-tecnologias-y-nuevas-formas-de-trabajo/.

De Stefano, Valerio, *The rise of the "just-in-time workforce": on-demand work, crowdwork and labour protection in the "gig-economy"*, International Labour Office, Geneva: ILO, 2016.

Drahokoupil, J., and Brian, F., The platform economy and the disruption of the employment relationship, ETUI Policy Brief No. 5/2016.

Finck, Michèle, *Blockchains and data protection in the European Union*, Max Planck Institute for Innovation and Competition Research Paper Series No. 18-01.

International Labour Organisation (ILO), *Non-standard employment around the world, understanding challenges, shaping prospects*, International Labour Organisation, Geneva, 2016.

ILO, *Ensuring decent working time for the future, General Survey concerning working-time instruments*, International Labour Office, Geneva, 2018.

Korunka, C., and Hoonakker, P., (ed) *The impact of ICT on quality of working life*, Springer editions, 2014.

Lee, M.K., Kusbit, D., Metsky, E., and Dabbish, L., *Working with machines; The impact of algorithmic and data-driven management on human workers*, Carnegie Mellon University, 2015.

Luque Parra, M. and Camargo, A., *Teleworking and labor conditions: conclusions*, IUS Labor 2/2017.

Meda, D, *Le travail, Publications Universitaires de France,* PUF, Paris 2015.

Messenger, J., Vargas Llave, O., Gschwind, L., Boehmer, S., Vermeylen, G., and Wilkens, M., *Working anytime, anywhere: The effects on the world of work*, ILO and Eurofound, Luxembourg, 2017.

Reinsch, R. and Goltz, S., Big data: Can the attempt to be more discriminating be more discriminatory instead, *Saint Louis University Law Journal*, 61:35, 2016.

Rubery, J., Ward, K., Grimshaw, D., and Beynon, H., Working time, industrial relations and the employment relationship, *Time & Society*, 14:1, 2005.

Schumpeter, *Digital Taylorism, A modern version of "scientific management" threatens to dehumanise the workplace*, The Economist, September 2015.

Taylor, Matthew, Good work: the Taylor review of modern working practices, United Kingdom, Future of Work Commission report.

Wagner, B., *Algorithmic regulation and the global default: Shifting norms in Internet technology*, Centre for Internet & Human Rights, European University Viadrina, ETIKK I PRAKSIS NR.1 2016.

Williams, S., *Introducing employment relations: a critical approach*, Oxford, 2014.

Part two
Other new forms of work, new workforce and new skills

7 New forms of work and contractual execution

Towards the "smart labour contract"

Alicia Villalba Sánchez

I Introduction[1]

Over the last few centuries, technological innovation has changed the way in which we provide goods and services. Since the new means of transport have allowed the establishment of new trade routes, up to the invention of the steam engine, technological progress underlies historical and economic evolution. Social relations have not remained apart from transformation. This transformation has particularly affected labour relations, to the extent that they have contributed to changing the ways of working.

In the same way that the Fordist model has contributed to the employee's specialisation and the globalisation process has resulted in outsourcing, the implementation of new information and communication technologies has changed the way of hiring, organising and controlling workers. On the one hand, hiring of workers through digital platforms has called into question the usefulness of traditional indications of labour relations, such as subordination. On the other hand, new control procedures have made possible a continual and complete oversight of employees, which, in turn, jeopardises their privacy as well as their well-being at work.

Obviously, employers have taken full advantage of the aforementioned transformation in order to hire workers outside the labour legal framework and to subject them to a kind of technological servitude. Undoubtedly, the deficiencies of an obsolete regulation, contained in the Royal Legislative Decree 2/2015 of 23 October 2015, which approves the revised text of the Workers' Statute Act[2] - hereafter, WS - has not contributed to the protection of workers during this last industrial revolution.

If Spanish law still does not provide an answer to these problems, which have affected workers for years, even less has it addressed an emerging reality, which

---

1 This paper is one of many results of the National Research Project carried out by MINECO (Spain), entitled "New (newest) information and communication technologies and their impact on the labour market: emerging aspects at the national and international levels" (DER2016-75376-R), led by Prof. Lourdes Mella. Author's email: alicia.villalba@usc.es.
2 Text available in the link: www.boe.es/buscar/act.php?id=BOE-A-2015-11430.

is the implementation of mechanisms that allow the automatic execution of the labour contract. This paper deals with the possibilities and limitations of these technological innovations, still unknown by law and jurisprudence.

II The smart labour contract: The concept

The impact of new technologies on contracting was not an unknown phenomenon in our legal system, from the moment when it was necessary to articulate a special regulation of electronic contracting through Law 34/2002 of 11 July 2002 on information society services and electronic commerce. Articles 23 et seq. highlight the information duty of the service supplier, providing a legal framework applicable to the conclusion of contracts whose uniqueness was given by the medium in which they were concluded. The challenges posed at the time by the signing of these contracts of adhesion by electronic means are now overcome by those who propose the development of computer programmes, which also allow their automated execution. This is the manner in which the smart contract was created.

A smart contract is a computer protocol through which the elements of a legal relationship of change are formalised, with the purpose that their programmed terms are automatically demanded once a predefined condition has been fulfilled.[3] For this purpose, this "condition" could be defined an event, situation or circumstance indispensable for the existence of another event. The first event (so called "triggering event") can be an act carried out by one of the parties (for example, the delivery of a work, which causes automatic payment of the remuneration). But it can also be an event that does not depend on the actions of the parties (for example, the arrival of a date, at which the payment of the salary is scheduled). Once the programme has received confirmation of the arrival of the triggering event, the execution of the contract will be carried out automatically. In other words, signing the contract guarantees its compliance thanks to the computer protocol that automates its execution.

Although the smart contract is often based on blockchain technology, the principle of technological neutrality supports a broader concept of smart contract, including other self-executing agreements which use programmes – scripts – to execute the content of the contractual clauses after the arrival of the triggering events envisaged in them. Therefore, it would not be possible to modify, block or fail to perform the duty.[4]

Efficiency is therefore the main intrinsic advantage of this technology as well as the security provided to the party who has complied with the agreed terms by having the certainty that the software will execute the consideration

---

3 See Cuccuru, P., "Blockchain ed automatizacione contrattuale. Riflessioni sugli *smart contract*", *La Nuova giurisprudenza civile commentata*, ISSN 1593-7305, vol. 33, no. 1, 2017, p. 110.
4 Echebarría Sáenz, M., "Contratos electrónicos autoejecutables (smart contract) y pagos con tecnología blockchain", *Revista de Estudios Europeos*, no. 70, 2017, p. 70.

immediately. Consequently, the elimination of risks in contracting, a primary ambition of not only those who hire through electronic means, is another of the great virtues inherent to this ingenuity.

While these advantages are to the benefit of the employer, the smart contract seems appropriate to provide legal certainty for the employee. Notably, blockchain technology offers transparency as it is a shared digital ledger which allows the operations monitoring, taking into account the subjects who perform them.[5] The inability to alter the history of transactions carried out by users[6] increases the reliability of this technological innovation, even if the ledger is cryptographically sealed and makes the intervention of intermediaries superfluous.[7] All these reasons have justified the fact that blockchain technology is now considered to be inseparable from the smart contract concept, to the extent that it has been defined as a "manifestation" of blockchain technology.[8]

However, the fast-paced technological evolution recommends not limiting the legal considerations set out in this study to the implementation of blockchain, given the expected technological evolution of what is, in the end, only the most developed support for a trend towards contractual automation. Whether through blockchain technology or the implementation of other IT tools, the efficiency and security provided by the transposition of the traditional contract into a computer language capable of executing pre-designed decisions makes the construction and future development of smart contracts one of the greatest challenges facing current law.

III Towards the "smart labour contract"

It is not difficult to deduce the variety of legal business likely to benefit from this technology, which has been considered particularly suitable to replace those in which a notary or another kind of attesting official is involved. Its suitability for application in sectors where standardised contracting is frequent, where it regulates measurable conditions for possible translation into code and insertion into decentralised databases, explains its success in the financial sector.[9] Nonetheless, it is also useful in any other contract where there is an automatable transaction. It is thus used to channel a sale, remitting the payment once the system has been informed of the delivery of the committed consideration and also the payment

---

5 Keidar, R. & Greenbaum, E., "Blockchain: the power to reinvigorate law firms", *The lawyer*, vol. 31, no. 28, 2016, p. 23.
6 Davara Fernández de Marcos, E., "Los smart contract", *Actualidad dministrativa*, no. 7, 2017, p. 1.
7 Keidar, R. & Greenbaum, E., *op. cit.* p. 23.
8 Ibidem.
9 Cuccuru, P., *op. cit.*, p. 1.

of intellectual property rights, paying the amount to the author for each reproduction of his work.[10]

More difficult seems to be the adjustment of the above-mentioned technology to the peculiarities of a synallagmatic contract, where what is offered in exchange for an economic consideration is not a thing but a service provided on a continuous, voluntary, personal and direct basis by a person on behalf and within the scope of the organisation and management of the counterparty.[11] Certainly, the provision of work cannot be automated as long as it cannot be provided by entities endowed with artificial intelligence and even then, one might legitimately doubt that its activity should be the subject of attention for labour law. However, since new technologies have become the service provider's usual tool and even the means by which to execute the aforementioned provision, it is feasible to apprehend data which, once processed and included in the corresponding databases, can give rise to an automated response. If the correct performance of the service is disclosed, the response will consist of a remuneration whose calculation and payment may well be scheduled, as may the contributions and taxes to be deducted from the employee's payroll. If there is evidence of the employee's non-compliance, a penalty may be imposed and the contract may even be terminated.

It is possible to deduce that the contractual automation is presented on the horizon as the next step to advance in this process of immersion in new technologies that companies are carrying out. A few lines should be devoted to recalling the rights and guarantees of workers that could be compromised in this process, in order to highlight the risks that could arise from the lack of foresight of a legislator on whose response depends the protection of a worker whose subordination has been greatly aggravated. To this end, it is considered appropriate to begin by dealing with the problems intrinsic to the formalisation of the employment contract in the form of a smart contract, in order to then weigh up the impact that it could have on its content. Only when these issues have been addressed will it be necessary to deduce the possibilities that automated execution can offer within the applicable legal framework.

1 Drafting of the smart labour contract

As far as form is concerned, civil law does not preclude the drawing up of a contract directly in code. In the interests of legal certainty, labour law has largely departed from this freedom, as enshrined in art. 1278 of the Civil Code,[12] especially in the contractual modalities most likely to be used in an abusive manner

---

10 Keidar, R. & Greenbaum, E., *op. cit.* p. 23.
11 Article 1 WS.
12 Echebarría Sáenz, M., *op. cit.*, p. 72.

or in fraud, such as training contracts,[13] a large number of fixed-term contracts[14] or those concluded on a part-time basis, among others.[15]

The requirement for a written form raises serious doubts as to the admissibility of an employment contract expressed directly in computer code, at least as regards the wide range of contractual modalities referred to in article 8.2 WS. Computer code can only be written down, even if this operation is necessarily carried out on a virtual medium. In the face of this argument, one could argue against the reason for the requirement for the written conclusion of these types of employment contract. And this is none other than guaranteeing access to the content of the contract that is signed.

It is well known in sectors of the legal system intended for the protection of the weak contracting party such as consumer law that the accessibility of the contractual content is an indispensable prerequisite for the validity of the consent of the adherent. This is why article 80, of the Royal Legislative Decree 1/2007 of 16 November 2007, approving the consolidated text of the General Law for the Defence of Consumers and Users and other complementary laws, requires the accessibility and readability of non-individually negotiated clauses incorporated in contracts with consumers and users, so that they can know the existence and content of the contract prior to its conclusion. The legislature's zeal in this area goes so far as to require a reasonable font size, which is not "less than one and a half millimetres", or a contrast which makes it easy to read the contract documents. The Law 7/1998 of 13 April 1998 on general terms and business conditions, however, penalises by not incorporating into the contract those general conditions when the "adhering party" has not had a real opportunity to know in full at the time of the conclusion of the contract or those that are "illegible".

The fact that the subjects protected by this legislation do not participate in the elaboration of the contractual content, whose acceptance is compelled by the need to have access to certain goods and services, justifies the interest of the legislator in ensuring their access to the contract. It is no different, in substance, from the situation in which the worker, who also adheres to the employment contract offered to him in order to earn a living, finds himself. Certainly, the technological advances that serve as the main thread of this

---

13 Internships, training and apprenticeships (article 11 WS) to be agreed in an official model (article 17 Royal Decree 488/1998 of 27 March 1998), implementing article 11 WS on training contracts.
14 At least those for temporary work and for specific works or services as well as those that may be required due to production circumstances must be formalised in writing when their duration exceeds four weeks or when they are arranged on a part-time basis (article 6 Royal Decree 2720/1998, of 18 December 1998, implementing article 15 WS in relation to fixed-term contracts).
15 The imposition of written form abounds in new types of contract, such as the indefinite employment contract to support entrepreneurs (article 4 of Law 3/2012 of 6 July 2012 on urgent measures to reform the labour market) as well as in fashionable types such as the distance employment contract (article 13 WS).

study have not contributed to mitigating the economic need that compels the worker to seek employment. On the contrary, job losses have only aggravated the situation of those who are seeking employment, which today more than ever can be considered a necessary and scarce asset. The strengthening of the employer's bargaining power is the logical consequence of the situation described. By virtue of this position, the company will be able to issue a job offer that naturally will meet its needs, proposing to those interested in it the signing of contractual terms that safeguard its interest. Although there is no legal obstacle preventing the worker from discussing this offer and proposing an alternative contractual wording, the scarcity of alternatives recommends accepting the agreement as presented.

It is known that the above-mentioned provisions do not apply to the employment contract.[16] Even though the WS avoids recognising the limited role played by the autonomy of both parties in the formation of the employment contract that, the secondary role that it assigns to it, recognised as a source of law postponed to the one represented by state regulation and collective autonomy[17] implies the admission of the worker's scarce participation in the negotiation. This system is established in order to limit the unilateral imposition of abusive conditions by the employer, to which the game of market rules leads.[18]

It is also evidenced from another perspective by the articulation of various channels through which the aim is to guarantee access to the contract's essential conditions, if not to the entire contract, to the worker and his legal representatives. This is shown by article 8.5 WS, which requires the employer to inform the employee in writing of the essential elements of the contract and the main conditions for performance of the work, provided that the contractual relationship is for more than four weeks. Specifically, information must cover: (a) the identity of the parties; (b) the date of commencement of the employment relationship and, in the case of a temporary employment relationship, its foreseeable duration; (c) the registered office of the undertaking and the place of employment where the employee habitually provides his services; (d) the category or occupational group of the post held by the employee or a description or summary description thereof; (e) the amount of the salary and the frequency of its payment; (f) the periods of notice to be observed by the employer and the worker in the event of termination of the contract or the arrangements for determining such periods of notice; and (g) the applicable collective agreement.

---

16 Excluded from its scope by article 4 of Law 7/1998 of 13 April 1998 on general terms and business conditions, and implicitly left outside the scope of application of Royal Legislative Decree 1/2007 of 16 November 2007, approving the consolidated text of the General Law for the Defence of Consumers and Users and other complementary laws, which is limited to the protection of a consumer or user who acts for purposes other than his or her business, trade or profession (article 3).

17 D'antona, M., "La autonomía individual y las fuentes del Derecho del Trabajo", *Relaciones Laborales*, no. 2, 1991, p. 284.

18 Durán López, F. & Sáez Lara, C., "Autonomía colectiva y autonomía individual en la fijación y modificación de las condiciones de trabajo", *Relaciones Laborales*, T. II, 1991, p. 385.

An insurmountable obstacle to the possibility of drawing up the contract in a computer code could be deduced from this rule, but this assessment seems to be contradicted by the provision itself, when it allows the information required to be included in a separate document from the contract. Specifically, the Royal Decree 1659/1998 of 24 July 1998 implementing article 8.5 of WS on information to workers on the essential elements of the employment contract, authorises employers to fulfil their duty to provide information by means of a written declaration signed by them and any other written document.

Nothing would prevent, in accordance with these regulations, the formalisation of the employment contract in computer code, as long as the employer complies with his obligation to inform the worker in writing of these conditions and elements within a maximum period of two months from the start of the employment relationship.[19] And much less the wording under such conditions of a contract of four weeks' duration or less, in which case the employer does not have to provide any information.

The penalty for failure to observe the written form does not contribute to strengthening the worker's consent. When this infringement should make it impossible to consider the contractual content as accepted, the legal system is satisfied with the fact that the contract has been concluded for an indefinite period of time and full time, unless it is possible to prove its temporary nature or the part time nature of the services.[20] Nor do the powers granted to workers' representatives, who are not required to receive the basic copy of all contracts to be concluded in writing, strengthen the workers' consent. Without wishing to underestimate this guarantee, the role of which is crucial when it comes to establishing the legality of the content subscribed, it should be ruled out that it is considered a sufficient mechanism to reinforce the worker's consent.

Notwithstanding the previous aspects, it should be noted that the shortcomings of this legal framework not only affect relations in which some type of contractual automation has been implemented, with the deficient accessibility to the regulation of the rights and obligations of the worker. On this issue, it should be clarified that the "accessibility" refers to the availability of the contract's content. For example, it is common that the employment contract does not reflect some rights and obligations applicable to the parties. Instead, reference is made to the collective bargaining. It must be recognised that this problem already created considerable legal uncertainty in the traditional employment contract, but it has now become an obstacle to scheduling the automatic execution of the contract.

The weakness of this guarantee of accessibility to the contractual content is evidenced by this legal regime, whose slight improvement is predicted by the Proposal for a Directive of the European Parliament and of the Council on transparent and predictable working conditions in the European Union.[21]

---

19 Article 6.1 Royal Decree 1659/1998 of 24 July 1998.
20 Article 8 WS.
21 Text available in the link: http://eur-lex.europa.eu/legal-content/EN/TXT/?uri=CELEX: 52017PC0797.

2 Content of the smart labour contract

Every contract requires the concurrence of consent, object and cause to be considered as existing.[22] The employment contract does not constitute the exception to this rule. Although neither its object nor its cause is significantly different due to the above-mentioned process of contractual automation, it is appropriate to dedicate some lines to the consent of the parties. Its valid issuance requires as an essential prerequisite that the contract be drafted in terms that are understandable to the parties.

Scientific doctrine has noted that the drafting of smart contracts in computer code would create a semantic barrier impossible to overcome, even for jurists.[23] While there is no shortage of people waiting for the predicted generalisation of programming knowledge in future generations, the fact is that today it is rare for a citizen, much less for a jurist, to have any programming knowledge. As long as programming knowledge is not widespread, the validity of the smart contract depends on whether the contractual terms have been expressed either in writing or merely orally in a language understandable to the parties to the contract. Another way to circumvent this language barrier would be to develop computer technology to translate legal language into code and vice versa.[24] However, the ideal option to ensure a full understanding of the contractual clauses would be the first one, given the doubts that the accuracy of the translation carried out by the programme might raise.

As specified above, the emergence of the smart contract does not mean the creation of a new type of contract, but a new way of drawing up, concluding and implementing the existing types of contract, based on the code wording. Thus, the conception of the smart contract as the translation into computer code of contractual terms, whose execution – programmable – depends on the occurrence of an event, would serve to overcome the previous barrier.

A corollary of the foregoing point is the resolution of any discrepancies that may arise between computer language and the common language in which the contractual terms have been agreed always in favour of the latter, since it is the one that is understandable to the party that has expressed its consent.[25] Any act performed as a result of a rule incorrectly translated into computer language, for example, the payment to the worker of a lower remuneration than he would be entitled to due to the non-inclusion of a supplementary salary to which he would be entitled, deserves to be treated as a breach of the agreed terms and even as an infringement, but never as an alternative contractual wording to be taken into account for interpretative purposes.

The foregoing discussion suggests that the technology used in the automatic execution of the employment contract seems to have little impact on its own

---

22 Article 1261 Civil Code.
23 Cuccuru, P., *op. cit.*, p. 113.
24 Cuccuru, P., *op. cit.*, p. 114.
25 Art. 1261 Civil Code. See ECHEBARRÍA SÁENZ, M., *op. cit.*, p. 72.

configuration. Nothing could be further from the truth, given the need to adapt language to the requirements and limits imposed by the "digital ecosystem" itself.[26] The drafting of the protocol allowing the automatic performance of the contract requires the transposition into computer language of terms drafted with an unknown degree of precision in a labour law, where moreover there is an abundance of indeterminate legal concepts such as "normal performance", "good faith", "trust" and so on.

The undisputed advantage of such a development would be the certainty that the parties would derive from the removal of the discretion inherent in the interpretation of such concepts. In this regard, its contribution to legal certainty has been commended.[27] The smart contract, as a translation of the contract into code, cannot be used for interpretative purposes. Thus, the condition that makes possible the execution of the programmed order must be expressed in terms which allow it to be activated without human judgement. This will come into play in a previous stadium, coinciding with the moment of drafting the contract in common language. It is then that the parties have to make the effort to anticipate any factual event which might give rise to the legal consequence whose implementation is to be automated, and to do so in such a way that the occurrence of the event can be detected and recognised by the software used.

The smart contract, as a translation of the contract into code, cannot be used for interpretative purposes. Thus, the condition that makes the execution of the programmed order must be expressed in terms that allow it to be activated without human judgement. This will come into play in a previous stage, coinciding with the moment of drafting the contract in common language. It is then when the parties have to make an effort to anticipate any factual event that might give rise to the legal consequence whose implementation is to be automated, and to do so in such a way that the occurrence of the event in question can be detected and recognised by the software used.

This transcends a merely formal level, introducing a change which is difficult to implement into our legal culture. Although not without obstacles, this development has been possible in sectors where contracting is based on measurable data or on arithmetic operations that can be easily translated into computer language such as finance.[28] However, such obstacles grow until they become insurmountable in areas of law where the correct performance of the service is usually assessed on the basis of standards of behaviour. It occurs in the ordinary law of obligations and contracts, when it mentions "the diligence of a good father of a family",[29] and in labour law, as long as the worker commits himself to comply with the specific obligations of his job "in accordance with the rules of good faith and diligence"[30] and the employer to a "regular exercise of his managerial

---

26 Cuccuru, P., *op. cit.*, p. 118.
27 Cuccuru, P., *op. cit.*, p. 113.
28 Cuccuru, P., *op. cit.*, p. 117.
29 Art. 1.094 Civil Code.
30 Article 5. a) WS.

powers".[31] The same applies when the employee's failing consists of a breach of contractual good faith and a breach of trust in the performance of the work.[32]

This is evidence of the transformation that the new technologies will introduce into the very content of the employment contract, which will otherwise become less and less individualised. The above statement is based on an essentially economic reason. Given the lack of programming skills affecting both employers and employees, the involvement of computer experts is essential in order to translate legal terms into computer language. However, this intervention is not free of costs for the employer, since it implies either including programming experts in its own staff or contracting this service to external companies or freelancers, the latter being the option that the company is likely to embrace. It is not unreasonable to assume how convenient it will be to translate contractual models which can be applied to a plurality of workers once and for all.

It was not necessary to wait until this point to find arguments suggesting the convenience of standardising the employment contract.[33] For decades, labour law has been aware of the use of contractual models used by the company to recruit workers who, lacking bargaining power, simply subscribe to their full content to access employment. Cost savings in legal advice and the standardisation of working conditions are behind a process of standardisation that moreover deserves to be viewed with caution, since it is intended to supplant a role once attributed to collective bargaining.

Although this process of automation may prevent any modification of the contract not based on mutual agreement[34] and eliminate those contractual clauses which are deliberately inconsistent and which have increased the employer's powers through the specification of an indeterminate duty to provide work, it also constitutes a double-edged sword. There is, therefore, a "tension between efficiency and justice".[35] Thus, although it will eliminate legal uncertainty and even judicial discretion, it must be borne in mind that, as a simple computer translation of terms conceived by the mind of the contracting party whether or not he is a lawyer, this contract will be as smart or intelligent as the person who conceived it.[36]

IV Conclusion

After a legal analysis of the changes introduced by the technological innovation that allows for self-execution in the employment contract, it can be inferred that, as a premise around which to build its legal framework, the smart labour contract does not constitute a new contractual modality. On the contrary, it is an

---

31 Article 5. c) WS.
32 Article 54.1. d) WS.
33 Echebarría Sáenz, M., *op. cit.*, p. 95 y Keidar & Greenbaum, *op. cit.*, p. 23.
34 Cuccuru, P., *op. cit.*, p. 116.
35 *Ibidem.*
36 Keidar & Greenbaum, *op. cit.*, .

invention that can be adapted to both open-end and fixed-term contracts and is suitable for use with workers who provide a service in the traditional way as well as for current smart workers. This is because this technological innovation does not alter the provision of services, which may or may not take place in a virtual environment, although if it is carried out there it may facilitate the automation of the contractual consequences.

In terms of its legal impact, this technology can accentuate the power of corporate control but also channel it, achieving the greater concreteness of the rights and obligations of the parties that the translation into computer language requires. It is also an innovation that could aggravate the process of contractual standardisation, which is the source of the imposition of abusive conditions on the worker as a weak party in the legal relationship. For this reason, it is advisable for the worker to anticipate the undesirable consequences which might arise from this process by setting up a system of preventive control of the contractual content aimed at guaranteeing, on the one hand, the information received by the worker and the acceptance of a non-abusive contractual content, on the other.

IV Bibliography

Cuccuru, P., "Blockchain ed automatizacione contrattuale. Riflessioni sugli *smart contract*", *La Nuova giurisprudenza civile commentata*, ISSN 1593-7305, vol. 33, n° 1, 2017.

D'antona, M., "La autonomía individual y las fuentes del Derecho del Trabajo", *Relaciones Laborales*, n° 2, 1991.

Davara Fernández de Marcos, E., "Los smart contract", *Actualidad administrativa*, n° 7, 2017.

Durán López, F. & Sáez Lara, C., "Autonomía colectiva y autonomía individual en la fijación y modificación de las condiciones de trabajo", *Relaciones Laborales*, T. II, 1991.

Echebarría Sáenz, M., "Contratos electrónicos autoejecutables (smart contract) y pagos con tecnología blockchain", *Revista de Estudios Europeos*, n° 70, 2017.

Keidar, R. & Greenbaum, E., "Blockchain: the power to reinvigorate law firms", *The Lawyer*, vol. 31, n° 28, 2016.

8 Spanish telework and Italian "agile" work

A comparison

Ana Murcia Clavería

I Introduction: the "surge" of telework in the digital era and the need for regulation that complies with the demands of decent work

The definition of "telework" which will be used in this study is one providing a European context that "for the first time sets the foundation for a clear and specific regulatory framework for teleworking".[1] The reference is from the European Framework Agreement on Teleworking (hereinafter AMET), signed by the European social partners[2] on 16 July 2002, according to which

> Telework is a form of organisation and/or realisation of work using information technology in the framework of a contract or working relationship, in which a job that could be performed equally on the company's premises is preformed off the premises on a regular basis.

As this definition makes clear, it is a complex task to regulate telework from a labour point of view. As noted, a few years ago by Gaeta, teleworking "breaks down the jurist's certainty",[3] because it breaks away from the two central concepts around which labour legislation has revolved since its inception: space (the factory, the company's site, the office) and time (working hours and consequently, the right to breaks and vacations). In this sense, telework shares many of the uncertainties that labour doctrine is already confronting when it analyses new forms of providing work. These uncertainties are arising as a consequence of the spectacular development of information and communication technologies (ICT), above all since the digitalisation of the means of production and the globalisation of the economy. Such is the case of work offered through digital

---

1 Vid., Thibault Aranda, J. "El impacto laboral de la descentralización tecnológica: el teletrabajo", en Lahera Forteza y Valdés Dal-Ré (dirs.) *Relaciones laborales, organización de la empresa y globalización*, ed. Cinca, 2010, Madrid, p. 90.
2 For the CES, UNICE/UEAPME and CEEP.
3 Gaeta, L. "Teletrabajo y derecho: la experiencia italiana", *Documentación laboral*, núm. 49/1996, p. 50.

platforms and their numerous variants.[4] Unlike this new phenomenon – a direct result of the digitalisation that is "revolutionising" not only the world of work but society in general – telework is certainly not so recent. It arose in the middle of the twentieth century[5] and had a non-technical classification; it was called "work at home" and existed well before the work contract was first regulated. Historical studies have confirmed these circumstances in Spain,[6] and the same could be said of Italy. To date, both countries are places where the option of telework is seldom chosen. Neither has telework in these countries had the expansion predicted a few decades ago. This was noted in Spain by researcher Thibault[7] and in Italy by researchers Serrani y Tiraboschi, who indicate that despite it being difficult to rely on official data, telework "has not yet taken off".[8]

Nevertheless, as found in more recent studies in both Spain and Italy,[9] the intensification of telematic systems and their spectacular digital development are producing a "surge" of telework. These studies make it possible to predict that, in the coming years, the use of telework will increase with no foreseeable

---

4 Among the already copious bibliography, vid., recent collective studies Mella Méndez (dir.) and Serrani, L. (coord.), *Los actuales cambios sociales y laborales: nuevos retos para el mundo del trabajo. I Cambios tecnológicos y nuevos retos para el mundo del trabajo (Portugal, España, Colombia, Italia, Francia)*, ed. Petr Lang, 2017, Suiza; and Rodríguez-Piñero Royo, M. and Hernández Bejarano, M. (dirs.) *Economía colaborativa y trabajo en plataformas: realidades y desafíos*, ed. Bomarzo, Albacete, 2017, and the monographic works of Mercader Uguina, JR. *El futuro del trabajo en la era de la digitalización y la robótica*, ed. Tirant Lo Blanch, Valencia, 2017; and Todolí Signes, A. *El trabajo en la era de la economía colaborativa*, ed. Tirant Lo Blanch, Valencia, 2017.

5 Gallardo Moya, R. *El viejo y el nuevo trabajo a domicilio De la máquina de hilar al ordenador*, ed. Ibidem. 1998, Madrid. González-Posada Martínez, E., *El teletrabajo*, ed. Junta de Castilla y León, 2006, Valladolid, y GARCÍA ROMERO, B., *El teletrabajo*. Ed. Civitas, Thomson Reuters, 2012, Navarra.

6 Vid., de la Villa de la Villa, L.E., en "Trabajo a distancia", en AAVV (Coord. Goerlich Peset) *Comentarios al Estatuto de los Trabajadores. Libro homenaje a Tomás Sala Franco*, ed. Tirant Lo Blach, 2016, Valencia. In this work, the author calculates the origin of work at home as the fifteenth century, developing from the mid-nineteenth century on, particularly in the textile industry.

7 Thibault Aranda, J. "El impacto laboral de la descentralización tecnológica (…)", *op. cit.*, p. 82. Thus, with data from 2002, only 4.9% of Spanish employees telework at least one day a week compared to 26.4% in the Netherlands, 17% in Germany, 18% in Great Britain and 24% in the United States.

8 Serrani, L. E Tiraboschi, M., "Il futuro del telelavoro in Italia", en Mella Méndez (ed.) y Villalba Sánchez (coord.) *Trabajo a distancia y teletrabajo*, ed. Aranzadi, 2015, Navarra. According to "unofficial" data, it is estimated that the use of teleworking is less than 2%. A more detailed analysis completed in 2006 analyses this issue by sectors and collects the following data: in postal services and telecommunications, 24.63% of the companies in the sector use one or more types of telework; in the chemical sector, 14.39%; and in wholesale and retail trade, 18.39%. In terms of company size, in 2006, 31.18% of the large companies (more than 250 workers) used telework, while only 2.9% of the companies with between 10 and 49 workers used telework (p. 332 and 333).

9 In Italy, it is also a firm commitment, above all to large companies. For example, between March and April 2017, the company Enel, increased from 500 to 7,000 workers, offered that they could work outside the office one day a week if they chose to. Vid. Taschini, L., "Smart working: la nuova disciplina de lavoro agile", en Massimario di *Giurisprudenza del Lavoro* n. 6/2107.

setbacks[10]. This prediction applies, above all, to the "regular" telework modality as defined in the AMET, where the teleworker performs his work more often outside the company premises than inside and does so on a permanent basis, which is common in most countries.[11]

Based on the existence of this "surge" and the prediction that this style of working will be expanding in the not-too-distant future, in this study we will analyse whether or not teleworking is regulated in Spain and Italy. If it is regulated, besides making a comparison, we will attempt to assess whether such regulations guarantee the following two conditions: (a) that teleworking fulfils the expectations of employer and worker when they agree to work in this manner; and (b) that the teleworker's working conditions are not only the same as other workers in the company who have similar professional positions, but that they also have specific rules dealing with labour needs stemming from working outside the premises of the company – in their home or in a place chosen by the worker. To do this, we will contrast the existing regulations with the minimum regulatory framework contained in the aforementioned AMET of 2002, with which the European social partners intend to promote collective bargaining on teleworking in the different countries that make up the European Union. In addition to the definition of telework mentioned above, in this important Agreement the principle of the voluntariness of telework is established for both employer and worker as well as conditions of "reversibility". The Agreement also sets forth the following: the equality of teleworkers and the rest of the company's workers; the need to regulate rules on data protection that guarantee the teleworker's privacy; rules on equipment and assumption of expenses; health and safety regulations; organisation of work; training; and collective rights.

The existence of good legislation and its control by public authorities, especially by labour authorities, is of great relevance since there is well-founded suspicion of a systematic breach of legislation on "work at a distance". The work in question could be of a non-technological kind – that is, the "old" work at home – which is frequent in sectors such as textiles, assembly, crafts and so on, or it could be of the technological version – teleworking – which is accomplished using ICT. It could also be working relationships that are concealed, a concept well captured in the image of the "false self-employed", or simply in the hidden

---

10 Quintanilla Navarro, R.Y., "El teletrabajo: delimitación, negociación colectiva y conflictos", en AAVV (Dir. San Martin Mazzucconi) Tecnologías de la información y la comunicación en las relaciones de trabajo: nuevas dimensiones del conflicto jurídico, ed. Eolas, 2014, Madrid, collects the following data. On the one hand, he points out that "57% of Spanish workers say they would like their company to offer them the option of teleworking". And on the other, "the reality shows that only 26% of Spaniards develop some type of work from home, while in Europe the average is 35%". In this sense, the author continues, "the White Paper on teleworking in Spain concludes that the levels of teleworking observed in Spain are low in relation to the European Union and even more so with the United States". The White Paper on Teleworking in Spain is from June 2012 and is prepared by Global Place and the Mas Familia Foundation (pp. 331 and 332).

11 Luque Parra, M y Camargo R., "Teleworking and labor conditions conclusions", en *IUSLabor* 2/2107.

or informal economy. These work situations are not only predictable in Spain and Italy, but also in many other countries both inside and outside the European Union. The International Labour Organisation (ILO) demonstrated its awareness of the situation in 1996, when it expressed concern about the working conditions of "teleworkers" and approved Collective Agreement 177 on "Work at Home", which entered into force in 2000 along with Recommendation n.184 of the same name and date, comprising a minimum set of rules governing basic labour conditions for homeworkers. Likewise, the aforementioned AMET of 2002 is the result of the same concerns. As de la Villa recalls:

> already a Communication of the Service of the Spokesman of the Union, of May 27, 1998, denounced that only a small percentage of the workers at a distance received conditions of remuneration and work comparable to those of internal workers, and therefore, most of them were poorly paid and virtually excluded from social security benefits, annual leave and compensation for dismissal, and in precarious conditions for health and safety.[12]

II The Spanish regulation of telework and the Italian regulation of "agile work": similarities and differences in some essential aspects

The first pertinent idea to point out is that neither Italy nor Spain have a specific law governing telework in the private sector. In Italy, there is state legislation for the public sector dating back to 1998[13] as well as the Inter-Confederal Agreement applicable to the Public Administration approved in 2000. In the private sector, a 1973 law regulates the so-called "work at home", similar to regulations under French law,[14] and does not permit inclusion of the telework concept that we are dealing with here. In the Italian private sector, telework has developed mainly through collective bargaining, addressing its typologies and legal regime depending on the sector or the applicable business. This relevant negotiation took place before the AMET of 2002 and has continued with much more intensity since its implementation by the Agreement of 9 June 2004.[15] This "special" "manner of executing the subordinate work relationship", called "agile work", has emerged from conventional experiences as Tiraboschi[16] states. Also identified by some authors using the English expression "smart working",

---

12 de la Villa, LE. En "Trabajo a distancia", en AAVV (...), *op. cit.*, p. 231.
13 Law n.191 of 16 June 1998.
14 Vid., such references in Dominguez Morales, A., "El tratamiento en la negociación colectiva del teletrabajo como modalidad de gestión del cambio", en AAVV (Dir. Cruz Villalón), *La negociación colectiva como instrumento de gestión del cambio,* ed. Cinca, Madrid, 2017, pp. 294 y 295.
15 Prior to the AMET, vid., Gaeta, L. "Teletrabajo y derecho", *op. cit.;* later, Tiraboschi, "Il lavoro agile tre legge e contrattazione colletiva: la tortuosa via italiana verso la modernizzazione del diritto del lavoror", WP CSDLE "Massimo D´Antona", *IT.* Núm. 335/2017.
16 Vid. Tiraboschi, M., "Il lavoro agile tre legge e contrattazione colletiv", *op. cit.*

it is the one that is the subject of study here and which is regulated in articles 18–23 of the Law of 22 May 2017, n. 81 – *Measures for the protection of non-entrepreneurial self-employment and measures to encourage flexible articulation in the time and place of subordinate work*[17] – hereinafter called Law 81/2017. It should be pointed out that, under the terms set out in article 18-3 of Law 81/2017, the application of "agile work" is also foreseen in the public sector.[18]

For its part, Spanish legislation has no specific law regarding "telework", neither for the public nor the private sectors. In the public sector, the regulation of telework has developed by means of regulations enacted by the autonomous communities. There are currently several regulations in existence; some[19] even prior to the current article 13 of the Workers' Statute (ET) after its reform in 2012 by Royal Decree-Law 3/2012 and subsequently Law 3/2012. Prior to the 2012 reform, article 13 regulated the "home work contract"; after the reform, it is referred to as "telework". The analysis of the Spanish regulations falls exclusively on article 13 of the reformed ET. With less intensity than in Italy, teleworking in Spain has been the subject of conventional treatment, both through sectoral and company collective bargaining. The bargaining has occurred, above all since the signing of the AMET in 2002, which was first incorporated into an Annex of the Inter-Confederal Agreement for Collective Bargaining (AINC) of 30 January 2003 acknowledging it in its entirety. Subsequently, the AMET and its full acceptance are reiterated in the ensuing Agreements, included in the last AINC from 2015 to 2017.[20] Despite this acceptance, many agreements limit themselves

---

17 (17G00096) (GU General Series n.135 of 06-13-2017). A commentary on the whole law, including also the "agile work" and giving an account of its "specialties", vid. Perulli, A. "Il Jobs Act del lavoro autónomo e agile: come cambiano i concetti di subordinazione e autonomía nel diritto del lavoro", en WP CSLE "Massimo D'Antona", *IT.* 341/2017.
18 In addition, in the public sector, the Directive of 1 June 2017 aims to encourage the use of "agile work", aspiring to achieve in 3 years' time that at least 10% of the civil servants who request it can carry it out (vid., Martone, M., "El Smart working o trabajo ágil en el ordenamiento italiano", *Revista Derecho de las Relaciones Laborales,* núm.1/2018. p. 88).
19 This is the case of the Autonomous Community of Castilla y León through Decree 9/2011 of 17 March, which regulates the day of non-contact work through telework in the Administration of Castilla y León. Decree 9/2011 was repealed and replaced by the current Decree 16/2018 of 7 June. The new decree incorporates interesting developments that will facilitate better and increased use of teleworking in the field of public employment.
20 In the AINC of 2004 (which extended the 2003) in the 2005, 2006 (which extended the 2005) and 2007, last extended for 2008. Subsequently signed the II AINC of 2010–2012 and currently governs the III AINC 2015–2017. In all of them, the following text is reiterated: "One of the innovative forms of organization and execution of the work performance derived from the advancement of new technologies is teleworking, which allows the realization of the work activity outside the company's facilities. Starting from the recognition by the social partners of telework as a means of modernizing the organization of work, we consider it appropriate to establish some criteria that can be used by companies and by workers and their representatives: The voluntary and reversible nature of teleworking, both for the worker as for the company. The equal rights, legal and conventional, of teleworkers with respect to comparable workers who work in the company's facilities. The convenience of regulating aspects such as privacy, confidentiality, risk prevention, facilities, training, etc."

to reproducing the directives of successive NCCAs, which, in turn, reproduce the AMET provisions in a generic way, without taking the initiative to articulate and thereby develop the rules set out in the AMET. With some exceptions,[21] it can be affirmed that teleworking in Spanish collective bargaining is still a pending issue.[22]

Having pointed out the above, there are only two normative bodies on which the comparison will be made: the "agile work", ex articles 18–23 of Law 81/2017, and article 13 or the ET. Of these two, for the obvious reasons of space, the exposition of their similarities and their differences will be made taking into account only two groups of materials: (a) purpose, legal concept and formal requirements, and (b) the rights and responsibilities of the teleworkers and the obligations of the business owner, especially the right to disconnection governed by Italian regulations.

1 Purpose, legal concept and formal requirements of Spanish telework and of Italian agile work

For the worker, reconciling working life with personal and family life is the purpose (not the only one, but the principle and most frequent) of teleworking. For the business owner, this manner of organising the provision of labour is designed to provide companies with flexibility and above all reduce labour costs, thereby increasing productivity and as a result, competitiveness. In essence, these are the objectives that motivate the regulation of teleworking, and this is how they appear in all the normative texts that we have mentioned, whether collective agreements, regional regulations, in the AMET[23] or others that are more recent.[24] These are also the objectives called for by the proposal for a Directive of the European Parliament and the Council of 2017 on the reconciliation of family life and professional life of parents and caregivers.[25] They also appear, of course, in the two regulations that are the object of our analysis. Thus, article 18-1 of Law

---

21 Vid. Mella Méndez, L. "Configuración general del trabajo a distancia en el derecho español", en Mella Méndez (Dir.) *El teletrabajo en España: aspectos teórico-prácticos de interés,* ed. Wolters Kluwer, Madrid, 2017, pp. 347 y ss.
22 Dominguez Morales, A., "El tratamiento en la negociación colectiva", *op. cit.,* p. 294 y ss.
23 "The social partners consider teleworking as both a means of modernizing the organization of work for companies and public service organizations, and for workers to reconcile professional life and social life and give them greater autonomy in carrying out their tasks. If Europe wants to extract the best part of the information society, it must confront this new way of organizing work, so that flexibility and security go hand in hand, the quality of employment is improved and that people with disabilities have better access to the labor market."
24 Vid. Declaration on teleworking by the European social partners in the insurance sector on 10 February 2015, in which, together with previous declarations, is also included "that of producing a positive impact on the environment and the community public by reducing pollution caused by transport (...) which brings benefits for the whole society".
25 Repealing Directive 2010/18/EU of the Council of 26 April 2017 (COM 2017) 253 final. Vid., A comment about it, Mella Méndez, L. "El trabajo a distancia como medida de flexibilidad y conciliación laboral", *IUSLabor* 2/2017.

81/2017 expressly states that "The provisions of this chapter, with the aim of increasing competitiveness and facilitating the balance between working hours and personal hours, promote agile work (...)". This is also the purpose in the Spanish regulation, as can be read, not in article 13 of the ET, but in the Statement of Motives of the Law upon which article 13 is drawn (Law 3/2012). According to this Statement, this "particular way of organising work" that is "teleworking" is intended to favour "the flexibility of companies in the organisation of work, increase employment opportunities, and optimise the relationship between work time and personal life and family".[26]

Regarding the legal concept of "teleworking", as one can deduce from what has been noted up to now, both normative codes present an important problem that we are only pointing out here, without being able to develop further. As of now, neither of the two normative orders uses the term "teleworking" nor does it define teleworking according to the guidelines offered by the 2002 AMET. As previously mentioned, there are two elements that characterise telework according to the definition offered by the AMET: (a) form of organisation or realisation of "labour" with the use of ICT; and (b) work that can be done in the company but is done outside the premises of the company "on a regular basis". Thus, the Italian regulation uses the expression "agile work" (rather than "telework") and defines it as "a way of carrying out the labour relationship established through agreement between two parties, also having forms of organisation by stages, cycles and objectives and without precise limitations of time or place", not necessarily requiring the use of ICT ("with the possible use of technological tools for the realisation of work activity"). Furthermore, it establishes that this way of working, agreed upon by the parties, can be carried out "partly within the company's facilities and partly outside the company, without a fixed location, within the limits of the maximum duration of daily and weekly working hours derived from the law and collective bargaining".[27] The Spanish regulation, as already indicated, publishes article 13 under the expression "Work at a distance" and does not mention expressly in any of its sections the use of

---

26 "The desire to promote new ways of developing work activity means that this reform also seeks to accommodate, with guarantees, teleworking: a particular form of work organization that fits perfectly into the productive and economic model pursued, by favoring the flexibility of companies in the organization of work, increasing employment opportunities and optimizing the relationship between work time and personal and family life. The organization of the traditional work at home is thus modified to welcome, through a balanced regulation of rights and obligations, work at a distance based on the intensive use of new technologies" (emphasis mine).
27 Article 18-1 Ley 81/2017: "The provisions of this chapter, with the aim of increasing competitiveness and facilitating the reconciliation of work and life time, promote agile work as a way of carrying out the employment relationship established through agreement between the parties, also with forms of organization by stages, cycles and objectives and without precise constraints of time or place of work, with the possible use of technological tools for the performance of work. The work performance is carried out, partly within company premises and partly outside without a fixed location, within the limits of maximum daily and weekly working hours, deriving from law and collective bargaining".

ICT. In such extremes, it concurs with the Italian regulation, except to state that the external place can be "the work address or in the place freely chosen" (article 13 ET),[28] a precision obviated in the Italian regulation by the words "without a fixed location". However, although teleworking is not expressly mentioned, Spanish regulation is closer to the telework concept included in the AMET than to the Italian regulation of agile work. Despite the obvious silences regarding the expression "teleworking" and ICT, which paradoxically are expressly included in the Motivation Statement, as we have already indicated,[29] the doctrine considers that article 13 regulates the category "Work at a distance". Within the category are two modalities: (a) non-technological or home work (without the use of ICT); and (b) technology or teleworking carried out through ICT.[30] Article 13 establishes a general or minimum framework applicable to all modalities.[31]

Regarding the "quantum" of the work performed by the worker inside and outside the company, Spanish legislation differs markedly from agile work, and does so with a regulation that is certainly "confusing".[32]

On the one hand, it is required that the work provided outside the company (either at the worker's home or in any other place chosen by the worker) is carried out "in a preponderant manner", adding at the end "in an alternative manner to his/her on-premises development at the company's workplace".[33] It is clear that, and in this there is doctrinal unanimity, unlike "agile work" in which occasional or sporadic teleworking is allowed as well as working for the company both on-premises and off-premises during the same workday,[34] both suppositions are discarded in the case of Spain. The discussion focuses on whether article 13 regulates "partial" teleworking, as Mella Mendez argues, indicating that, although the legislator does not say it literally, a teleworking model is configured

---

28 Article 13: "The work in which the provision of the labor activity is carried out predominantly in the home of the worker or in the place freely chosen by him, in an alternative to his on-site development in the center of work, will be considered remote work".
29 Vid., previous note in which part of the Motivation Statement is transcribed.
30 As Mella underlines to differentiate both figures: "all teleworking is teleworking, but not all teleworking is teleworking" ("Configuración general...", *op. cit.*, p. 26).
31 Such a broad approach has the advantage of encompassing everything and the inherent disadvantage of the impression regarding critical points of the legal regime for each type of teleworking. Therefore, "for greater precision, it will be necessary to investigate the clauses of the collective agreements or specific pacts, individual or collective, that the employer can negotiate in his company for each case" (Mella Méndez, L., "Configuración general...", *op. cit.*, p. 25).
32 Vid., On the conceptual and terminological difficulties of telework, García Romero, B., El teletrabajo..., *op. cit*. Thibault Aranda, J., El teletrabajo, *op. cit.* y "El impacto laboral...", *op. cit.* Mella Méndez, L., "Configuración general (..), *op. cit.*
33 Work at a distance is "one in which the provision of work is performed predominantly in the home of the worker or in the place freely chosen by him, in an alternative to his face-to-face development in the workplace of the company" (article 13-1 ET).
34 This is one of the reasons why some authors consider that agile work should be differentiated from teleworking, which in the absence of legal regulation (except for civil servants) in Italy is governed by collective agreements in a manner very similar to that of AMET since it was passed on by the Agreement of 9 June 2004. Vid. Dominguez Morales, A., "El tratamiento en la negociación colectiva (...)", *op. cit.* pp. 293 and 294).

in which "the worker performs work outside of the traditional work centre, not exclusively, but in an alternative way to his/her presence-based development in the company" (article 13.1 ET).[35] Regarding "preponderance", this author interprets it to mean that the required off-premises period "must be greater than fifty percent of the total working day in weekly, monthly or annual computation".[36] Other authors, also critical of the "extreme dose of uncertainty created" by the use of the word "preponderant", understand that at least 51% of the work must take place off company premises. Sierra Benítez agrees with Mella that the current regulation seems to support exclusively a remote telework model called telependurismo, that is, "one that alternates on-premises work in the company and teleworking". But the idea is unconvincing, because "digital reality allows full activity at a distance". And although it has been claimed that being present at the workplace prevents isolation – isolation being one of the psycho-social risks for teleworkers – this author points out that these risks can be avoided through other means, and not only by requiring the alternation between on-premises periods and distance periods.[37]

Finally, with regard to formal requirements, both legal codes require that the pact or agreement which governs teleworking be set down in writing. In the Spanish regulation, and without prejudice to other conventional requirements, a basic copy of the pact must be given to the legal representatives of the workers (article 8-3 ET). At this point it will be transferred to the public employment office for its deposit, which is also true in case there are no representatives in the company. In the Italian legislation, the agreement regarding the modality of agile work is stipulated in writing "for the purposes of administrative regularity and proof". Except that both standards require the written form of the telework agreement or the agile work agreement *ad probationem*, the rest of the issues related to the agreement differ greatly between one regulation and another. In Italy, the legislator regulates the agreement in detail by determining the list of matters to be included in it as well as its duration, which may be temporary or indefinite, and the rules of extinction.[38] On such extremes, the regulation of article 13 of the ET does not stipulate anything, limiting itself to reproducing some of the basic principles established in the AMET, as indicated in the following section.

---

35 Mella Méndez, L. "Configuración general (...)", *op. cit.*, p. 31.
36 Ibidem, p. 32.
37 Vid., Sierra Benítez, EM., "Valoración crítica y propuesta de mejora de la regulación del trabajo a distancia en la normativa estatal y autonómica", en *Trabajo y Derecho*, núm.29/2017, p. 5.
38 Article 19-2 Ley 81/2017: "The agreement referred to in paragraph 1 may be complete or indefinite; in the latter case, withdrawal may take place with notice of not less than thirty days. In the case of disabled workers pursuant to article 1 of the Law of 12 March 1999, n. 68, the period of notice of termination by the employer can not be less than ninety days, in order to allow an adequate reorganization of the work paths with respect to the needs of life and care of the worker. In the presence of a justified reason, each of the contracting parties may withdraw before the expiry of the term in the case of fixed-term agreement, or without notice in the case of permanent agreement".

2 Rights and duties of teleworkers and obligations of the employer. In particular, the right to disconnection determined by the Italian regulations

There are three groups of rights which are included in both legislations and in similar terms: (a) the principle of equal rights for teleworkers with respect to workers who provide their services in the workplace (article 13-3 ET); (b) the right to professional training for the employment of workers at a distance, and the corresponding managerial duty to facilitate their access and to inform them about vacancies "for their on-premises development in their work centres" (article 13-3, paragraph 2 ET); and (c) the right to adequate protection in terms of safety and health in accordance with the specific regulations on occupational risks in each country.[39] To these rights, article 13 ET expressly prescribes the right to representation of workers at a distance, indicating that for this purpose, they must be assigned to a specific work centre (article 13-5 ET), a precaution that is not included in the regulation of agile work. However, the Italian regulation contains specific rules on limits to the employer's supervision over the activity that the worker carries out outside the premises of the company (article 21-1 of Law 81/2017),[40] specific rules relating to the social security of agile workers (article 23-1 and 2) and expressly contemplates the accident *in itinere* (an accident occurring during the commute to or from one's place of work) (article 23-3). Unlike the Spanish, the Italian regulation adds a precept relating to "the responsibility of the employer regarding the safety and proper functioning of the technological tools assigned to the worker for the development of their productive activity" (article 18-2 of Law 81/2017), which refers to a clear element of employment that, for cases in question, may contribute to test the validity of the labour relation.

A principal difference must be added to this "contrast" summary of the rights and obligations contained in the respective regulations. This difference is the relationship between the law and the contract or agreement for telework and/or agile work. Unlike the Spanish legislation where nothing is said on the subject, the Italian legislation highlights the call to contract and therefore, the autonomy of will for the regulation of aspects expressly contemplated in the law relating to the power of direction and disciplinary power (article 21 of Law 81/2017). Among these matters, it is obligatory that the contract determines "the rest periods of the worker, in addition to the technical and organisational measures necessary to ensure the disconnection of the worker from the technological tools of work" (article 19-1 *in fine*). These measures refer to the systems that will allow these breaks to be effective; or that the established working day be fulfilled by a more flexible, irregular or regular schedule as preferred.

---

39 Article 20, article 22 y article 23 de la Ley 81/2017, respectively.
40 Article 21-1 Ley 81/2017. "The agreement concerning the modality of agile work governs the exercise of the power of control of the employer on the performance rendered by the worker outside the business premises in compliance with the provisions of Article 4 of the Law of 20 May 1970, n. 300, and subsequent modifications".

This "call to the pact" supposes a "revaluation" of the autonomy of the will that, in principle, has been indicated as what is wrong with the asymmetry that characterises the working relationship.[41] From this perspective, the Italian regulation differs greatly from the French legislation, both in what refers expressly to telework, a recently reformed ordinance,[42] as well as to the new regulation on the right to disconnection. In both cases, the French law refers to collective bargaining and, failing that, to the elaboration by the employer of a "letter" (charte) in which such matters are regulated.[43] However, as Martone recognises, and we agree, the "individualisation" designed by the Italian legislator is not an attempt to "evict" the collective agreement from these flexible formulas of contract:

> Rather, the very intention to individualise the discipline of labour benefits carried out in an agile modality in function of the specific demands of the unique work (referring to 'work-life balance'), and within the same business organisation, would be almost like creating a tailor-made suit.[44]

Indeed, the agile work contract allows an "individualised" regulation that satisfies the conflicting interests of both parties – something it is already accomplishing. Additionally, it incorporates the obligation that work contracts include the "right to disconnection" contemplated in the law as well as the consequences of its non-compliance – something equally relevant and necessary.

III Conclusions

The previous pages have exposed the similarities and differences of what is known in Spain as "remote work", ex. article 13 of the ET, and in Italy "agile work", ex. article 18–23 of Law 81/2017. These articles coincide in objectives intended to establish this way of working, expressly contemplated in the Italian regulation in legal diction as: "Increase competitiveness and facilitate the balance between life and work" (article 18-1 of Law 81/2017). Additionally, it is established in

---

41 Vid., Martone, E., "El Smart working o trabajo ágil (…)", *op. cit.*, y Perulli, A., "IL Jobs Act del lavoro (…)", *op. cit.*
42 Ordinance no. 2017-1387 of 22 September 2017 on the predictability and the security of working relations. For the amendment of the articles L-1222-9 to L-1222-11 of the Labor Code.
43 Vid. Article L. 2242-8 of the Code du Travail, a section 7 that establishes that in the framework of the annual negotiation on "professional equality and quality of life at work" should be about "modalities for the full exercise by the employee of their right to disconnect and the establishment by the company of devices to regulate the use of digital tools, in order to guarantee respect for rest and leave periods, as well as personal life and family In the absence of a pact, the employer draws up a letter (Charte), after consulting the works council or, failing that, the staff delegates. This letter defines the modalities for exercising the right to disconnect and also provides for the implementation, for employees and management staff, of training and awareness-raising actions for the reasonable use of digital tools". Article L.2242-8 of the Labor Code, amended by LOI No. 2016-1088 of 8 August 2016 on the work, the modernisation of the social dialogue and the securing of career paths.
44 Vid. Martone, E., "El Smart working (…)", *op. cit.*, p. 90.

both legislations that teleworking/agile work will be carried out by "agreement" between the parties in writing, and must comply with a minimum of formalities regarding registration and control. They also concur in mentioning three imperative rules included in the AMET: (a) the principle of equality between teleworkers and other workers; (b) the teleworkers' right to training; and (c) adequate protection in terms of safety and health.

They differ, however, in their regulatory legal concept, since agile work allows work to be performed both on and off company premises during the same workday and does not insist that the time worked off-premises is superior to the time worked on-premises, as does Spanish regulation. They also differ in the set of rights regulated – the Italian regulation being more complete, in general, than the Spanish. Unlike the Spanish regulation, the Italian expressly defines the duration of the agreement (temporary or indefinite) and the forms of termination; it provides specific rules on disciplinary power and limits what the contract must contain (article 21 of Law 81/2017). It also contemplates specific social security rights, in particular the accident *in itinere* (article 23 of Ley 81/2018), as well as the obligation to establish "rest periods" and the right to disconnect (article 19-1 of Law 81/2017). However, the Italian regulation omits any mention of the collective rights of "agile" workers, unlike the Spanish regulation, which in this case follows the indications of the AMET (article 13-5 ET).

Having pointed out similarities and differences, here are some criticisms of the two regulations. The first is that both agreements are mute on very relevant aspects of teleworking: in the Italian, collective rights; in the Spanish, provisions for work-related accidents produced at home or in the place of work chosen by the worker as well as the regulation of the accident *in itinere*, an accident suffered on the journey from home to the worker's chosen place of work, or from home or the chosen place to the company's premises. Also, there are no rules on who assumes the costs of teleworking (equipment, supplies etc.), leaving this question, in the absence of legal and/or conventional regulation, to agreement between the parties. There is also a lack of specific regulation on the effectiveness of the principle of willingness and the "reversibility" of teleworking required in the AMET. Spanish regulation also lacks specific rules on the duration of the telework agreement and its causes for extinction.

Finally, lacking in both legislations are specific regulations aimed at guaranteeing effective compliance with working hours and therefore, the right to rest and vacations. Without this "not working" time, there is no rest nor is it possible to achieve the objective that teleworking aims to offer the teleworker – that of balance between personal/family life and work. It is true that the Italian directive incorporates the right to disconnect as indicated, but it is not a sufficient or complete regulation. The obligation to contemplate in the contract "rest periods", and "technical and organisational measures necessary to ensure the disconnection of the worker from the technological tools of work", is not enough. This being important, specific sanctions should be set out in the event of non-compliance with these requirements on the part of the employer.

Occasions of non-compliance should be considered violations, not only of the rules on the right to rest for workers, but also of other constitutional rights such as personal life and privacy. Also, to the extent that "non-disconnection" causes "overload" of work and therefore stress, employer breaches of agreement on the prohibition of "connection" in non-work periods should also be considered violations of the rules that guarantee the health of the workers.[45] In this sense and due to the fact that technology enables workers – both teleworkers and non-teleworkers – to be connected "at any time and anywhere", we fully agree with the idea expressed by DAGNINO. He states that this right of disconnection should be regulated for all workers and contractual modalities, because the risks of work overload and "hyper-connection" today affect the vast majority of workers, not only those who work at a distance or have flexible arrangements such as "agile" work.[46] We would add here that this prohibition of "connection" should also be extended to the workers themselves, an issue that should be the responsibility of the employer, with the obligation to establish "technical measures" by which one could avoid any connection outside working hours, both the employer with the worker and *vice versa*, excluding exceptional cases or force majeure. The introduction of the aforementioned "technical measures" in the tools used by workers would also be a clear indication of dependence in the case of needing to prove the legitimacy of the labour relationship against allegations of "non-labour" or autonomy.

All the legal gaps outlined can and should be covered by collective bargaining, as is already being done. Specifically, the right to disconnect has recently been included in the latest agreement of the Axa Group in Spain, but only in terms of "freedom" or "right to not respond to work-related emails or messages outside of working hours".[47] It does not prohibit the sending of messages by the company, nor does it set out sanctions for the breach of such prohibitions.[48]

---

45 Molina Navarrete, C., "Derecho y trabajo en la era digital: ¿"Revolución industrial 4.0" o "economía sumergida 3.0"? en AAVV El *futuro del trabajo que queremos. Conferencia Nacional Tripartita (OIT) de 20 de marzo 2017*. Ed. Mess, Madrid.

46 Dagnino, E., "Il diritto alla disconnessione nella legge n. 81/2017 e nell'esperienza comparata", Diritto delle Relazione Industriale, no. 4/2017.

47 Collective agreement for the Axa Spain Group (BOE 20 October 2017). Article 14, right to digital disconnection: "The technological changes produced in the last decades have caused structural modifications in the field of labor relations. It is undeniable that nowadays the phenomenon of 'digital interconnectivity' is affecting the forms of work execution, changing the scenarios of the development of labor occupations towards external environments from the classic productive units: companies, centers and jobs. In this context, the place of job provision and working time, as typical elements that shape the framework in which the work activity is carried out, are being diluted in favor of a more complex reality in which permanent connectivity prevails, affecting, without doubt, the personal and family environment of the workers. That is why the signing parties of this Agreement agree on the need to promote the right to digital disconnection once the working day has ended. Consequently, except for reasons of force majeure or exceptional circumstances, AXA recognizes the right of workers not to respond to emails or professional messages outside of their work schedule".

48 Molina Navarrete, C., "Derecho y trabajo en la era digital: (..)", *op. cit.*

Here are three concluding ideas. First, it is necessary to update existing legislation, both international and community (the AMET of 2002 and the ILO Convention of 177), as well as national (article 13 of the ET in 2012 – besides being incomplete and generic, it was obsolete at inception). Second, collective bargaining is decisive when regulating telework, establishing a minimum framework within which this mode of working will be made compatible to individual workers and employers, and complying with the working conditions regime established in the law and in the collective agreement. Finally, "the work of public authorities is decisive, especially that of the labour authority, through inspections designed to control teleworkers' working conditions, without which the legal prescriptions would not be worth the paper they are written on.[49]

IV Bibliography

AAVV (Dir. Mella Méndez, coord. Villalba Sánchez) (2015) Trabajo a distancia y teletrabajo, ed. Aranzadi, Navarra.

CERVILLA GARZÓN, Mª J, (2017) "Avances en Italia y España hacia la regulación del derecho a la desconexión tecnológica y el nuevo 'lavoro agile'", en MELLA MÉNDEZ, Lourdes (Dir.), SERRANI, L. (Coord.) Los actuales cambios sociales y laborales: nuevos retos para el mundo del trabajo. I. Cambios tecnológicos y nuevos retos para el mundo del trabajo: (Portugal, España, Colombia, Italia, Francia), Petr Lang, Suiza, pp. 433 a 463.

DAGNINO, E. (2017), "Il diritto alla disconnessione nella legge n. 81/2017 e nell'esperienza comparata", Diritto delle Relazione Industriale, n° 4/2017.

DE LA VILLA, L.E. (2016) "Trabajo a distancia", en AAVV (Coord. Goerlich Peset) Comentarios al Estatuto de los Trabajadores. Libro homenaje a Tomás Sala Franco., ed. Tirant Lo Blach, Valencia.

DE LAS HERAS GARCÍA, A. (2016) *El teletrabajo en España: un análisis crítico de normas y práctica*, ed. CEF, Madrid.

DOMINGUEZ MORALES, A. (2017) "El tratamiento en la negociación colectiva del teletrabajo como modalidad de gestión del cambio", en AAVV (Dir. Cruz Villalón) La negociación colectiva como instrumento de gestión del cambio, ed. Cinca, Madrid, pp. 290 a 315.

ESCUDERO RODRÍGUEZ, R. (2000) "Teletrabajo", en AAVV Descentralización productiva y nuevas formas organizativas del trabajo, ed. MTASS, Madrid.

GAETA, L. (1996) "Teletrabajo y derecho: la experiencia italiana", Documentación laboral, núm.49/1996.

GALLARDO MOYA, R. (1998) *El viejo y el nuevo trabajo a domicilio De la máquina de hilar al ordenador*, ed. Ibidem. Madrid.

GARCÍA ROMERO, B. (2012) El teletrabajo. Ed. Civitas, Thomson Reuters, Navarra.

GONZÁLEZ-POSADA MARTÍNEZ, E (2006) El teletrabajo, ed. Junta de Castilla y León, Valladolid.

LUQUE PARRA, M y CAMARGO R., (2017) "Teleworking and labor conditions conclusions," en IUSLabor 2/2107.

---

[49] de la Villa, LE. "Trabajo a distancia", (…), *op. cit.*, p. 321.

MARTONE, M. (2018) "El Smart working o trabajo ágil en el ordenamiento italiano", Revista Derecho de las Relaciones Laborales, núm.1/2018.
MELLA MÉNDEZ (Dir.) (2017) *El teletrabajo en España: aspectos teórico-prácticos de interés*, ed. Wolters Kluwer, Madrid.
MELLA MÉNDEZ, L. (2017) "Configuración general del trabajo a distancia en el derecho español", en Mella Méndez (Dir.) El teletrabajo en España: aspectos teórico-prácticos de interés, ed. Wolters Kluwer, Madrid.
MELLA MÉNDEZ, L. (2017, b) "El trabajo a distancia como medida de flexibilidad y conciliación laboral", IUSLabor 2/2017.
MELLA MÉNDEZ, L. (Dir.) y SERRANI, L: (Coord.) (2017) *Los actuales cambios sociales y laborales: nuevos retos para el mundo del trabajo. I. Cambios tecnológicos y nuevos retos para el mundo del trabajo: (Portugal, España, Colombia, Italia, Francia)*, Petr Lang, Suiza.
MERCADER UGUINA, J.R. (2017) *El futuro del trabajo en la era de la digitalización y la robótica*, Tirant lo Blanch, Valencia.
MOLINA NAVARRETE, C. (2017) "Derecho y trabajo en la era digital: Revolución industrial 4.0" o "economía sumergida 3.0"? en AAVV El futuro del trabajo que queremos. Conferencia Nacional Tripartita (OIT) de 20 de marzo 2017. Ed. MESS, Madrid.
NIETO, J. (2017) "Tendencias laborales y le futuro del trabajo", en Gaceta Sindical núm.29/2017.
PERULLI, A. (2017) "Il Jobs Act del lavoro autónomo e agile: come cambiano i concetti di subordinazione e autonomía nel diritto del lavoro", en WP CSLE "Massimo D'Antona", IT. 341/2017.
QUINTANILLA NAVARO, R.Y. (2017) "El teletrabajo: de la dispersión normativa presente a la necesaria regulación normativa europea y estatal futura", en AAVV El futuro del trabajo que queremos. Conferencia Nacional Tripartita (OIT) de 20 de marzo 2017. Ed. MESS, Madrid.
QUINTANILLA NAVARRO, R.Y. (2014), "El teletrabajo: delimitación, negociación colectiva y conflictos", en AAVV (Dir. San Martin Mazzucconi) Tecnologías de la información y la comunicación en las relaciones de trabajo: nuevas dimensiones del conflicto jurídico, ed. Eolas, Madrid.
ROCHA SÁNCHEZ, F. (2017) "La digitalización y el empleo decente en España. Retos y propuestas de actuación, en AAVV El futuro del trabajo que queremos. Conferencia Nacional Tripartita (OIT) de 20 de marzo 2017. Ed. MESS, Madrid.
RODRÍGUEZ-PIÑERO ROYO, M. y HERNÁNDEZ BEJARANO, M. (2017) (dirs.): Economía colaborativa y trabajo en plataforma: realidades y desafíos, Bomarzo, Albacete.
SELLAS I BENVINGUT, R. (2001) El régimen jurídico del teletrabajo en España, ed Aranzadi, Navarra.
SERRANI, L. E TIRABOSCHI, M. (2015) "Il futuro del telelavoro in Italia", en Mella Méndez (ed.) y Villalba Sánchez (coord.) Trabajo a distancia y teletrabajo, ed. Aranzadi, Navarra.
SIERRA BENÍTEZ, E.M. (2017) "Trabajo a distancia y relación individual: aspectos críticos" en Mella Méndez (Dir.) El teletrabajo en España: aspectos teórico-prácticos de interés, ed. Wolters Kluwer, Madrid.
SIERRA BENÍTEZ, E.M. (2017) "Valoración crítica y propuesta de mejora de la regulación del trabajo a distancia en la normativa estatal y autonómica", en Trabajo y Derecho núm.29/2017.
THIBAULT ARANDA, J. (2000) El teletrabajo. CES, Madrid.

THIBAULT ARANDA, J. (2010) "El impacto laboral de la descentralización tecnológica: el teletrabajo", en Lahera Forteza y Valdés Dal-Ré (dirs.) Relaciones laborales, organización de la empresa y globalización, ed. Cinca, Madrid.

TASCHINI, L. (2017) "Smart working: la nuova disciplina de lavoro agile", en Massimario di Giurisprudenza del Lavoro n.6/2107.

TIRABOSCHI, M. (2017), "Il lavoro agile tre legge e contrattazione colletiva: la tortuosa via italiana verso la modernizzazione del diritto del lavoror", WP CSDLE "Massimo D'Antona", IT. Núm.335/2017.

TODOLÍ SIGNES, A. (2017) El trabajo en la Era de la Economía colaborativa, ed. Tirant Lo Blanch, Valencia.

USHASKOVA, T. (2017) "Los modelos de la acción normativa de la OIT para regular el trabajo a distancia", en AAVV El futuro del trabajo que queremos. Conferencia Nacional Tripartita (OIT) de 20 de marzo 2017. Ed. Mº de Empleo y Seguridad Social, Madrid.

9 Robotics and work

Labour and tax regulatory framework

María Yolanda Sánchez-Urán Azaña and María Amparo Grau Ruiz

I Introduction[1]

A reflection on the labour law and financial implications of robotics must start with the technological context that is described today as the Fourth Industrial Revolution, which is more than a simple description of change driven by technology.

We jurists are obliged to comprehend the phenomenon. First, to understand, define and delimit it; second, to explain and analyse it; and third, to propose fair and equitable step-by-step solutions because this global concept encompasses multiple realities, each with their own characteristics and a particular impact. Of particular complexity are the impacts of the technologies on working life as a source of personal identity.

Thus, for example, we speak of Artificial Intelligence (AI) as a set of technologies devoted to replicating in machines' cognitive processes that are similar to those in humans, in order to enable the former to learn and adapt on their own to a specific environment (*FTI Consulting Report*). Or as "the ability of computer programs to produce results from reasoning equivalent to those obtained by natural human intelligence by means of artificial learning systems that are similar to natural ones".[2] And this differs from robotics in that robots may or may not be equipped with AI.

It is true that deep down there is a common element or feature that concerns society in general, social scientists and especially jurists from different areas of research: namely that of the social dimension of this phenomenon and the

---

1 CertificaRSE Project, DER 2015-65374-R (MINECO-FEDER); and INBOTS CSA, *Inclusive Robotics for a better Society*, Program H2020-ICT-2017-1, Project No. 780073, http://inbots.eu/.
2 Agote Eguizábal, R.: 'Inteligencia Artificial, Ser humano y Derecho', *Review Claves de Razón Práctica*, no. 237, 2018, p. 41. The Communication from the Commission, "Artificial Intelligence for Europe", Brussels 24.4.2018, COM (2018)237, describes AI: "Artificial intelligence (AI) refers to systems that display intelligent behaviour by analysing their environment and taking actions – with some degree of autonomy – to achieve specific goals. AI-based systems can be purely software-based, acting in the virtual world (e.g. voice assistants, image analysis software, search engines, speech and face recognition systems) or AI can be embedded in hardware devices (e.g. advanced robots, autonomous cars, drones or Internet of Things applications)".

necessary intergenerational responsibility, particularly the interrelationship between technological change, economic performance and employment.

On the one hand, the impact of these technological manifestations on free, personal human work or employment; in its configuration and definition and in the different models or forms of work, profoundly altered today by automation or digitalisation, globalisation and the increase in productivity of a small number of highly qualified professionals, and the impact on labour relations, that is, on the conditions in which the worker provides services, should be analysed. On the other hand, the practical effect of sound financial and tax regulations is common knowledge, especially in the pursuit of non-fiscal goals.

In order to analyse the subject in depth, particularly the impact of robotics on labour law and financial law, we must start with some reflections raised by ethics (Part 2); attempt to adopt a concept of robots and lay the foundations for legal regulation (Part 3); and last, resolve a number of issues which, from the perspective of these disciplines, are posed by the robotisation of the labour market (Parts 4 and 5).

II Ethics, law and inclusive robotics

Law needs ethics as a foundation for its rules and ethics needs law to give more force to its conclusions. Roboethics, understood as the set of criteria or theories which are formulated as a response to the ethical problems arising from the design, creation, development and use of robots,[3] warns us that robotics gives rise to unique issues that go beyond those which are common to all the so-called "emerging technologies". These include the relationship or interaction between human beings and machines (uses and limits of robotics) and the moral status of robots, that is, their possible consideration as moral agents. There is also a debate as to whether, when robots possess certain characteristics which make them similar to humans, they cease to be an object and can be considered a subject.[4] Robotics presents several issues or problems that affect its political and legal implications. On the one hand, these implications should guide public authorities in their job to oversee the introduction of robots in a socially responsible manner in such a way that society perceives that they are necessary and useful to people and are accepted by them. On the other hand, they should facilitate a situation whereby those authorities and the many groups with a social and economic stake in the matter can work towards legislation, which addresses not so much (or not only) the specific characteristics intrinsic to robots but the type of problems they pose.

---

3 Veruggio, G.: *The EURON Roboethics Roadmap*, 2006, available at: www3.nd.edu/~rbarger/ethics-roadmap.pdf. Also, Veruggio, G. and Operto, F.: 'Roboethics: Social and Ethical Implications of Robotics', in *Handbook of Robotics*, Siciliano, B. and Khatib, O. (eds.), 2008. By the same authors: 'Roboethics: a bottom-up interdisciplinary discourse in the field of applied ethics in robotics', *International Review of Information Ethics*, Vol. 6, No. 12, 2006, pp. 2–9.
4 De Asís, R.: *Una mirada a la Robótica desde los Derechos Humanos*, Edit. Dykinson, 2014, pp. 41–43, 74, 75.

As part of the process of eliminating existing barriers, the need to legally regulate robotics is obvious, although there is no unanimous position as regards the manner and scope of that regulation because there is, as yet, no common position regarding the ethical framework required to deal with the challenges posed by robotics. Whether we follow the path of regulation, which we can call *hard law*, or whether we opt for the path of *soft law*, in both cases we need to ensure transparency and accountability regarding the social and economic costs and benefits.

Should the path of mandatory regulation be the one finally chosen, it will be necessary to bear in mind not only the multiplicity of technological applications, but also the range of legal problems they generate and the difficulty of fitting them all into a uniform paradigm. That is why approaches which until recently were different, those of the United States (CALO et al.[5]) and Europe (PALMERINI et al.[6]), can now come together around regulations or minimum mandatory rules which establish the necessary balance between facilitating robotic technological development and protecting the values desired by humans. National reports in various countries, some in the general context of digitalisation, others related more specifically to AI and others relating even more specifically to robotics in connection with AI (e.g. Economic and Social Council in Spain; Italy; France; United States; Great Britain; and Japan) stress the interaction between robotics and human being and the social impact thereof by reminding us that "we are creating systems to help us; we are not creating life".[7]

For this reason, the response to issues relating to when the law should intervene, how to intervene and what form of regulation would be necessary requires that we not only take into account the specificity of the context (in particular, the different characteristics of robots, especially when they are endowed with systems of AI), but above all that we precisely identify the significant challenges arising from the profound underlying problems. In order for the law to be able to adopt measures in this regard, we need to clearly define the problem and the challenges that have to be addressed based on the set of common general principles in the acquis of the European Union (which help to construct

---

5 Calo, R., Froomkin, A.M. and Kerr, I. (Eds): *Robot Law*, EE Elgar, 2016; CALO, R. described Robots some time ago as 'entities' and consider them to be artificially intelligent devices with 'cognitive' faculties, in Calo, R.: 'La robótica y las lecciones del Derecho cibernético', *Review Privacidad y Derecho Digital*, núm.2, 2016, pp. 155–157.

6 Palmerini, E.: 'Robótica y Derecho: sugerencias, confluencias, evoluciones en el marco de una investigación europea', *Review de Derecho Privado*, Universidad Externado de Colombia, n.º32, January–June 2017, p. 80; Leenes, R., Palmerini, E., Koops, B.J., Bertolini, A., Salvini, P. and Lucivero, F.: 'Regulatory challenges of robotics: some guidelines for addressing legal and ethical issues', *Journal Law, Innovation and Technology*, 2017, Vol. 9, No. 1, 1–44, p. 12.

7 As discussed in Nisa Ávila, J.A.: 'Robótica e Inteligencia Artificial ¿legislación social o nuevo ordenamiento jurídico', El Derecho.com, Lefebvre, 2016, http://tecnologia.elderecho.com/tecnologia/internet_y_tecnologia/Robotica-Inteligencia-Artificial-legislacion-social-nuevo-ordenamiento_11_935305005.html (consulted in March 2018).

what has started to be called "fully-fledged digital citizenship").[8] Today the framework of the European Pillar of Social Rights pays special attention to human abilities; those abilities which are affected by robots and those which, though it may seem paradoxical, can be fostered by robots so that people can devote themselves to performing activities which can be described as inherently human, that is, those related to characteristics associated with humans such as emotions, awareness, reflection, abstract processing, personality and free will. It is a question of moving forward on the basis of what technology has called "the principle of caution"[9] as applied to freedom of scientific investigation and beyond rules of "technological neutrality"[10] (which cannot become an end in itself), to implement the principle of socially and legally responsible technological innovation.

Whether we talk of "Robot Law"[11] or "Robotics Law" or whether we consider this to be a branch of the broader Digital Law, the first issue to resolve (to define both the object and subject) is that which concerns the characterisation and classification of robots. We can take a specific technical definition (the one provided by the *Industrial Federation of Robotics* [IFR]) as a starting point; move forward towards a more general technical definition; and conclude that the characteristics which define robots are autonomy, corporeality and intense physical and/or cognitive interaction with humans. Hence an initial distinction can be made between CoBots (mainly interactive in industrial and manufacturing sectors) and Inclusive Robots (predominantly interactive in services sector and others, i.e. healthcare), characteristics which have been described as the ability to gather data via sensors; to process raw data; and to plan and perform actions by means of knowledge and information acquired, generally on the basis of pre-established objectives (described as *sense-think-act*). Bear in mind that the following are also occasional characteristics: the ability to communicate with an operator with other robots or with an external network and the ability to learn.[12] Conversely, the existence of life in a biological sense would never be a characteristic of a robot.[13]

---

8 Cortina, A.: 'Ciudadanía digital y dignidad humana', opinion article in *El País*, 26 March 2018, which considers it to be a fair and essential requirement that digital citizenship be at the service of autonomous and vulnerable people.
9 "Which supports the adoption of protective measures with regarding to certain products or technologies which are suspected of posing a serious risk even though there is no scientific proof of this", De Asís, R.: *Una mirada a la Robótica…, cit.*, p. 68.
10 Leenes R., et al.: 'Regulatory challenges of robotics…', *cit.*, p. 12.
11 Barrio Andrés, M. (Ed.): *Derecho de los Robots*; Edit. La Ley, Wolters Kluwer, 2018.
12 García-Prieto Cuesta, J.: 'Qué es un Robot'? in Barrio Andrés, M. (dir.): *Derecho de los Robots, cit.*, p. 38, describes a robot as "a machine, endowed with a certain complexity both in its components and its design or in its behaviour, which manipulates information about its environment in order to interact with it".
13 Richards, N.M. and Smart, D.: 'How should the law….', *cit.*, p. 6. They describe robot as "a constructed system that displays both physical and mental agency, but is not alive in the biological sense".

As people enablers (so that individuals can devote themselves to developing abilities inherent to human beings), whether they be *CoBots* or *Inclusive Robots* (which share the characteristics indicated previously, especially autonomy, corporeality and physical and/or cognitive interaction with human beings), what is now being called "botsourcing" (the replacement of human jobs by robots) can have a positive effect on the labour market, as analysed below.

III Labour law implications of robotics

One of the fundamental problems posed by robotics is its effect on the labour market, and this reflection encompasses the challenges posed by technology in general and automation in particular in the world of work.[14]

From this perspective, studies and reports have adopted varying approaches. Two expressions have become generalised: techno-pessimism,[15] which identifies the risks posed by robotics to employment and concludes with a drastic prediction of job disruption or destruction; and techno-optimism (Mckinsey Global Institute, 2017; PwC, 2018), which identifies the challenges and opportunities presented by the robotisation of the labour market.

In any event, we should bear in mind that the studies are carried out in a socio-economic context of employment precariousness (we speak of "the precarious" in sociological and economic terms[16] as an emerging social class which lives in a state of economic and professional insecurity), together with a high level of unemployment, and in a demographic context of an ageing population and high levels of life expectancy.

In spite of all this, the fundamental question is whether the increase in company productivity and competitivity (which does not appear to be in doubt) will also be accompanied by an increase in the quantity and quality of human employment. And in this respect, apart from the "replacement" effect, problems arise in relation to the transitional period we are still going through, including those which affect the working conditions of humans: pressure on salaries, particularly

---

14 From ILO, Nieto, J.: 'El futuro del trabajo que queremos y el Derecho del Trabajo', in *Ius Labor* 3/2017, www.upf.edu/documents/3885005/140470042/1.+Editorial.pdf/406c3008-6ef9-7ed6-f4ee-8f754c9adc31 (last access March 2018). The ILO Initiative for the Future of Work can be consulted in www.ilo.org/global/topics/future-of-work/lang--es/index.htm; and the national syntheses in www.ilo.org/global/topics/future-of-work/WCMS_591507/lang--es/index.htm.

15 For example, from the United States, Acemoglu, D. and Restrepo, P.: 'Robots and Jobs: Evidence from US Labour Market', *NBER Working Paper* No. 23285, 2017, in www.nber.org/papers/w23285 (last access March 2018); also, Frey, C.B. and Osborne, M.A.: 'The Future of Employment: How susceptible are Jobs to Computerisation', *Technological Forecasting and Social Change*, Vol. 114, No. C, 2013, pp. 254–280, which analyses 702 jobs and claims that 47% of jobs in the United States are at risk of being computerized or robotized. The projections of these authors are used in the 2018 BBVA report; Doménech, R. et al.: How vulnerable is employment in Spain to the digital revolution? www.bbvaresearch.com/wp-content/uploads/2018/03/Cuan-vulnerable-es-el-empleo-en-Espana-a-la-revolucion-digital.pdf (last access March 2018).

16 Standing, G.: *The Precarious: a new social class*, Edit. Pasado y Presente, 2013, Barcelona, 2013. Founder of the Basic Income Earth Network that postulates universal basic income.

on those of less skilled workers; the move towards decentralised production; the reallocation of jobs and tasks; and the effect of technological unemployment.

There is no snapshot available that covers all sectors, all kinds of work, every skill level, all markets or all countries.[17] Therefore:

- The analysis requires a temporal perspective but should avoid making long-term projections exclusively. We need to promote a situation in which the absence of constraints on technological innovation goes hand in hand with the principle that automation and robotics must permit employment to be focused on "jobs that add greater value"; this means committing ourselves now to the development of technological competencies and balancing the two needs, one which stems from growth and competitivity and consequently the adoption of technology and the other which minimises disruption in the labour market to prevent social inequalities.
- The digital breach and the associated social cost must be dealt with, paying special attention to the vulnerability of certain groups (based, among other factors, on gender and age).
- A "safety net" for the transition period is required, and it demands the proposal of related political and legislative measures.

To solve these problems, is it necessary to make changes to the labour law (and also the social security law), that is, in the regulatory framework of labour relations in the robotised neo-technological context? The answer must take into account the multi-functionality of the legal definition of robots (autonomy, physical configuration and ability to interact with workers)[18] and the involvement of entrepreneurs and workers' representatives, especially trade unions, in order to make decisions, which are based on consensus between them and accepted by the public authorities. Last, a minimum, albeit necessary, mandatory legal intervention is needed to ensure a balance between entrepreneurial freedom and the function and purpose of labour law, especially with regard to the protection and guarantee of human work. This last part affects two areas: the concept of "worker" and forms of employment in the robotised labour market (1) and the working conditions (2). For both of these, we need to reflect urgently on some of the problems and the possible legal solutions in the transition phase.

---

17 United Nations: *Trade and Development Report*, 2017; in particular, Chapter III, *Robots, Industrialization and Inclusive Growth*: "This discussion shows that disruptive technologies always bring a mix of benefits and risks. But whatever the impacts, the final outcomes for employment and inclusiveness are shaped by policies", p. 60.
18 Del Rey Guanter, S.: *Robótica y su impacto en los Recursos Humanos y en el marco regulatorio de las Relaciones Laborales*, Edit. Wolter Kluwer, 2018, Chapter 3, describes these elements in the following way: autonomy, acquired by means of sensors and/or data sharing and analysis (interconnectivity); physical configuration, that is, a minimum physical materialisation, which entails the possibility of physical movement applied to the work with the possibility of total or partial displacement; and interaction with the environment with reponse capability by means of the appropriate programming.

1 Concept of worker and forms of employment in the robotised labour market

Let us pose these issues in question form and briefly indicate a solution:

1. Impact on the concept of salaried employee? There is no direct reconsideration; however, it could indirectly affect "labour law evasion" (especially as regards the solution to the problem of liability for damages).
2. Reconsideration of the concept of disabled worker? The concept of disability may change in the future, and this means it will be necessary to rethink the legal concept of occupational integration based on the distinction between therapy and the improvement of capabilities.
3. Due to the replacement effect, will there be a change in the traditional forms of work, whether the person has an employment contract or is self-employed? Contractual diversity should be maintained, although it should be committed to guaranteeing social, economic and labour rights, that is, by adopting measures to prevent and correct regressive segregation. It is precisely this which is, or should be, a priority of the regulatory framework of labour relations in this phase of robotisation for the purpose of preventing worker polarization or digital polarisation as a synonym for precarious employment, even if it is necessary to accept a new division of labour – between digital labour and human labour.
4. As far as "robot workers" are concerned (electronic personality or Impersonal Capable Entities; the original Spanish term is *Entes Capaces No Personales*, ECNP),[19] labour law allows us to take a critical position regarding a robotic personality or ECNP, that is, regarding legal recognition of a new category of capable subjects or entities, and even more so when it comes to defining a relationship, such as a labour relationship, which is both proprietary and personal in nature, an exchange which is permanent and stable and above all voluntary. Voluntariness and awareness are something that robots will never achieve, even if they are endowed with AI.
5. If this was the case, could they have employment status? For this to be possible, we would have to stop considering them as a mere instrument of work and start considering them as technologically complex tools. They would not, however, be subject to labour rights and obligations due to the absence of the characteristic of "voluntariness".
6. With regard to the change in the model of work and the polarisation of workers, we would counteract the digital breach (and the effects thereof on specific groups of workers) by means of actions and measures geared towards safeguarding the distribution of work and the protection of the most vulnerable workers within the framework of the principle of equality and non-discrimination in employment. Would it be necessary to go further in

---

19 García Mexía, P.: 'Entes Capaces No Personales. ¿Hacia una personalidad para los robots', in www.automatas.tech/pablo-garcia-mexia-colabouracion.html (last access March 2018).

the principle of *equality and robotic non-discrimination*, which would also require as preventive and corrective measures the implementation of rules on positive or affirmative action in favour of human workers? This would require us to address the following issues, among others:

- A "human quota" in companies? A measure which could be implemented in the transition period on an exceptional, extraordinary and temporary basis.
- Financial incentives for entrepreneurs? Incentives for retraining and relocating workers could be adopted.
- Technological requirements during the selection process, that is, can these conditions or the technological adaptability (robotics) of the workers be used as selection criteria? This means considering whether the assessment of such requirements in the framework of the right to equality and non-discrimination should be applied restrictively during the transition period and progressively extended for companies which exhibit a high level of robotisation in their production processes or in those which are immersed in a process of robotisation.

2 Working conditions and the impact of robotics

There are two aspects to be analysed here: one is related to the "replacement effect" of robotics and the other is related to collaborative or cooperative work with robots.

If we analyse the impact of robotics from a negative perspective, that is, the replacement of the human workforce by robots (botsourcing)[20] and if we maintain that this effect will be inevitable in the short term, it is worth considering whether or not robotics is a technological phenomenon which impacts on the right to non-discrimination in terms of working conditions, the main legal "safety net" for workers. And this, in our opinion, allows us to assess not only arbitrary behaviour on the part of entrepreneurs, but also those forms of behaviour which can "aseptically" be considered as linked to an entrepreneurial right to technological-robotic innovation in the company. If this impacts on certain groups of workers for reasons which include gender and age, robotisation could be considered as a cause of indirect discrimination (with robotisation being identified as a neutral criterion which has or can have an adverse impact on or prove detrimental to one of the vulnerable groups identified for one of the causes where discrimination is prohibited) and would activate the guarantee process provided for in European Union regulations, particularly Directive 2000/78.

This leads us immediately to analyse the "technical cause" arising from robotisation in such a way that measures are devised which are geared towards workers'

---

20 Waytz, A. and Norton, M.I.: 'Botsourcing and Outsourcing: Robot, British, Chinese, and German Workers Are for Thinking – Not Feeling – Jobs', *Emotion,* 2014, No. 2, pp. 434–444.

remuneration (which is none other than the effective and real application of the right to equal pay for equal work; *human work as work of equal value to that of the robot*). And also in relation to eliminating vacant positions (or dismissals or job changes) arising from robotisation.

From this latter perspective, we need to analyse *botsourcing* and its labour implications, bearing in mind that the robot is or can be considered to be a "technical improvement" in the company, which affects aspects of internal and external flexibility. This will require the legislator to specify, at the regulatory level, the technical reason arising from robotisation (in the sense of a massive incorporation of robots and replacement of workers) – the implementation of well-thought-out and balanced measures which limit the impact of dismissal (need for preventive measures, prior to termination, and immediate corrective measures, need to relocate the worker affected). As far as the preventive measures are concerned, one of the issues posed in this respect is the definition of "reasonable adjustment" as regards the necessary readjustment of the job of the worker who has been replaced by robots with the subsequent problem of whether these adjustments can be considered an "excessive burden" for the entrepreneur. In our opinion, it would be necessary to assess the reasonableness or otherwise of the adjustment in relation to tax incentives and subsidies for innovation which have been granted to entrepreneurs. And last, a highly controversial aspect is the issue of "auxiliary aids", particularly the use exoskeletons which able-bodied people could request of entrepreneurs in order to improve their personal skills.[21]

If we analyse the perspective of collaboration, cooperation, interaction of human workers and robots, a number of issues arise, particularly in connection with:

- Health and safety at work, new psycho-social risks, professional retraining of workers and working time (assessment of the digital disconnection of the robots and its influence on pay and the calculation of working time).
- The worker's right to privacy and, in particular, "robotic" surveillance.
- Intellectual property rights/patent right when the worker "trains" the robot.
- Advanced perspective of entrepreneurial secrecy (Spanish draft bill).

IV Financial and tax law implications of robotics

There is an obvious need to adapt the financial and tax rules to face the legal, economic, ethical and social challenges posed by robotics.[22] This process of adaptation has just begun and will have to be maintained in the future. Apparently, as a machine includes new functions – similar to human capabilities – it is

---

21 Hoder, C. et al.: 'Robotics and law: Key legal and regulatory implications of the robotics age (part II of II)', *Computer Law & Security Review*, No. 32, 2016, pp. 557–576.
22 Grau Ruiz, M.A.: 'La adaptación de la fiscalidad ante los retos jurídicos, económicos, éticos y sociales planteados por la robótica', *Nueva fiscalidad*, No. 4, 2017, p. 35.

referred to as "robot"; once we differentiate them from the ones attributable to humans, it is called again "machine".[23] As a consequence, those functions, for the purpose of our study, may help to dynamically define a job.

In this changing environment, an interactive robot (with different levels of complexity) may supplement or substitute a human being for the development of some tasks.[24] In the coming years, the economy and the appearance of various jobs will possibly experience alterations, particularly regarding the remuneration and/or the number of required personnel in a specific field. Hence, the design of new public policies will surely have an impact on the financial legal order; conversely, the latter will probably impose restrictions of the formers' feasibility in light of the expected qualitative and quantitative transformations.[25]

Undoubtedly the types of work have been changing along history hitherto. From now on, the degree of robot's penetration may be gradually increased in a given job (considering the total, partial or nil reservation of some tasks for human participation). As the use of robotics in our society evolves, the legislation will have to consider how individuals and companies use robots.[26]

Nowadays, the world trends already show a continued proliferation in the use of robots.[27] In this context, many questions arise: should taxation intervene to slow down the spread use of robots or to finance new labour opportunities? Should the companies that invest in robots substituting workers pay taxes and social security contributions for the benefits obtained due to the increase of productivity?[28] Which would be the competent authority to receive those payments? In the case where several States are involved, because the robot interface may act in a multiple off-line real (on top of virtual) environment, these States will have to cooperate in the design of coherent measures to safeguard social protection, taking advantage of the pace and volume of information flowing across borders.

The main issue, in the middle of this digital revolution, is how to allocate rights and responsibilities among human beings for the actions of no-human beings, fighting inter-personal and inter-national inequality (as intellectual and financial capital providers are supposed to enjoy the greater benefits).[29]

---

23 Professor Bernard Roth elaborated this variable concept at Stanford. García-Prieto Cuesta, J. '¿Qué es un robot?' (Chapter I), in Barrio Andrés, M. (dir.): *Derecho de los robots*, La Ley-Wolters Kluwer, 2018, p. 33.
24 García-Prieto Cuesta, J.: '¿Qué es un robot?', cit., p. 39.
25 Froomkin, A.M.: 'Prologue', in Barrio Andrés, M. (dir.): *Derecho de los robots*, La Ley-Wolters Kluwer, 2018, p. 22.
26 Barrio Andrés, M.: 'Del Derecho de Internet al Derecho de los robots', in Barrio Andrés, M. (dir.): *Derecho de los robots*, La Ley-Wolters Kluwer, 2018, pp. 71–73.
27 Available at https://ifr.org/news/world-robotics-survey-service-robots-are-conquering-the-world-/ (last access 1 April 2018).
28 Segura Alastrué, M.: 'Los robots en el Derecho Financiero y Tributario' (Chapter VII), in Barrio Andrés, M. (dir.): *Derecho de los robots*, La Ley-Wolters Kluwer, 2018, p. 173.
29 Gupta, S.; Keen, M.; Shah, A.; Verdier, G. (eds.): *Digital revolutions in public finance*, International Monetary Fund, Washington DC, November 2017, pp. 11–12. Available at www.elibrary. imf.org/view/IMF071/24304-9781484315224/24304-9781484315224/Other_formats/ Source_PDF/24304-9781484316719.pdf (last access 1 April 2018).

The risks of job destruction and structural unemployment have propitiated the discussions around the universal basic income.[30] The International Monetary Fund (IMF) states that this instrument allows facing the acceleration of the decline in income and the uncertainty due to the impact of the technological evolution on the employment. However, there are doubts regarding the affordability and its costs, if they are displacing other priority expenditure programmes that actually promote inclusive growth. Additionally, some critics argue that separating this income from the participation in the workforce would be problematic.

A number of experiments, considering distinct features of the universal basic income, are being carried out by the private and the public sector to find out its impact on the individual and the society.[31] This movement may be understood as an extension of the social security network, an alternative to bureaucracy and public intervention or a manner to maintain social peace. Evidently, behind the supporters of universal basic income one may find completely different views, but they all face the same problem: how to finance it?[32] For instance, in Switzerland, the proposal of universal basic income was rejected by citizenship because of its costs, among other reasons.[33]

Clearly, the way to finance this measure will influence its net redistributive impact. The IMF has recently declared that the possibility to replace the current system of social protection with a basic universal income will depend on the performance of that system, the governmental administrative capacity and the prospects to improve targeting. Presently, in developed countries, it seems preferable to reinforce the existing systems, directly eliminating the gaps in the coverage nets caused by the participation rules or the incomplete take-up and pay attention to the proper design of salary subsidies to incentivise the work of low-income workers.

The IMF has recognised that a sound motivation to adopt a universal basic income could be "enhancing income insurance in the context of rising job insecurity due to technological change and automation or building public and political support for structural reforms, such as eliminating food or energy subsidies and broadening the consumption tax base".[34]

---

30 No country has approved a UBI for the entire population to date. International Monetary Fund: 'Tackling Inequality', *IMF Fiscal Monitor*, October 2017, pp. 3–4. Executive summary available at www.imf.org/en/Publications/FM/Issues/2017/10/05/fiscal-monitor-october-2017 (last access 1 April 2018).
31 E.g. 'Y Combinator' in San Francisco, or Canada (Ontario), Finland and the Netherlands.
32 A 70% of Finnish say that they are in favour of a basic income, however this percentage is 35% when they are told that taxes would be raised to finance it. As the cost of the experiment is limited to 20 million euros, it is impossible to guess how the taxpayers' incentives could change, if the model would become general. *El coste de mantener las prestaciones de un Estado como Noruega*, BBVA, June 2017.
33 Segura Alastrué, M.: 'Los robots...', *cit.*, p. 178.
34 International Monetary Fund: 'Tackling Inequality', *IMF Fiscal Monitor*, October 2017, p. X. Executive summary available at www.imf.org/en/Publications/FM/Issues/2017/10/05/fiscal-monitor-october-2017 (last access 1 April 2018).

Other voices claim for modelling the technology instead, for policies to increase economic growth and improve jobs for all by investing in education, research and development and infrastructures.[35]

Noticeably, the effects of UBI will vary depending on the country. The developing countries may use it to reinforce quickly their safety nets, but this would require efficient and equitable increases in taxes or cuts in spending. Whilst in developed countries, the UBI might result in a reduction of benefits for low-income households.

The UBI, financed through the general budget, might become a disincentive for the employment search and also produce a call effect. Therefore, reality imposes its transformation into a conditional basic income, limited subjectively (e.g. a specific group of beneficiaries depending on age), quantitatively or temporally. Others believe that a specific tax on robots could be a collateral effect, and defend that it should be only a transitional tax with earmarked revenue.[36] An alternative could be a negative tax on income, to substitute the benefits not depending upon contributions, for all the citizens below the poverty line.[37]

The legislator should not look for extreme solutions when the social alarmism may put at risk traditional legal institutions whose continued existence must be preserved. It is necessary to find a consensus on the extension of the solidarity principle while shaping the relation among technology, social processes and regulation.

V Conclusions

In view of the legal problem for which a solution is sought, there are various conceptual approaches to robotics and robots. Although a certain consensus exists as to the characteristics which these devices must possess in order to be considered robots, their functionality (we could say multi-functionality) and the degree of interaction with humans allow us at this stage to adopt a more restrictive concept (geared towards the industrial sector) and a broader concept (with regard to AI systems added to robots).

The legal problems spill over into various disciplines or areas of knowledge, which come together to seek solutions to the effect of robots in the labour market. When robotisation in the labour market means the replacement of

---

35 Brynjolfsson, E.; Mcafee, A.: *The Second Machine Age: Work, Progress, and Prosperity in a Time of Brilliant Technologies*, W. W. Norton & Company, New York, 2014. Taxing robots seems easier to include in an electoral programme than an increase of investment in R+D+i and education. Segura Alastrué, M.: 'Los robots...', *cit.*, p. 183.
36 This could lead to double taxation of capital and should not be admitted to remain unmoved. Alastrué, M.: 'Los robots...', *cit.*, pp. 174, 176 and 184.
37 Rodríguez Márquez, J.: 'La justicia tributaria. ¿Cómo puede el sistema fiscal contribuir a disminuir la desigualdad?', *VI Encuentro de Derecho Financiero y Tributario* (on 'Tendencias y retos del Derecho Financiero y Tributario'), Instituto de Estudios Fiscales, Madrid, 27 February 2018.

human jobs, tasks and activities by robots, ethics should be used as a starting point to reflect on the principles, scope and methods of regulatory intervention needed to safeguard human rights, that is, those inalienable rights which derive from human dignity.

Nevertheless, regulation, in its most continental sense, that is, hard law, cannot be designed from a perspective as defence or barrier against robotic technological innovation, but should rather be geared towards formulating measures which provide certainty to all those involved on the basis of the principle of socially and legally responsible robotic innovation. To this end, based on the fundamental rights enshrined in the EC and now in the European Pillar of Social Rights, it is necessary for everybody – public authorities and social partners – to promote legislation which balances the guarantee of entrepreneurial freedom with that of workers' rights.

From this dual perspective, legislation should go further in guaranteeing the employability of humans and balance the incentives for launching highly technologised activities and companies against the loss of workers in sectors which are reconverting from their traditional model towards more technologically based activities. In this respect, it will be necessary to offer, at least in the transition phase, financial incentives for those companies that truly and effectively invest in the technological training of their workers.

Furthermore, with regard to the labour relationship, labour law needs to consider the possibility that a ("intelligent") robot can be considered as a worker. It may be endowed with a certain employment status, but it cannot be legally considered as a salaried or self-employed worker. Labour law is based on human work and a robot, even one with a high dose of AI, cannot be considered as such.

If we use this fundamental fact as a starting point, robotics has many implications for the direct or indirect regulation of working conditions, for rights and obligations, for both the entrepreneur and the worker and from both a labour and fiscal perspective.

The starting point for the analysis is the principle of equality and non-discrimination, that is, the real and effective equality of people, of the groups of people who are vulnerable to automation or robotisation. Thus, these cannot become a direct or indirect cause of discrimination; technological neutrality cannot entail a disadvantage or barriers for certain groups of workers. In this respect and also in the transition phase, as an exceptional, limited and conditional measure, it is necessary to reflect on the quota of humans in companies and reasonable adjustment measures for those groups which are especially vulnerable, including older workers.

On the basis of this first reflection, we need to adapt labour legislation as it applies to workers' rights and obligations, both from the perspective of guaranteeing people's employability more than jobs themselves (which will affect the direction taken by legislation relating to the replacement effect, i.e. the replacement of humans by robots) and of guaranteeing the rights of workers in their interaction with robots in the workplace (cooperation between them).

All the expected public policies will probably have an impact on the financial and tax law, but at the same time, this discipline will condition their actual applicability in practice. The States will have to allocate rights and responsibilities among human beings for the actions of no-human beings, fighting inter-personal and inter-national inequality through strengthened cooperation. The high costs of a universal basic income, now at an experimental phase, could be publicly funded (through tax measures or cuts in spending) and/or even privately (if there could be a particular interest, i.e. in eliminating candidates for another competitor). In parallel, the idea of a more limited conditional basic income emerges for practical budgetary reasons. However, it will entail the need of proportionate justification in order not to breach constitutional or EU principles. The financial and tax regulation should always look for a balance between technological and social progress.

VI Bibliography

Acemoglu, D., Restrepo, P.: 'Robots and jobs: evidence from US labour market', *NBER Working Paper* No. 23285, 2017, available at www.nber.org/papers/w23285.

Adecco-Cuatrecasas: Informe, 2018, available at https://adecco.es/wp-content/uploads/2018/02/Estudio-cualitativo-sobre-la-percepcio%CC%81n-de-la-robo%CC%81tica-industrial-en-Espan%CC%83a.pdf.

Agote Eguizábal, R.: 'Inteligencia Artificial, Ser humano y Derecho', *Revista Claves de Razón Práctica*, No. 237, 2018.

Arranz de Andrés, C. (Dir.): *Aspectos fiscales de la dependencia y la discapacidad*, Thomson Reuters Aranzadi, Cizur Menor, 2017.

De Asis, R.: *Una mirada a la Robótica desde los Derechos Humanos*, Dykinson, Madrid, 2014.

Barrio Andrés, M. (Dir.): *Derecho de los Robots*, La Ley - Wolters Kluwer, Madrid, 2018.

Brynjolfsson, E.; Mcafee, A.: *The Second Machine Age: Work, Progress, and Prosperity in a Time of Brilliant Technologies*, W. W. Norton & Company, New York, 2014.

Calo, R., Froomkin, A.M. and Kerr, I. (Eds.): *Robot Law*, Edward Elgar, Cheltenham, 2016.

Calo, R.: 'La robótica y las lecciones del Derecho cibernético', *Revista Privacidad y Derecho Digital*, No. 2, 2016.

Cortina, A.: 'Ciudadanía digital y dignidad humana', *El País*, 26 March 2018.

Doménech, R., García, J.R., Montañez, M. and Neut, A.: *¿Cuán vulnerable es el Empleo en España a la revolución digital?*, BBVA, Madrid, March 2018. www.bbvaresearch.com/wp-content/uploads/2018/03/Cuan-vulnerable-es-el-empleo-en-Espana-a-la-revolucion-digital.pdf.

International Monetary Fund: 'Tackling inequality', *IMF Fiscal Monitor*, octubre 2017, p. 3–4. Available at www.imf.org/en/Publications/FM/Issues/2017/10/05/fiscal-monitor-october-2017.

Frey, C.B. and Osborne, M.A.: 'The future of employment: how susceptible are jobs to computerisation', *Technological Forecasting and Social Change*, Vol. 114, No. C, 2013.

FTI Consulting: *The global policy response to AI Report*, February 2018, available at http://brussels.ftistratcomm.com/wp-content/uploads/sites/5/2018/02/The-global-policy-response-to-AI-snapshot.pdf.

García Mexía, P.: 'Entes Capaces No Personales. ¿Hacia una personalidad para los robots', available at www.automatas.tech/pablo-garcia-mexia-colabouracion.html.

García-Prieto Cuesta, J.: '¿Qué es un Robot?, in Barrio Andrés, M. (Dir.): *Derecho de los Robots*, La Ley – Wolters Kluwer, Madrid, 2018.

Grau Ruiz, M.A.: 'La adaptación de la fiscalidad ante los retos jurídicos, económicos, éticos y sociales planteados por la robótica', *Nueva fiscalidad*, No. 4, 2017.

Gupta, S., Keen, M., Shah, A. and Verdier, G. (Eds.): *Digital revolutions in public finance*, International Monetary Fund, Washington DC, 2017, available at www.elibrary.imf.org/view/IMF071/24304-9781484315224/24304-9781484315224/Other_formats/Source_PDF/24304-9781484316719.pdf.

Holder, C., Khurana, V., Hook, J., Bacon, G. and Day, R.: 'Robotics and law: Key legal and regulatory implications of the robotics age (part II of II)', *Computer law & Security Review*, No. 32, 2016.

IBA Global Employment Institute, 'Artificial intelligence and robotics and their impact on the workplace', April 2017.

International Federation of Robotics (IFR): *The Impact of Robots on Productivity, Employment and Jobs*, April 2017; available at https://ifr.org/ifr-press-releases/news/position-paper.

Leenes, R., Palmerini, E., Koops, B-J., Bertolini, A., Salvini, P. and Lucivero, F.: 'Regulatory challenges of robotics: some guidelines for addressing legal and ethical issues', *Law, Innovation and Technology Review*, Vol. 9, No. 1, 2017.

Mercader Uguina, J.R.: El future del trabajo en la era de la digitalización y la robótica; tirant lo blanch, Valencia, 2017.

McKinsey Global Institute, 'A future that works: automation, employment and productivity' 2017, available at www.mckinsey.com/mgi/overview/2017-in-review/automation-and-the-future-of-work/a-future-that-works-automation-employment-and-productivity.

Nieto, J.: 'El Futuro del trabajo que queremos y el Derecho del Trabajo', *Ius Labour*, No. 3, 2017, available at www.upf.edu/documents/3885005/140470042/1.+Editorial.pdf/406c3008-6ef9-7ed6-f4ee-8f754c9adc31.

Nisa Ávila, J.A.: 'Robótica e Inteligencia Artificial ¿legislación social o nuevo ordenamiento jurídico', El Derecho.com, Lefebvre, 2016, available at http://tecnologia.elderecho.com/tecnologia/internet_y_tecnologia/Robotica-Inteligencia-Artificial-legislacion-social-nuevo-ordenamiento_11_935305005.html.

ILO: The future of work, available at www.ilo.org/global/topics/future-of-work/lang--es/index.htm; a summary of the national dialogues is available at www.ilo.org/global/topics/future-of-work/WCMS_591507/lang--es/index.htm.

Palmerini, E.: 'Robótica y derecho: sugerencias, confluencias, evoluciones en el marco de una investigación europea', *Revista de Derecho Privado*, Universidad Externado de Colombia, No. 32, 2017.

PwC: *Will robots really steal our jobs? An international analysis of the potential long-term impact of automation*, 2018, available at www.pwc.es/es/publicaciones/tecnologia/assets/international-impact-of-automation-2018.pdf.

Del Rey Guanter, S.: *Robótica y su impacto en los Recursos Humanos y en el marco regulatorio de las Relaciones Labourales*, La Ley – Wolters Kluwer, Madrid, 2018.

Richards, N.M. and Smart, D.: 'How should the Law think about Robots', in CALO et al.: *Robot Law*, Edward Elgar, Cheltenham, 2016.

Segura Alastrué, M.: 'Los robots en el Derecho Financiero y Tributario' (Chapter VII), in BARRIO ANDRÉS, M. (dir.): *Derecho de los robots*, La Ley – Wolters Kluwer, Madrid, 2018.

Standing, G.: *El Precariado: una nueva clase social*, Edit. Pasado y Presente, Barcelona, 2013.

United Nations: *Trade and Development Report*, 2017, available at http://unctad.org/en/PublicationsLibrary/tdr2017_en.pdf.

Veruggio, G.: *The EURON Roboethics Roadmap*, 2006, available at www3.nd.edu/~rbarger/ethics-roadmap.pdf.

Veruggio, G. and Operto, F.: 'Roboethics: social and ethical implications of robotics', in *Handbook of Robotics*, Siciliano, B. y Khatib, O. (eds.), 2008.

——— 'Roboethics: a bottom-up interdisciplinary discourse in the field of applied ethics in robotics', *International Review of Information Ethics*, Vol. 6, No. 12, 2006.

Villar Ezcurra, M. (ed.): *State Aids, Taxation and the Energy Sector*, Thomson Reuters Aranzadi, Cizur Menor, 2017.

Waters, R.: 'Do androids dream of personal deductions?', The big read, *Financial Times*, 25 February 2017, available at www.ft.com/content/597fff44-fa78-11e6-9516-2d969e0d3b65.

Waytz, A. and Norton, M. I.: 'Botsourcing and Outsourcing: Robot, British, Chinese, and German Workers Are for Thinking – Not Feeling – Jobs', *Emotion*, Vol. 14, No. 2, 2014; available at www.hbs.edu/faculty/Publication%20Files/waytz%20norton_a358958c-3b94-4f25-bb8c-7d10605738d8.pdf.

National reports

France 2017, Ministère Économique et Financiers: "France Intelligence Artificielle".

Italy 2017, Senato della Republica: "Impatto sul mercato del lavoro della quarta rivoluzione industriale".

Japan 2015, Headquarters for Japan's economic revitalization: "New Robot Strategy. Japan's Robot Strategy. Vision, Strategy, Action Plan".

Spain 2017, Consejo Económico y Social de España (CES): "Digitalización de la Economía".

United Kingdom 2016, House of Commons: "Robotics and AI".

The USA 2016, Executive Office of the President, National Science and Technology Council, Committee on Technology: "Preparing for the Future of AI".

10 Technology and jobs
Has what was old become new?*

Matthew W. Finkin[†], Albert J. Harno and Edward W. Cleary

I Introduction

> Will the digital revolution, and its current manifestations in cloud computing and platform-based work, inexorably lead to the elimination of jobs and work due to automation[?]
>
> (John Zysman & Martin Kenney, 2016)[1]

Contemporary anxiety about crowd work, robotisation and automation is connected by a common thread – that modern technology will render work more precarious: the former straightaway as more workers live from task to task, taking work from a multiplicity of taskmasters, and the latter less immediately as human workers are displaced by machines over time. They share a common sense of immediacy, however, even urgency, derived from the idea that this state of affairs is unprecedented, even startling.

The claim of novelty in the former instance has been addressed. It has been argued that the crowdsourcing of work is a modern manifestation of the hoary "putting out" system, the roots of which go back to ancient Mesopotamia and which thrived into the twentieth century, contemporaneous with industrialisation; the farming out of some work continued when it was cost effective compared to factory manufacture.[2] What is new today is that electronic technology allows employers to retain the economic advantages of the putting-out system without its historical drawbacks.

What follows addresses the claim of novelty vis-à-vis the latter. It is the case that technology has augmented and even eliminated human labour for millennia. Even so, public concern for the displacement of labour by technology grew with

---

* To appear in Regulating the Platform Economy: International Perspectives on New Forms of Work (Lourdes Mella Mendez, ed.) (Routledge, in press) with appreciation to the editor and the publisher.
[†] Professor of Law, the University of Illinois.
1 John Zysman & Martin Kenney, Where Will Work Come from in the Era of the Cloud and Big Data? Berkeley Roundtable on the International Economy, BRIE Working Paper 2014-6.
2 Matthew Finkin, Beclouded Work, Beclouded Workers in Historical Perspective, 37 *Comp. Lab. L. & Pol'y J.* 603 (2016).

the metamorphosis of wage labour into a foundational element of society[3] and the invention and deployment of ever more labour displacing technologies.[4] The question is whether there is anything radically new in this today.

II Creative destruction

"It is often assumed", Eric Hobsbawm wrote, "that an economy of private enterprise has an automatic bias towards innovation, but this is not so. It has a bias only towards profit".[5] An enterprise will substitute machinery for labour when more profits are to be made thereby. If not, not. Glass bottle makers in late nineteenth-century Pittsburgh, for example, resisted the introduction of mechanised bottle manufacture because it was more profitable for them to rely on cheap child labour. They succeeded in doing this for some time by opposing the enactment or blunting the administration of child labour laws.[6]

Some of the historiography of industrialisation, especially in earlier writings, assumed that the substitution of technology for labour was a process of an "orderly progressive character".[7] It was anything but.[8] First, the invention and perfection of technology was usually a painstaking and costly process – of trial and error, of false starts and arrested development.[9] Development may have to await innovation in cognate technologies as well as requiring significant institutional change – in marketing, management and leadership.[10] In hard rock mining, for example, the machine drill was developed in the 1870s, but struggled to convince mine operators of its superiority to hand drilling for almost two decades, sometimes losing public contests of man against machine.[11] The mechanisation of

---

3 In 1589, the Reverend William Lee invented a frame for the knitting of stockings. Using Lee's frame, a knitter could make 600 stitches a minute. The average for a good hand knitter was 100. When Lee's patron, Lord Hundson, sought a patent for him of the Queen, she declined thusly:

> I have too much love for my poor people who obtain their bread by the employment of knitting, to give my money to forward an invention that will tend to their ruin by depriving them of employment, and thus make them beggars.
>
> *Quoted in* Brian Bailey, *The Luddite Rebellion* 3 (1998)

4 The classic work is David Landes, *The Unbound Prometheus: Technological Change and Industrial Development in Western Europe From 1750 to the Present* (1969) (2nd ed. 2003).
5 Eric Hobsbawm, *Industry and Empire: The Birth of the Industrial Revolution* 18 (1968).
6 James Flannery, *The Glass House Boys of Pittsburgh: Law, Technology, and Child Labor* (2009).
7 Merritt Roe Smith & Robert Martells, Taking Stock of the Industrial Revolution in America, in *Reconceptualizing The Industrial Revolution* 169, 175 (Jeff Horn, Leonard Rosenbrand & Merritt Roe Smith eds. 2010).
8 *Id*. at 187.
9 See generally, David Hounshell, *From the American System to Mass Production 1800–1932: The Development of Manufacturing in the United States* (1984). A case study is the development of the steam engine which, to many scholars, *was* the Industrial Revolution. William Rosen, *The Most Powerful Idea in the World: A Story of Steam, Industry, and Invention* (2010).
10 For example, Ross Thomson, *The Path to Mechanized Shoe Productions in the United States* Ch. 16 (1989).
11 Mark Wyman, *Hard Rock Epic: Western Miners and the Industrial Revolution, 1860–1910*, 87–89 (1979).

underground coal production took almost 25 years.[12] The potential superiority of containerised shipping over the manhandling of cargo was obvious by 1957; but it took decades to surmount engineering, political, financial and managerial obstacles for containers to stride the globe.[13]

Second, inasmuch as the drive to mechanise is fuelled by the desire to reduce labour costs – of wages and "inefficient" work practices – deployment must sometimes have to surmount the opposition of those whose wages and work would be adversely affected, opposition most often institutionally embodied in unionisation. Skilled coal miners, for example, paid by the ton, were free to substitute leisure time for work: once their work yielded what they considered to be an adequate sum, they could simply leave the mine. The traditional methods of longshoring, which necessitated the unpacking and repacking and stowage of the goods to be shipped, sometimes assisted by forklifts but more often done by sheer physical strength, were so labour intensive that the wages of longshoremen could amount to half the total expense of a shipment. In both cases, unionised workers resisted mechanisation not only because of obvious loss of jobs, but also due to the consequent submission to factory-like discipline in the former and the loss of a traditional culture of work in the latter.[14]

That feature in the drive towards mechanisation is well illustrated in the processed food industry. With the invention of the pressure cooker in 1870, the market for canned produce grew apace. The canning process required the work of a capper, who sealed each tin with a soldering iron. The work was skilled, complex and to the consternation of the processor, strategically situated. Cappers could and often did walk out on strike, sometimes with little or no notice. Processors sought:

> an affordable and workable machine which would not necessarily replace labor in the capping of cans, but would, by lowering the skill requirements of this task, make cappers more easily replaceable from the general pool of unskilled labor and consequently force down wages.[15]

In 1887, J.D. Cox seized the opportunity, as Figure 10.1 shows.

---

12 Kenneth Dix, *What's a Coal Miner to Do? The Mechanization of Coal Mining* 77 (1988).
13 Marc Levinson, *The Box: How the Shipping Container Made the World Smaller and the World Economy Bigger* (2nd ed. 2016).
14 A radical view argues that the managerial drive towards automation today may have as much to do with the desire to wrest the control of work away from the workers as the desire to maximise profits. David Noble, *Progress without People: In Defense of Luddism* (1993). There is a deeper root in this view. See Stephen Marglin, *What Do Bosses Do? The Origins and Functions of Hierarchy in Capitalist Production*, 6 Rev. Radical Pol. Econ. 60 (1974). But thus far that argument has failed to have much persuasive effect. See David Landes, What Do Bosses Really Do, 46 *J. Econ. Hist.* 585 (1986).
15 Martin Brown & Peter Philips, Craft Labor and Mechanization in Nineteenth-Century American Canning, 46 *J. Econ. Hist.* 743, 749 (1986).

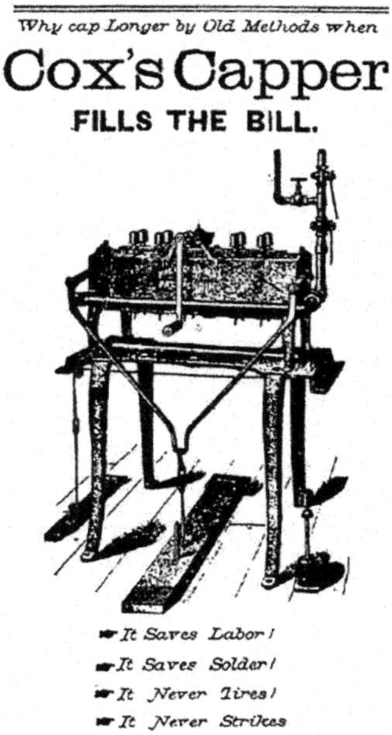

Figure 10.1 Cox's cap.
Source: The Canning Trade (1887).

The italicised portion of the advertisement proclaims Cox's capper *never went on strike*; it deskilled the job, lowered wages and increased profits.

Other, more drastic instances not only of job deskilling but job displacement abounded in an industrial tableau at the turn of the twentieth century of what Joseph Schumpeter was later to call "creative destruction"[16] – a continuous process wherein old jobs are destroyed to be replaced by new jobs requiring different, sometimes greater skills.[17] In 1910, there were over 63,000 hostlers in the United States, primarily employed by horse-drawn trolley ("street traction") companies, the major means of urban transport at the time.[18] The training and care of these horses was highly skilled work.[19] But, the electrification of street rail transport eliminated the need for hostlers even as it created jobs "such as electricians, linemen, and powerhouse workers which more than made up for job

---

16 Joseph Schumpeter, *Capitalism, Socialism and Democracy* (1942). The concept, which has generated volumes of economic analysis, is taken up for the non-specialist by Pierre Cuhac & André Zylberby, *The Natural Survival of Work: Job Creation and Job Destruction in a Growing Economy* (William McCraig trans. 2006).
17 Steven Davis, John Haltiwanger & Scott Schuh, *Job Creation and Destruction* (1998).
18 Bureau of Census, *IV Thirteenth Census of the United States Taken in the Year* 1910, 53 (1914).
19 Scott Malloy, *Trolly Wars: STREETCAR Workers on the Line* 63 (1996).

losses in the obsolete horse stables".[20] Hostlers and dray horses disappeared; we are not told what became of them.

III The stratigraphy of an anxiety

The year 1868 was a pivotal year in American history, for in that year the number of waged workers exceeded the self-employed. The shift from independent proprietorship to employment drove towards a radical reversal in public attitude – from a civic ideology of economic proprietorship that denigrated wage labour as a near servile condition to labour market participation – having a job – as the indicum of citizenship.[21] As that was becoming to be so, a question that disconcerted social observers was what would come of a democracy grounded in waged work if there were an insufficiency of work to do?

By the third quarter of the nineteenth century, the substitution of machinery for labour could be seen all about and which instinctively triggered that anxiety, if not fear. In 1876, the Boston Eight Hour League's convention was held under a banner reading "Machinery is discharging *labor*, better than new employments are provided".[22] In 1887, the jurist Henry Booth saw the replacement of men by machines as "the revolution we are called upon to face".[23] In 1895, John Swinton, editor of America's most well-respected labour newspaper, sounded the same note: he said that the deployment of "new mechanical appliances... that have... reduced man's service", is "the most serious problem that has ever confronted mankind...."[24]

The issue intensified in the 1920s when the term "technological unemployment" was coined in the wake of "a mechanization boom that resulted in the displacement of large numbers of workers".[25] As Sanford Jacoby explains, the issue pressed to the fore by the "slow rate of absorption of displaced workers into expanding industries".[26] No less a figure than Rexford Tugwell, later to be a member of President Franklin D. Roosevelt's New Deal "brain trust", saw in this the prospect of unprecedented progress, if not quite "a new industrial revolution".[27] Because of the enormous advances in productivity afforded by machines, he thought it practical that "machinery be made to work for us longer and faster than it characteristically does" to reduce the hours of work down to

---

20 *Id.* at 79.
21 Rosanne Corrarino, *The Labor Question in America: Economic Democracy in the Gilded Age* (2011).
22 Quoted in David Zonderman, *Uneasy Allies: Working for Labor Reform in Nineteenth Century Boston* 145–146 (2011) (italics in original).
23 Henry Booth, The Labor Question, 1 *Chicago Law Times* 11, 15 (1887).
24 John Swinton, *A Momentous Question* 18–19 (1895).
25 Sanford Jacoby, *Employing Bureaucracy: Managers, Unions, and the Transformation of Work in American Industry*, 1900–1945, 168 (1985).
26 *Id.* at 169.
27 Rexford Tugwell, *Industry's Coming of Age* 26 (1927).

four a day.[28] As industry "comes of age", he opined, it should be "socialized": industry should be made to serve "social ends rather than individual ones".[29]

The debate intensified with the Great Depression, the very cause of which some attributed to technological unemployment.[30] Mainstream economists scoffed at the proposition that there was anything new to call for political address.[31]

The technological employment debate ended with America's entry into the World War, only to revive in the post-war period stimulated, again by a worrisome level of persistent unemployment in tandem with the deployment of a new mode of technological labour displacement – automation – and a new catch-phrase, "structural unemployment".[32]

What automation was, how it differed from the mechanisation of the past, was itself a subject of debate. To John Diebold, automation was about integrated systems.[33] To Walter Buckingham, it involved four discrete factors: mechanisation, feedback, continuous processes and rationalisation.[34] To the editors of the *Scientific American*, it was the regulation of production free of human control.[35] The latter was seconded by a prominent labour law academic: automation encompassed an entire productive process programmed to perform without human intervention.[36] The thread running throughout was whether and in what way the impact of automation differed from the labour-displacing technologies of the past.[37]

---

28 *Id.* at 222–223.
29 *Id.* at 230–231.
30 Industry no doubt abetted the popular perception. With execrable timing, for example, in the depth of the Depression a company announced the development of a mechanical pretzel-twisting machine that could do the work of 15 "expert pretzel-bending girls". *Popular Mechanics*, November 1936. It is unclear how well it worked. A pretzel-bending technology was rolled out by American Machine and Foundry (AMF) in 1949 that replicated the mechanics of the human arm and hand. Its machine rolled out 50 pretzels a minute, twice as fast as a skilled twister. *Popular Science*, August 1949 at p. 138.
31 Leverett Lyon et al., *The National Recovery Administration: An Analysis and Appraisal* 6 (1935) ("that the introduction of machines causes at least temporary unemployment is at least as old as the Industrial Revolution").
32 See generally, Gregory Woirol, *The Technological Unemployment and Structural Unemployment Debates* (1996). The debate over automation was particularly rich. A bibliography of bibliographies was supplied at the time by Norman Pauling. Some Neglected Areas of Research on the Effects of Automation and Other Technological Change on Workers, 37 *J. Bus.* 261, n. 1 at 261 (1964).
33 *Quoted in* Reuben Slesinger, The Pace of Automation: An American View, 6 *J. Indus. Econ.* 241, no. 1 at 241 (1958).
34 *Quoted in* Slesinger, *id.*, no. 2 at 241.
35 *Automatic Control* (Scientific American Editors 1955).
36 Merton C. Bernstein, A Challenge to Enterprise: How to Put Automation to Work Making Jobs, *Challenge*, October, 1964 at p. 23.
37 The debate is reviewed by Gregory Woirol, *supra* n. 32. W. Willard Wirtz, then Secretary of Labor, took a categorical view:

> The myth that automation is only a new stage on an old process is akin to the thinking that splitting the atom represented only an evolutionary development in the dynamics of war, a projection of the first use of the crossbow or the Trojan horse.
> W. Willard Wirtz, *Labor and the Public Interest* 182 (1964)

Some saw in automation a Second Industrial Revolution,[38] in which new specialties and more high skilled jobs would be created; those displaced "will move to other sectors of the economy where their relatively low skill level will be wanted"[39] or will be retrained; but those who "work in the future will have more leisure than workers do today".[40] Others were more sceptical or alarmed. A study conducted by the Upjohn Institute for Employment Research concluded that "The impact of automation on the content of a job, on the existing skill hierarchy, and on employment opportunities is apt to be extensive".[41] It feared that "some workers will never fit or be placed into the new production system", notwithstanding extensive efforts at retraining.[42] Charles Killingsworth argued that the analogy to the past was erroneous, an error of "magnitude", because of the lower rate of economic growth in a mature economy,[43] an analysis echoed more recently.[44]

A study of the impact of automation on management by the American Foundation on Automation and Employment concluded that much work done by middle managers could be automated, that is, that computers could be programmed to make some managerial decisions.[45] It attributed the lack of the more widespread use of computers to managerial resistance,[46] ironically echoing the resistance to mechanisation by blue-collar workers – the coal miners and stevedores encountered above.[47]

Others saw less cause for concern. Early on, in 1964, the economist Robert Heilbroner saw no reason *a priori* why we should be any more concerned of a dollar's worth of automated equipment replacing labour than a dollar's worth of any other piece of labour-displacing equipment.[48] The 1966 report of the

---

38 Robert Dubin, *The World of Work* Ch. 11 (1958).
39 *Id.* at 201.
40 *Id.* at 208.
41 William Haber, Louis Ferman & James Hudson, *The Impact of Technological Change: The American Experience* 8 (1963).
42 *Id.* This, they recognised, in the face of incomplete evidence.
43 Charles Killingsworth, Automation, Jobs and Manpower, in *Automation and Public Welfare* 1 (1964).
44 Robert J. Gordon, *The Rise and Fall of American Growth: The U.S. Standard of Living Since the Civil War*, Ch. 17 (2016).
45 American Foundation on Automation and Employment, *Automation and the Middle Manager: What Has Happened and What the Future Holds* (1966).
46 *Automation and the Middle Manager*, *supra* n. 45 at 39.
47 To get a bit ahead, the Foundation's prediction has proven prescient. The World Bank, *The Changing Nature of Work* 21 (2019) (noting the displacement of financial analysts and lawyers by automation). See also, Noam Schreiber, Unorthodox Hires, And Maybe Lower Pay, *The N.Y. Times*, 7 December 2018, at P. B1 (on the use of algorithms to do some of the work of human resource managers).
48 Robert Heilbroner, Men and machines in perspective, in *The Triple Revolution* 27 (1964). He also noted that all the angst was being devoted to manufacture, even as the economy was shifting to services which were more resistant to automation at the time. Heilbroner became less sanguine 2 years later after the report the National Commission on Technology, Automation, and Economic Progress, to be taken up below. In a foreword to a polemic on the impact of automation, more

Congressionally mandated National Commission on Technology, Automation, and Economic Progress was equally cautious on the basis of voluminous studies it commissioned. What it saw was put in a nutshell by a review:

> Unemployment is caused, not by technological change per se, but by the failure of the economy to grow with rapidity sufficient to keep up with increases in output per man hour and with increases in the size of the labor force. Persons with certain social characteristics are found in disproportionately large numbers among the unemployed, not because they are unemployable in a highly technological economy, but because there are not enough jobs to go around, and these persons are the least attractive to employers. Level of education is a good example…Criteria for employment are not set by the demands of the job to be done, but by the educational level of the labor force. This is not, of course, an argument against increasing the education attainment of all workers. Instead, it is a plea that unemployment not be blamed on the characteristics of the labor force.[49]

The Commission made several recommendations to buffer the impact of job displacement: for provision of adequate notice of job loss; for a better system of job matching for the displaced; and for programmes for education and job retraining of the displaced in which private actors – employers and unions – should play an important role. It also recommended that serious thought be given to income maintenance, a "negative income tax", to provide a "floor of adequate minimum incomes" unconnected to participation in the labour market.[50]

"By the time the commission's report was released", a study by the National Academies observed a generation later, "the economic and political outlook had changed dramatically".[51] With a fall in the unemployment rate and the country's engagement in the Vietnam War, the administration put the Commissioner's

---

on workers than on work – on the "social order" – Heilbroner termed the Commission's work "thoughtful" but near-sighted. Robert Heilbroner, Foreword to Ben Seligman, *Most Notorious Victory: Man in an Age of Automation*, ix (1966). He argued that the Report's prescriptions might be good for a decade, the Commission's actual time horizon, but not for a half century – that is, today.

49 Frank Breul, Review, 40 *Social Service Review* 240, 241 (1966). A study by the National Academies a generation later observed of the Commission's analysis that it "echoed the reports of the 1930s in expressing concern over a 'glut of productivity'" that increased productivity would reduce the demand for labour unless offset by growth in the demand for output, which, it agreed, is what governmental policy should focus on. *Technology and Employment: Innovation and Growth in the U.S. Economy* 88 (Richard Cyert & David Mowery eds. 1987) (Panel on Technology and Employment Committee on Science, Engineering, and Public Policy of the National Academy of Sciences, National Academy of Engineering, and Institute of Medicine) (National Academies Report).

50 *Technology and the American Economy*, Report of the National Commission on Technology, Automation, and Economic Progress Ch. 3(C) (1966).

51 National Academies Report, *supra* n. 49 at 89.

Report on the shelf.[52] The perceived threat of structural unemployment disappeared.

There the issue rested until stirred to life a generation later and made subject of another federal study of, not Congressionally mandated but similarly composed, academics, business leaders and union officials.[53] It, too, associated technology with economic growth. It, too, found that new technologies were only gradually adopted, which pace of adoption moderated job-displacing effects. It, too, found no relationship between the deployment of technology per se to change in the level of needed job skills or to limit the job opportunities of "individuals entering the labor force with strong basic skills". Nevertheless, it found that 20%–30% of displaced workers lacked basic skills and that federal jobs training programmes did not serve the interests of many displaced workers. It called for labour-management cooperation in the adoption of technology, greater employee involvement – recommending "best practices" as exemplified in collectively bargained agreements – and the use of severance payments where best labour/management practices to assure job security could not be observed. It called for improvements in assistance to displaced workers in job training and for income support while in job training. But the recommendation made a generation before that thought be given to income maintenance more broadly was not pursued.

IV Technological change: The agony and the ecstasy

I believe that an artist, fashioning his imaginary worlds out of his own agony and ecstasy, is a benefactor to all of us, but that the worst error we can commit is to mistake his imaginary worlds for the real one. H.L. Menken (1930).[54]

Yesterday's fiction finds its parallel in today's fact. A century which dawned on an industrial revolution that saw men concerned about becoming slaves has reached its high noon in a revolution of technology haunted rather by the specter of men's becoming robots. W. Willard Wirtz (1964).[55]

Today, the impact of the deployment of sophisticated technology, of devices capable of acting interactively with others – even of "learning" in the process – independent of human supervision is drawing rising attention[56] along with ris-

---

52 Gregory Woirol attributes the lack of later debate on automation to the Vietnam War. Woirol, *supra* n. 32 at 127.
53 National Academies Report, *supra* n. 49.
54 H.L. Menken, *What I Believe*, Forum and Century (September 1930). I am indebted to Heather Simmons of the Albert E. Jenner, Jr. Memorial Law Library for tracking down this and other places where the phrase "agony and ecstasy" is used. The origin of it remains unknown to me.
55 W. Willard Wirtz, *Labor and the Public Interest*, *supra* n. 37 at 181.
56 For example, Jerry Kaplan, *Humans Need Not Apply: A Guide to Wealth and Work in the Age of Artificial Intelligence* (2015); Martin Ford, *Rise of the Robots: Technology and the Threat of a Jobless Future* (2015); Erik Brynjolfsson & Andrew McAfee, *The Second Machine Age: Work, Progress, and Prosperity in a Time of Brilliant Technologies* (2014); Simon Head, *The New Ruthless Economy: Work and Power in the Digital Age* (2003). Special Report: Artificial Intelligence, 419 *The Economist* (25 June 2016).

ing angst for the future of employment.[57] The Pew Research Center's Spring 2018 Global Attitudes Survey of ten countries showed that in all of them, a majority believe that robots and computers would "definitely" or "probably" take over many human tasks in the next 50 years; that people would have a harder time finding work; and that inequality would rise.[58]

The state of academic research on the threshold proposition confirms the popular perception: there is a professional consensus that technology will replace human skills and so supplant human labour, though the pace and sectors of displacement – which the National Academies' study a generation ago saw to be critical to social impact and so to needed social response[59] – are not and are unlikely to be either in tandem or uniform.[60] But even as some jobs will be lost, others will be created.

1 The agony

The impetus for the 1964 congressional mandate for a commission to study automation derived from a seemingly persistent and unacceptably high level of unemployment. The Commission zeroed in not on the prospect of joblessness, but on the lack of job growth. The Commission concluded that there was no reason for there to be any significant concern for labour displacement if the economy was generating jobs to take up the labour of those displaced. As Robert Gordon observed more recently:

> "[T]he replacement of human jobs by computers has been going on for more than five decades, and the replacement of human jobs by machines in

---

57 Pierre Cahuc & André Zylberberg, *supra* n. 16.
58 Richard Wilke & Bruce Stokes, In Advanced and Emerging Economics Alike, Worries about Job Automation, *Pew Research Center*, 23 September 2018. In terms of skills preparation, the vast majority of those surveyed in the United States (72%) placed responsibility on the individual, with only 35% thinking the government bore responsibility. In this, the United States is an outlier. A majority of the citizens in the other nine countries held the opposite view.
59 National Academies report, *supra* n. 49. The shift of labour off the farm and into the factory, for example, was massive. In 1870, 46% of employed labour in the United States was on the farm; in 2009, it was 1.1%. Robert Gordon, THE RISE AND FALL OF AMERICAN GROWTH, *supra* n. 44, Table 203 at p. 53. The shift was driven by the centrifugal force of labour-saving machines and innovations in farm chemicals and the centripetal force of opportunities in the factory. Apropos the former, in 1870 the McCormick Reaper company sold a total of 9,033 pieces of farm equipment. In 1885, it sold 49,902. David Houndshell, *supra* n. 9, Table 4.1 at p. 161. The point is that that shift, massive over time, did take time to be massive and that the rate of displacement was not uniform. In 1910, 32.6% of the working population was on the farm. A generation later, in 1930, it was 23.4%. The US Bureau of the Census, *Historical Statistics of the United States Series* D 11–15 at p. 127 (1975).
60 World Economic Forum, *Eight Futures of Work* (January 2018); Pricewaterhouse Coopers (PWC), *Will Robots Really Steal Our Jobs? An International Analysis of the Potential Long-Term Impact of Automation* (January 2018); McKinsey Global Institute, *A Future that Works: Automation, Employment, and Productivity* (January 2017); Morgan Stanley Research, *Process Automation: The Rise of the Machines* (24 September 2017); OECD, Employment Outlook, 2016 (Box 2.3 at p. 78) (2016).

general has been going on for more than two centuries. Occupations such as financial advisers, credit analysts, insurance agents, and others are in the process of being replaced, and these displaced workers follow the footsteps of victims of the web who lost their jobs within the past two decades...Yet these previous job losses did not prevent the U.S. unemployment rate from declining to a rate near 5 percent in 2015, because new jobs were created to replace the jobs that were lost".[61] As this is written, the unemployment rate in the United States is just below 4%.[62]

However, Gordon points to a consequence beyond the Commission's field of vision at the time: the problem created by automation is not mass unemployment, but the loss of "good, steady, middle-level jobs".[63] Several factors have contributed to this state of affairs, not the least the offshoring of manufacturing and so good, steady and middle-level manufacturing jobs. Nevertheless, technology has come in to play as well, for these reasons:

> In general, automation (computerization, introduction of robots and AI) predominantly affects routinized work in stationary, predictable environments, typically found in the middle-skilled jobs, particularly whenever tasks merely concern executing rules rather than require cognitive processing of information....The non-routine and cognitive tasks typically are executed by high-skilled employees with high wages, while the routine tasks generally are conducted by medium-skilled employees with medium wages.... Jobs which require refined perception and physical dexterity, creative intelligence/improvisation, or social intelligence, regardless of whether they are low-skilled, are less at risk of replacement....Thus, technological substitution of jobs does not necessarily displace low-skilled work, but rather routinized work. As routinized work is often executed by medium-skilled work, this substitution effectively "polarizes" or "hollows out" the labor force, with fiercer competition and thereby wages stagnation, particular for middle and lower skilled work.[64]

This analysis is concordant with David Autor's and Anna Salomens's that productivity growth, which robotisation and information technology promises, will add to employment in the aggregate; but the jobs added will be bimodally distributed: the jobs retained or created will be those most resistant to machine

---

61 Robert Gordon, *supra* n. 44 at 602–603.
62 It needs to be stressed that this figure discounts the number of able-bodied prime-age males who have existed in the working population. Didem Tüzemen, *Why Are Prime-Age Men Vanishing from the Labor Force?* 103 Econ. Rev. 5 (2018).
63 Robert Gordon, *supra* n. 44 at 604.
64 Ben Vermeulen, Jan Kesselhut, Andreas Pyka & Pier Paolo Saviotti, *The Impact of Automation on Employment: Just the Usual Structural Change?* 10 Sustainability 166 at ms. p. 3 (2018) (references omitted).

displacement, that is, well-paid, high-skilled jobs and low-paid, low-skilled jobs.[65] Their analysis was echoed by a National Academies' study in 2017[66] and by the World Bank in 2019.[67]

In other words, the deployment of today's technology portends the prospect of a working population whose earned income is not displayed in a bell curve, with a robust middle class, but bimodally. The future is presaged in a paper of the Federal Reserve Bank of New York, a snapshot addressing job generation in high-wage, middle-wage and low-wage jobs in recent years. The top, bearing earnings above $60,000 a year, were in high-skilled jobs – management, engineering, finance. The bottom, earning below $30,000, were in low-skilled service jobs – food preparation, building maintenance, healthcare, mostly requiring face to face service. The middle group, earning between those two, are jobs in production, transportation, administrative support and the like; that is, in routine work of medium skill more capable of being automated. The result is displayed in Figure 10.2.

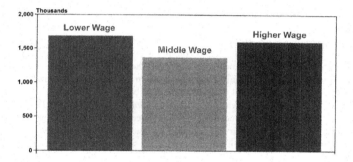

Figure 10.2 Net job gains in the United States by wage category (2015–2017) (in thousands).
Source: Federal Reserve Bank of New York, *Labor Market Conditions in the Region* (4 December 2018). In New York City, an increasingly "high tech" job market, jobs in the middle category actually declined in absolute terms.

---

65 David Autor & Anna Salomens, Does Productivity Growth Threaten Employment? "Robocalypse Now?", (European Central Bank Annual Conference Paper) (27 June 2017). This is concordant as well with earlier predictions. Michael Katz & Mark Stern, *One Nation Divisible: What America Was and What It Is Becoming* 179–181 (2006).
66 National Academes of Sciences, *Information Technology, and the U.S. Workforce: Where Are We and Where Do We Go From Here?* (2017).
67 World Bank Report, *supra* n. 47 at 24:
   In advanced economies, employment has been growing the fastest in high-skill cognitive occupations and low-skill occupations that require dexterity. By contrast, employment has shifted away from middle-skill occupations such as machine operators. This is one of the factors that may translate into rising inequality in advanced economies. Both middle- and low-skill workers could see falling wages – the former because of automation and the latter because of increased competition.

The 1966 Commission attended primarily to the effect of automation on those displaced. It urged greater attention to efficient job matching[68] and programmes for retraining by public and especially private action – by collective bargaining[69] – as well as legally mandated advance notice and severance pay. But it did more. Anticipating a need to restore earnings automation would hollow out, the Commission floated the idea of basic income maintenance unconnected to workforce participation. The National Academies' study a generation later endorsed all the Commission's proposals, save the latter.

The persistent fear since the technological unemployment debate of the 1930s has been about permanent unemployment. The hope was that with such government intervention that might be needed enough jobs would be generated to accommodate those that automation displaced. Today, the consensus is that

---

68 The inadequacy of institutions to match workers having needed skill sets with the employers who need them has been argued to more recently. Andrew Weaver & Paul Osterman, Skill Demands and Mismatching in U.S. Manufacturing, 70 *H.R. Rev.* 275 (2017). The woeful inadequacy of public job retraining programmes, instituted in the wake of the 1966 Commission report, was noted in the National Academies' report in 1987 and more recently. Kathleen Thelen, *Varieties of Liberalization and the New Politics of Social Solidarity* 76–80 (2014) (reviewing the literature).

69 It is not surprising that the 1966 Commission would stress the role of union-management cooperation: union density at the time was about a third of the workforce and union leaders were members of the commission. It was commonly assumed by serious students of labour relations that unions and managements would resolve the problems automation would create for incumbent workers. George Schulz & George Baldwin, *Automation: A New Dimension to Old Problems* (1955). How successful unions had actually been in dealing with management about mechanisation was contested. Benjamin Kirsh, *Automation and Collective Bargaining* (1964). Return to the two instances of mechanisation discussed above – coal mining and longshoring. The Bituminous Coal Commission appointed by President Wilson to resolve the UMW strike of 1919 endorsed the operators' installation of labour-saving machinery, provided that the cost in labour-saving be disclosed and the worker be paid "a fair propesition of the labor-saving effected" in addition to his wage. Keith Dix, *supra* n. 12 at 133. Resolutions of the union's convention in 1936, 1938 and 1940 called for "a tax on the output from machines, with the funds generated used to aid those laid off when the machines were installed" *Id.* at 214. The union's autocratic president, John L. Lewis, who favoured mechanisation, took no action on it. The union did negotiate a welfare fund paid by a tonnage royalty on coal for health and welfare benefits. Morton Baratz, *The Union and the Coal Industry* 115–116 (1955). That was all it did.

Agreements in longshoring on the west coast guaranteed a class of senior workers a guaranteed income plus a pension. In the port of New York, a similar guarantee was negotiated paid by a royalty on the containers. Marc Levinson, *supra* n. 13 at Ch. 6. The former secretary-treasurer of the New York longshoremen's union later groused that the union had given up more than it should. *Id.* at 167.

In 1981, a group assembled by the Machinists Union promulgated a Technology Bill of Rights. It demanded that the gains of productivity and the cost savings of labor be shared with the workers. *Reported in* David Noble *supra* n. 14 at 127–128. Nothing came of it. But this is neither here today for the simple reason that unions have imploded: private sector union density today is under 7%. Consequently, there is no longer any formal institutional presence in the workplace by which workers can deal collectively with the prospect of automation, to secure on-going training, for example, which employers are ever more reluctant unilaterally to provide. Andrew Weaver's survey of US manufacturing found that 50% of employers provide formal training for production makers. This contrasts with the provision of formal training to 70%–80% in the 1990s. Andrew Weaver, *The Myth of the Skills Gap*, 120 MIT Tech. Rev. 76, 79 (2017).

technology will generate enough jobs, but the jobs produced drive inexorably towards widening inequality within the working population.[70]

2 The ecstasy

Concern for the implications of ever widening income disparity has drawn attention anew to the provision of a basic income for everyone. The idea has achieved some popular attention,[71] political agitation[72] and scholarly study[73]; but it is generally acknowledged that providing for a basic income, at least in any meaningful amount, will be a reach.[74]

Even so, the idea has deep historical roots. From Crates of Athens in the fifth century B.C.E., scores of writers have dreamt of a world in which machines relieved man of the need to work.[75] It took the Second Industrial Revolution (as mechanisation was called in the 1920s and 1930s) to make the prospect seem real. Rexford Tugwell thought the abundance of production wrought by mechanisation should drive inexorably towards the reduction of work hours and the socialisation of industry – to plenty and leisure for all. It did not.

The prospect of a workless world revived with automation in the 1950s and 1960s, which some thought this time really to *be* the Second Industrial Revolution. The prospect even of "too much" leisure generated by increased productivity was actually taken seriously.[76] The Twentieth Century Fund commissioned a study by the political scientist and philosopher, Sebastian de Grazia. He thought it plausible that:

> There will either be the same number of jobs—but with their hours cut down drastically and legislation to prevent overtime and moonlighting—or,

---

70 Sylvain Ledoc and Zheng Liu point out that the percentage of national income that goes to workers – the "labor share" – has declined from 63% in 2000 (and had held steady at that level for quite some time) to 56% in 2018. They attribute the decline and the anomaly of stagnant wages during a period of low unemployment as well to automation. Sulvan Leduc & Zheng Liu, *Are Workers Losing to Robots?* Federal Reserve Bank of San Francisco, Economic Letter (30 September 2019).

Cynthia Estlund's estimate of the impact of automation is concordant with that set out here, but she places it in the larger context of change in business structure and practice that, when added in, calls for a more encompassing engagement with social protections. Cynthia Estlund, What Should We Do After Work? Automation and Employment Law, 128 *Yale L.J.* 254 (2018).

71 For example, Andrew Stein's, *Raising the Floor: How a Universal Basic Income Can Renew Our Economy and Rebuild the American Dream* (2016). Vermeulen and his colleagues, *supra* n. 1, list the proposal for a guaranteed basic income as a policy implication of the income disparity resulting from the display of jobs in a highly automated economy, though they do not treat the follow-on issues of financing and administration.

72 A Swiss referendum in 2016 in which the proposal – of 2,500 Swiss francs per month for every adult – received almost a quarter of the vote. Raphael Minder, Guaranteed Income for All? Switzerland's Voters Say No, *The N.Y. Times*, 5 June 2016.

73 Philippe van Parijs and Yannick Vanderborght, *Basic Income: A Radical Proposal for a Free Society and a Sane Economy* (2017) and Guy Standing, *Basic Income* (2017).

74 See the collection, Basic Income, 40 *Comp. Lab. L. & Pol'y J.* 151–161 (2019).

75 Some of these are collected in *The Oxford Book of Work* 577–583 (Keith Thomas, ed. 1999).

76 Herbert Simon, *The Shape of Automation* 4–6 (1965). ("A Glut of Goods and Leisure").

more likely in view of the first possibility, a relative few will work, and the rest will live on Easy Street.[77]

Today, most of working age are working and few have a life of ease.

V Conclusion

The fear of persistent, long-term unemployment wrought by the replacement of humans by machines is a recurring motif in American history. If history is instructive, the fear is without foundation.

Today, the agony of technology is growing economic inequality, social marginalisation and political discord, the prospect of which is real. The ecstasy of technology is a life of universal comfort and leisure, the prospect of which is fictional still.

VI Selected bibliography

Given the wealth of material this chapter draws on, only the most salient are set out below.

David Autor & Anna Salomens, Does Productivity Growth Threaten Employment? "Robocalypse Now?" (European Central Bank Annual Conference Paper) (June 27, 2017).

Pierre Cuhac & André Zylberby, *The Natural Survival of Work: Job Creation and Job Destruction in a Growing Economy* (William McCraig trans. 2006).

Matthew Finkin, Beclouded Work, Beclouded Workers in Historical Perspective, 37 Comp. Lab. L. & Pol'y J. 603 (2016).

Robert J. Gordon, *The Rise and Fall of American Growth: The U.S. Standard of Living Since the Civil War* (2016).

David Hounshell, *From the American System to Mass Production 1800–1932: The Development of Manufacturing in the United States* (1984).

Sanford Jacoby, *Employing Bureaucracy: Managers, Unions, and the Transformation of Work in American Industry, 1900–1945* (1985).

David Landes, *The Unbound Prometheus: Technological Change and Industrial Development in Western Europe from 1750 to the Present* (2nd ed. 2003).

National Academes of Science, *Information Technology, and the U.S. Workforce: Where Are We and Where Do We Go from Here?* (2017).

Symposium, Basic Income, 40 Comp. Lab. L. & Pol'y J. No. (2019).

Technology and the American Economy, Report of the National Commission on Technology, Automation, And Economic Progress (1966).

Technology and Employment: Innovation and Growth in the U.S. Economy, 88 (Richard Cyert & David Mowery Eds., 1987) (Panel on Technology and Employment Committee on Science, Engineering, and Public Policy of the Academy of Sciences, National Academy of Engineering, and Institute of Medicine).

Gregory Woirol, *The Technological Unemployment and Structural Unemployment Debates* (1996).

The World Bank, *The Changing Nature of Work* (2019).

World Economic Forum, *Eight Futures of Work* (Jan. 2018).

---

[77] Sebastian de Grazia, *Of Time, Work, and Leisure* 329 (1962) (references omitted).

11 Technologies and powers
Marginal notes on the Amazon wristband

Rosa Di Meo

I Introduction

It was in 1509 and in *Henry V* that William Shakespeare warned that the King should take note of all the intentions of his subjects with means that cannot even be imagined. In 1791, Jeremy Bentham theorised, with his *Panopticon*, a prison model in which, through a circular structure and a clever use of light and shadow, a single guard would be able to watch over all the prisoners, who would not be able to see those who watched them. In short, "the ideal of every powerful person has always been to see every gesture and to listen to every word of his subjects (possibly without being seen or heard)".[1]

These two examples are used by the author of this chapter to highlight the typical temptation of the employers to exercise unlimited forms of monitoring of their employees, in particular, during the time of "Industry 4.0". As recently underlined by the tenet:

> employers have always collected information on their employees, both in the pre-contractual phase, in order to select the contracting counterparty, and in the execution phase of the obligation, to protect their interest in the correct fulfillment and for other purposes that instead could not be considered among the legal effects of the employment contract, but had a relation to the enterprise organization as a power structure.[2]

The only difference is that, compared to the past, increasing levels of automation in the organisation of work have made it possible to refine the techniques through which it is possible to control employees.

However, there is a limitation in the power of the employers to supervise their employees. It is fundamental indeed to establish the threshold between the licit control of the work of the employee and the illicit one. The supervision of the

---

1 Norberto Bobbio, *Il futuro della democrazia* (Torino: Einaudi, 1984), 18.
2 Marco Barbieri, "L'utilizzabilità delle informazioni raccolte: il Grande Fratello può attendere (forse)", *Controlli a distanza e tutela dei dati personali del lavoratore*, ed. Patrizia Tullini (Torino: Giappichelli, 2017), 183.

employee's work is indeed licit only when it is directly related to the fulfilment of the performance, as provided for in the contract. This work inserts in the framework of the definition of the limitation of the employers, since this remains still an open debate.

Nowadays, this risk is increasing, since it is easier for the employers to monitor their employees by means of new technologies. As a matter of fact, the relationship between man and machine as well as between the operating methods and the technologies applied to the productive processes is becoming closer and closer. Consequently, it is fundamental to evaluate if the legislator (that can only chase these social phenomena) has brought about effective rules and limitations to the monitoring of the working service, which is potentially uncontrolled.

The relationship between man and machine ("M2M") could provide a double effect: on the one hand, the interaction between the two could be beneficial to the human being, as a relationship of complementarity could be established between them; on the other hand, it could be responsible of the complete replacement of the man by the machine.

However, even if in this second hypothesis it seems that man could benefit from the work of the machine alleviating his physical strain, it has to be noticed that the interchangeability between human and artificial intelligence represents a threat in the existing employment levels (already distressing).

In the hypothesis of the complementarity, indeed "the most immediate effect concerns the realisation of the object of the employment relationship: the fulfillment of the obligation",[3] meaning that the boundary between the obligations of the worker and his own rights risks to blur.

When the worker makes use of some technological instrument to carry out his working performance, if on the one hand he has the possibility of accomplishing faster and more efficiently to his obligations (benefiting his employer), on the other hand, the adopted instrument is able to collect more extra information than those necessary for the employer to monitor the employee's fulfilment of contractual obligations, as highlighted by the recent controversy about the use of the electronic wristband patented by Amazon for its employees.

In this perspective, the present study intends to treat the Italian regulatory framework (through the analysis of article 4 of the Workers' Statute, amended by article 23 of Legislative Decree no. 151/2015, in force since 24 September 2015) and the European law in light of the recent events involving the wristband patented by the well-known US e-commerce company, in order to understand if and eventually what are the legal instruments to face the corporate policies related to the electronic wristband, currently sporadic,[4] but potentially recurring.

---

3 Patrizia Tullini, "La digitalizzazione del lavoro, la produzione intelligente e il controllo tecnologico nell'impresa", in *Web e lavoro. Profili evolutivi e di tutela*, ed. Patrizia Tullini (Torino: Giappichelli, 2017), 6 ss., which reference is made for further details.
4 While reflecting on the matter, a few weeks ago in Italy, already in use in the city of Livorno is an electronic wristband that allows the company to check that the operators have correctly ecologically emptied the trash bins. One speaks of "Amazon style" (www.corriere.it/cronache/

A methodological clarification is necessary, even if it is trailblazing of the conclusions of this work. The article 4 of the Italian Workers' Statute originally forbade any form of monitoring of the employee's performance; nowadays, even if the same article 4 has become more flexible about this prohibition (allowing the direct monitoring of the worker's performance under certain thresholds), it is still finalised to the preservation of the worker's dignity.

If the modalities of execution of subordinate work performance become extremely flexible in times and in space due to the use of the new technologies, the ways in which the employer uses his supervision naturally experience a metamorphosis[5] (e.g. in Italy, there is open debate about the new form of *"agile work"*, regulated by the law n. 81/2017, which – by express legislative prevision – represents a particular modality of the subordinate work's execution, carried out partially inside and outside the company and possibly with the use of technological instruments (*ex* article 19, co. 1).[6]

The digital revolution is able to affect "the qualitative and quantitative dimension of the service, the way in which the tasks are performed, the relevance of the result of the employee's work for the interest of the employer, and so on".[7] However, if on the one hand the introduction of new information technologies in the organisation of the work inevitably has an impact on the structure of the company, on the other hand, this does not necessary translate in a rethought of the rules of the parties (employer and employee) in the fulfilment of the contract.

18_aprile_13/a-livorno-braccialetto-elettronico-gli-spazzini-polemica-f71bf40e-3f2f-11e8-876a-83c5b28c227f.shtml?refresh_ce-cp, http://iltirreno.gelocal.it/livorno/cronaca/2018/04/13/news/un-braccialetto-elettronico-controlla-spazzini-1.16708532, www.ansa.it/toscana/notizie/2018/04/13/braccialetti-elettronici-per-spazzini-a-livorno-e-polemica.-insorge-la-cgil_f4a417a1-76e0-4596-96b9-aafae0b55eb0.html), precisely to contest the use of such tools to make the performance. The Municipality soon pointed out that the tool does not include the satellite (GPS), thus implicitly excluding that the bracelet of the employees is a tool from which derives "also" a remote control of the activity of workers, pursuant to article 4, paragraph 1, l. 300/1970. However, even if we admit that AVR, a company contracted by AMS and wholly owned by the Municipality, which provides cleaning services, has installed a device without GPS on the wrist of its employees, there are still strong doubts surrounding the electronic bracelet as to the usability of the data that this new working tool can collect.

5 For a recent analysis, see Michele Tiraboschi and Francesco Seghezzi, "Il Piano nazionale Industria 4.0: una lettura lavoristica", *Labour and Law Issues*, 2, II, (2016), 25, according to which "a new phase seems to be opening in the debate on the characteristics and regulation of remote work, moving from the old teleworking, which maintains intact the elements of control and subordination to orders and directives, to a modern work remotely or in mobility, that is without any fixed location and without a precise working time. There would therefore be an evolution from the translation of office logic to another place to the actual overcoming of the same, opening space to a virtual office, made possible by Internet platforms, where the element of contact with the company is access to information useful to perform and that, with modern cloud technologies, can be done through any media connected anywhere on the planet and at any time".

6 For a recent analysis, see Luigi Fiorillo and Adalberto Perulli, *Il Jobs act del lavoro autonomo e del lavoro agile* (Torino: Giappichelli), 2018.

7 Mariella Magnani, "Il contratto di lavoro subordinato", accessed in 2018, n. 360, 3–4, http://csdle.lex.unict.it/docs/workingpapers/Il-contratto-di-lavoro-subordinato/5745.aspx.

In other words, if the pervasiveness of the new technologies allows to monitor *all* the behaviours of the employee during the working time (and not only the ones concerning the execution of the work), in the opinion of the author of this work, in article 4 of the Workers' Statute, there are rules allowing the introduction of new business technologies if they are under the *threshold* of the "legally permitted" (*threshold* that can be determined also through the reference to the Privacy Code and in general to the European standards).

In this framework, the recent event of the electronic wristband patented by Amazon is placed. To understand this, it is necessary to recall all the fundamental stages of the progressive evolution of the regulation of the remote monitoring of worker's activities.

II Article 4, Law n. 300/1970 between a new formulation and traditional protection requirements

In its original formulation, article 4 of the Workers' Statute opened with an express prohibition, contained in paragraph 1 of that provision, prescribing that "the use of audiovisual equipment and other equipment for purposes of remote monitoring of the activity of workers is prohibited".

The object of the prohibition was the use of technological equipment which had the sole purpose of controlling the performance of the employees' work since it was believed that such control was not justified by the criteria of objectivity and necessity which the law had already required since 1970. In this way, the legislator had individuated a fine threshold between opposing requirements, beyond which the power conferred on the stronger contracting party became recessive.

As the tenet has underlined, indeed "the absoluteness of the prohibition that accompanies the legislative provision is part of that line of protection of human values of the person of the employee engaged in the contractual relationship and that the Statute intends to protect".[8]

On this point, however, a clarification is necessary: the legislator of 1970 did not eliminate the monitoring power in general, because such power would derive and would be legitimised only from the simple insertion of the worker in the productive organisation.[9] The legislator indeed imposes on the employer to verify that the employee has committed a non-fulfilment of the contract before proceeding to the possible imposition of a sanction.

The Workers' Statute, therefore, does not in any way eliminate the employer's power to carry out checks, but:

> rationalizes the ways in which it is exercised in relation to all the requirements emerging from the relationship and therefore also those - previously

---

8 Bruno Veneziani, "Art. 4. Impianti audiovisivi", in *Lo Statuto dei Lavoratori. Commentario*, ed. Gino Giugni (Milano: Giuffrè), 1979, 19.
9 Bruno Veneziani, Article 4,18.

neglected - of the dignity, freedom and confidentiality of the employee, reconstructing the form of correct monitoring.[10]

The absoluteness of the prohibition concerned the possibility of installation of equipment aimed at a specific thing (the activity of the worker) and for a specific purpose (the mere purpose of monitoring), but it did not exclude a power of monitoring *tout court*. Indeed, having identified this area of prohibition, the legislator did permit in some cases predetermined by paragraph 2, that is, in the event of "organizational and production requirements" and/or linked to "safety at work", the installation of such instruments from which remote monitoring could also be carried out, but only subject to agreement with the trade union representatives within the company.

These hypotheses confirmed the power of the prohibition referred to in paragraph 1. Even in the case in which there was a need for the employer to install such equipment either for technical, organisational and productive reasons or related to the occupational safety (in practice, expressed as an illegal form of remote monitoring of the employee's activity), these instruments could be used only upon the agreement with the trade union, as they were specifically intended for satisfying the organisational need of the employer.[11]

The prohibition previously provided for in clause 1 has formally disappeared due to the so-called *Jobs Act*, which has introduced a new two-part subdivision.

It is now envisaged that audiovisual equipment and tools, "which *also* provide the possibility of remote monitoring of workers' activities", can only be used for specific purposes (organisational and production need, for safety at work and for the protection of company assets) and can only be installed following a prior collective agreement procedure stipulated by the employee's representatives (first possibility, clause 1). This provision does not apply "to devices used by the worker to carry out the work" (second possibility, clause 2). In this second case, the agreement with the trade union is not required.

The information collected pursuant to clauses 1 and 2 may be used "for all purposes connected with the employment relationship provided that the worker

---

10 Bruno Veneziani, Article 4, 18.
11 Riccardo Del Punta, "La nuova disciplina dei controlli a distanza sul lavoro" (article 23, d.lgs. n. 151/2015), *Rivista Italiana di Diritto del Lavoro*, 2016, I, 81 ss., stresses the "aporias" of the original wording of the rule and maintains that, insofar as it did not prejudice the possibility of remote control of workers' activity should the above technical requirements so require, the latter was misleading in that "asserting that control is lawful only when it is 'unintentional' should, for the sake of consistency, involve an investigation into the subjective element of the employer", an investigation of which there is no trace in the courtroom, "also because it would have no meaning". As the author points out, "the true implication of the rule was therefore another, and transpired as soon as the misunderstanding in question, in paragraph 1, of the concept of 'purpose' was eliminated: the installation of audiovisual systems and other equipment from which the possibility of remote control of the activity of the workers derived was allowed if it was required by qualified business needs. Therefore, we were faced with nothing more than the application of the most common technique limiting employer powers, that of the 'justified reason', even though integrated by the provision of an administrative procedure".

is given adequate information on the methods of use of the instruments and of carrying out the monitoring" (paragraph 3).

As is quite clear:

> the object of the prohibition and that of the permit do not coincide: in the first instance, it concerns the use of audiovisual equipment and other equipment 'for purposes of remote monitoring of the activity of workers', while the attention now immediately shifts to all those instruments 'from which the possibility of remote monitoring of the activity of workers derives', and therefore not specifically installed for this purpose.[12]

However, while previously the wording of the provision was clear as to the consequences of sanctions for employers who used such equipment for the purposes of remote monitoring of their employees, today the statutory provision does not expressly provide for a ban, but merely provides for the installation and use of such equipment.[13]

The division made by the statutory provision poses a problem for the interpreter, which concerns the choice of whether to frame *connected devices* as instruments from which the possibility of a remote monitoring *also* derives or whether these should be framed as instruments used to carry out one's job.[14] It is sufficient to think, for example, of clocking-in mechanisms, useful both to the company and to the worker (for the determination of working hours and therefore of remuneration).[15]

---

[12] Marianna Russo, "*Quis custodies custodiet?* I 'nuovi' limiti all'esercizio del potere di controllo a distanza", in *Labour and Law Issues*, 2, II, (2016), 5. See also Luigi Andrea Cosattini, "Le modifiche all'art. Stat. Lav. sui controlli a distanza, tanto rumore; per nulla?", *Il Lavoro nella Giurisprudenza*, (2015), 986, for a critique of the formal elimination of the prohibition previously contained in article 4, paragraph 1 of the Statute.

[13] In doctrine, see Arturo Maresca, "Controlli tecnologici e tutele del lavoratore nel nuovo art. 4 St. Lav", in *Controlli a distanza e tutela dei dati personali del lavoratore*, ed. Patrizia Tullini (Torino: Giappichelli, 2017), 6, which proposed an interpretation, so to speak, *in bonam partem* of the provision, claiming that "the first provision applied only to plants and equipment whose sole purpose was that of controlling the employees". In this case, however, the current rule has a broader scope of application, referring to all «audiovisual equipment and other instruments from which the possibility of remote control *also* derives». In this case, therefore, control is not necessarily the primary and typical function of the instruments to which the legislator refers, but it identifies the capabilities with which the instrument is also equipped. It is precisely this clarification that confirms the potential control function. In other words, the old art. 4 dealt exclusively with control instruments, while the new art. 4 concerns every instrument (except those of co. 2) that, in any case, is able to carry out control as well.

[14] Even Arturo Maresca, "Controlli tecnologici", 14, stated that "the legislator is based on a dual awareness of these instruments, which, on the one hand, fulfil the primary function of enabling the employee to render the service and, therefore, fulfil the contractual commitments that must comply with the organization of work as prepared by the entrepreneur, but on the other, have an undoubted and significant capacity for remote control of the work".

[15] Supreme Court, 13 May 2016, number 9904, for which a remote control of the entrances and exits can also be used to verify compliance with working hours and therefore the correctness of the performance of the service.

Commentators are in fact divided between those who opt for a restrictive interpretation of paragraph 2 and those who, on the contrary, do not see an ontological or structural difference between what is provided for in the first paragraph and what is provided for in the second.

In the first reconstruction,[16] it is necessary to establish a close connection between the "tools" used by the worker and his tasks, with the consequence that they would fall within the scope of paragraph 2 in all cases where there are technological tools assigned by the company to the worker which are used by them to carry out their work.

This reconstructive option is contrasted with another,[17] which instead considers that the device, in any case correlated to the fulfilment or even only to the facilitation of the work of the worker, would enable the employer to monitor employees without any authorisation limits. This interpretation, however, does not seem to be acceptable, because even the new formulation of article 4 suggests a distinction between tools that the worker uses in the performance of his work and tools from which the worker derives for potential monitoring, with the consequence that the legislator of the Jobs Act seems to have had in mind the reasons for protecting human privacy, which must not be weakened when crossing the gates of the company, also because otherwise the rule would risk being declared unconstitutional.

From this point of view, the words of Vezio Crisafulli are still relevant: More than sixty years ago, he wrote that the fundamental rights that the Constitutional Charter recognises for workers cannot be subject to "any limitations to their exercise other than those *strictly necessary* for the ordinary carrying out of their employment duties",[18] whose strict necessity would derive from the very instrumental nature of the technological means with respect to the work performance.

At this point, however, the axis of reasoning shifts to an understanding of the question of whether Amazon's electronic wristbands are strictly indispensable for the normal execution of performance or not.

---

16 It is the majority interpreting option in doctrine. See in particular, Riccardo Del Punta, "La nuova disciplina dei controlli a distanza", 100 ss.; Ilario Alvino, "I nuovi limiti al controllo a distanza", 23 ss., which analyses the characteristics provided by the provision (which speaks of "instruments used by the worker to make the performance of work") and considers that the second paragraph covers "only instruments used by the worker to make the performance of work. That is, those instruments whose functioning requires the active participation of the worker, who makes use of them to render the service".

17 Analysed by Patrizia Tullini, "La digitalizzazione del lavoro", 14–15, which however indicates that "the question of interpretation seems to be misplaced. The nodal point does not concern the difference between the first two paragraph of article 4 of Workers Statute, and therefore the ease or not of exercising remote control, but rather concerns the open space from the current discipline to the monitoring of and over workers, overcoming the prohibition originally established by the Statute which derived, as a logical corollary, the un-usability of any information acquired".

18 Vezio Crisafulli, "Diritti di libertà e poteri dell'imprenditore", *Rivista Giuridica del Lavoro*, I, (1954), 190.

III The Amazon electronic wristband as a "working tool"

The recent case of the electronic wristband patented in January 2018 by Amazon has immediately assumed such importance in Europe (including the media)[19] that it has imposed delicate problems on the legal commentator in terms of the legal effects of the American company's decision.

In practice, this instrument emits ultrasonic sound pulses and radio transmissions that allow the company to understand where the hands of the employee are. Compared to previous practices, when employees used a small scanner to check the company's inventory, Amazon recently decided to move such equipment to the wrists of employees, who in this way have their hands free and can therefore take the product from the warehouse and box it in less time.[20]

The wristband also locates[21] the employee and through a countdown that appears on the device (namely a green light) gives him the maximum time to reach the location of the next product to be taken from the shelves.

If the employee is "slower" than the time the company considers necessary to move from one location to another (when the time signal turns red), he or she could potentially be subject to a disciplinary sanction due to poor performance. The worker can also insert any breaks from work in the wristband, but even in this case the company assigns the maximum time of the break, depending on the reason for which the employee who registers it requests it. In short, the Amazon wristband seems to be one of those tools:

> in which technology directs, marks and records individual transactions, prevents errors and defects, corrects in real time the mode of performance: employees can be completely directed from the intelligent system that 'automatically knows the next step' and sets the next task with extensive predictive capabilities, calculating 'the operation to ensure quality and control and eliminate manual logging'.[22]

---

19 See, for example, the articles published in the most famous European newspapers and beyond; available at www.theguardian.com/technology/2018/jan/31/amazon-warehouse-wristband-tracking, www.handelsblatt.com/unternehmen/handel-konsumgueter/armbaender-fuer-angestellte-amazon-will-jeden-handgriff-seiner-mitarbeiter-ueberwachen/20921234.html, www.lesechos.fr/monde/europe/0301254982312-ca-se-passe-en-europe-en-italie-levee-de-boucliers-contre-le-bracelet-damazon-2151116.php, www.lanacion.com.ar/2109933-una-pulsera-para-controlar-los-movimientos-de-los-trabajadores, www.elmundo.es/economia/2018/02/02/5a74742f468aeb277a8b47e7.html.
20 Hopefully, "the time measured and paid must also be a time without impurities or defects, a time of good quality, along which the body remains applied to its exercise. Accuracy and application are with regularity, the fundamental virtues of disciplinary time". Thus Michel Foucault, *Sorvegliare e punire. Nascita della prigione* (Torino: Einaudi, 1975), 164.
21 On the device that allows locating the employee, see the reconstruction carried out by Arturo Maresca, "Controlli tecnologici e tutele del lavoratore", 16–17.
22 Patrizia Tullini, "La digitalizzazione del lavoro", 7.

However, in such a case should the technological device be framed in the first or second paragraph of article 4 of the Workers' Statute?[23]

The patent on this instrument, as mentioned, aroused media interest, and the previous Italian Minister of Labour Giuliano Poletti also called on the company to comply with Italian law and to provide for the use of such instruments only after an agreement with the trade unions. The Minister, therefore, seems to prefer an interpretative solution that brings this instrument back to the provision of paragraph 1 of article 4 of the Statute, as can be seen from the request for a concerted regulation with the trade unions.

A more detailed analysis reveals that this is not the case, because the issue actually appears to be much more complex than that proposed by the Minister and the trade unions, because the assignment to the employee of an electronic wristband forwards customer orders and measures the time it takes for the employee to move from one shelf to another and take the object to be sent is for the employee a device that can transmit directives to perform the work, although suitable to collect data that exceed this purpose.

This would mean that the use of the electronic device would not be covered by the article at paragraph 1 but in paragraph 2 of the same provision, because it seems that the configuration of this instrument is aimed at setting up more dynamic management procedures of work, responding to needs which, in the broadest sense, are organisational for the employer. Therefore, the information collected by the wristband "can be used for all purposes related to the employment relationship", provided that the employee is given adequate information about the methods of use and "in compliance with the provisions of Legislative Decree 30 June 2003, n. 196".[24]

---

23 See Emanuele Dagnino, "Tecnologie e controlli a distanza", in *Le nuove regole del lavoro dopo il Jobs Act*, ed. Michele Tiraboschi (Milano: Giuffrè, 2016), 109, for which "the interpretation of the expression 'instrument used to make the work performance', on which the real distinction is made, will be fundamental". As also underlined by Patrizia Tullini, "La digitalizzazione del lavoro", 13, "it is quite clear the difficulty of tracing a sure distinction – both on a theoretical and operational level – between the area of remote controls that can be subject to prior authorization for justified business reasons (…) and that of monitoring through work technologies that are exempt from constraints and considered legitimate *ex se*".

24 Marco Marazza, "Dei poteri (del datore di lavoro), dei controlli (a distanza) e del trattamento dei dati (del lavoratore)", accessed 2016, http://csdle.lex.unict.it/docs/workingpapers/Dei-poteri-del-datore-di-lavoro-dei-controlli-a-distanza-e-del-trattamento-dei-dati-del-lavoratore/5511.aspx, 7, "if the first two paragraphs of that provision establish the rules for the legitimate use of remote control instruments, the third and last paragraph lays down the conditions so that the data, if legitimately collected (art. 4, paragraphs 1 and 2), can, then, in practice be used '*for all purposes related to the employment relationship*'. (It follows that) full compliance with the first two paragraphs of art. 4 of the Workers' Statute is not in itself sufficient to allow the information acquired to be managed, for example, to introduce a bonus policy or to exercise disciplinary power. In order to use this data for '*all purposes connected with the employment relationship*', it is in fact necessary to comply with the provisions of art. 4, paragraph 3, and it is precisely from this specific point of view that the interpenetration between the right to work and the right to *privacy* emerges".

IV The employer's powers and the limits to the usability of the information collected

Following from the previous analysis, the electronic wristband can be considered as a working instrument aimed at the improvement of the business productivity. The point concerns the limits of usability of any additional information collected by the device.

The use of a wristband always connected to the internet indeed could abstractly allow the employer to exercise a continuous monitoring of the worker's activity, overcoming the boundaries of the contract fulfilment by the employee. The power to monitor, therefore, is not an end in itself, but it is instrumental with respect to a further (and possible) disciplinary purpose, since it is necessary to understand "which" among the employer powers is replaceable by the electronic wristband.

In the opinion of the author of this chapter, this instrument can legitimately replace at most the traditional directive power of the employer; that is, it could only tell the worker where to take the product and box it, with the consequence that a use of the electronic wristband that exceeds the legitimate purpose mentioned above is prohibited.

The directive power and the monitoring power indeed cannot be overlapped, and although the new formulation of article 4, l. 300/1970 has literally overcome the previous model, article 4 continues to be "functionalized to the need to safeguard the dignity of the employee".[25] The utilisation of the electronic wristband in a company indeed should be helpful for the employee to perform better his work (e.g. knowing place and activity to be done), without being a threat for his work.

In this second case, the wristband would replace both the executive and the monitoring power. However, the pure purpose of remote monitoring of workers' activity is not a generally lawful purpose for the employer, also considering the Privacy Code.

The Legislative Decree n. 196/2003 is not limited only to regulating the moment of data acquisition, but through a series of rules also determines the processing of personal data that, pursuant to article 114, are in addition to the substantive and procedural safeguards provided for by the Workers' Statute. In essence, the Italian legislator (in support of the European legislator) "intervenes *in addition* to the statutory regulations, in a combination of the special regulations of the Statute and the *general* regulation contained in the Privacy Code".[26]

---

25 Even Bruno Veneziani, "Art. 4", 20.
26 Pietro Lambertucci, "Potere di controllo del datore di lavoro e tutela della riservatezza del lavoratore: i controlli 'a distanza' tra attualità della disciplina statutaria, promozione della contrattazione di prossimità e legge delega del 2014 (c.d. Jobs Act)", accessed 2015, http://csdle.lex.unict.it/docs/workingpapers/Potere-di-controllo-del-datore-di-lavoro-e-tutela-della-riservatezza-del-lavoratore-i-controlli-a-di/5405.aspx, 7; according to Riccardo Del Punta, "La nuova disciplina dei controlli a distanza", 91, article 114, Legislative Decree n. 196/2003, formalized "a pact (...) that was resolved more in a mutual non-belligerence than in a complementarity. The two

In order to avoid the *Panopticon effect*, two provisions are the most relevant, to be read in combination with each other: on the one hand, the principle of purpose (article 11, paragraph 1, letter b, Legislative Decree n. 196/2003) on the basis of which "personal data may be collected and registered in order to pursue a predetermined and explicit, as well as legitimate",[27] under penalty of the unusability of the information collected (article 11, paragraph 2, of the Privacy Code); on the other hand, the principle of necessity (article 3, Legislative Decree n. 196/2003) which requires one to intervene upstream in the configuration of a wristband that does not allow the collection of data not necessary compared to those suitable to issue directives.[28]

If the instrument were to be programmed in such a way as to include additional information with respect to a lawful use, in this case it is believed that the data collected by the company would not be useable against the worker because they are disproportionate with respect to the purpose, and therefore not necessary and are thereby inadmissible because they are used for a monitoring purpose not allowed by law.

Along this direction, we are helped by the interventions of the Privacy Guarantor, which has helped over time to concretise these principles in the specific work environment, before the reform of article 4, Law n. 300/1970.

In one of the first decisions concerning the utilisation of personal data collected via email and the internet[29] in 2007,[30] Privacy Authority provided that in exercising the monitoring power of the employer, "it is necessary to respect the freedom and dignity of workers" (paragraph 4). This means that, in application of the *principle of necessity*, "the employer is called upon to promote all appropriate organisational and technological measures aimed at preventing the risk of improper use (...) and, in any case, at 'minimising' the use of data in relation to workers" (paragraph 5.2).

From an organisational point of view, therefore, the employer is called not only to carefully evaluate the impact of the introduction of the work tool on workers'

---

normative apparatuses, in substance, have continued to gravitate in their respective spheres, without developing particular interactions".

27 Vito Pinto, "I controlli 'difensivi' del datore di lavoro", 150–151. He continues by saying that "since this principle is rooted in supranational law (...), its derogation at national level must be excluded because of the primacy recognized by EU regulations. (with the consequence that) even if it were to be considered that the employer could legitimately pursue several purposes through the active collection of personal data, it could not be argued that he is free to establish the quantity and quality of data processed".

28 Pursuant to article 3, Legislative Decree no. n. 196/2003 (entitled "Data minimization Principle"), "information systems and software shall be configured by minimizing the use of personal data and identification data, in such a way as to rule out their processing if the purposes sought in the individual cases can be achieved by using either anonymous data or suitable arrangements to allow identifying data subjects only in cases of necessity, respectively".

29 In www.garanteprivacy.it/web/guest/home/docweb/-/docweb-display/docweb/1387522.

30 Which followed on from Opinion no. 8/2001 on the processing of personal data in the context of employment relationships, available at www.garanteprivacy.it/web/guest/home/docweb/-/docweb-display/docweb/1390186.

rights, but also, for example, to configure the tool with some filters which do not allow the company to collect information inconsistent with the purpose.

From the point of view of the purpose, however, it is perhaps appropriate to remember that the Privacy Guarantor has stressed that this principle does not only require the collection of data for a specific lawful and determinate purpose, but also that such data cannot be used for "further processing in a manner incompatible with the purpose mentioned above".[31] This means that personal data may be processed:

> for the purpose of fulfilling obligations arising from the individual contract (for example, to check that the service has been performed correctly or to determine the amount of remuneration, including overtime payments, or the premiums payable, to calculate holidays and leave, or to establish the existence of a legitimate reason for absence). (...) If these purposes are in general terms lawful, it is however necessary to respect the principle of compatibility between the purposes pursued (Article 11, paragraph 1, letter b) of the Code): the purpose pursued in practice by the employer on the basis of the processing of personal data must not be incompatible with the purposes for which they were collected.[32]

It is difficult to predict how this complicated event will be managed in the future.[33] In any case, it is more and more stringent the need for coordination both with the Privacy Code and with the legislation on the protection of personal data, because of the real risk that the boundaries between the optimisation of the work and the monitoring of the employees could blur.

The Legislative Decree n. 196/2003 has a general scope and is obviously not limited to the field of work, but on this point it is interesting to note that the Regulation (EU) 2016/679 on the protection of personal data, in force since 25 May 2018, contains a rule, article 88, expressly dedicated to the processing of data in the context of the employment relationship.[34] The provision under paragraph 1 is without prejudice to more favourable provisions of the law or collective agreements to ensure "the protection of rights and freedoms with regard to the processing of personal data of employees in the context of employment relationships", and paragraph 2 specifies that these rules (legal or contractual) must include "appropriate and specific measures to safeguard human dignity, the legitimate interests and fundamental rights of those concerned".

31 We read again in Opinion no. 8/2001.
32 http://194.242.234.211/documents/10160/2097030/Linee+guida+sul+trattamento+di+dati+personali+dei+lavoratori%C2%85.pdf, 4.
33 It will be necessary to wait for the first decisions of the judges and of the Authority for the protection of personal data, a fortiori because Regulation 2016/679 has provided in articles 54 ss. for the rules on the establishment of a supervisory authority with the task of supervising the application of the aforementioned Regulation.
34 For a comment, please see Anna Trojsi, "Controllo a distanza (su impianti e strumenti di lavoro) e protezione dei dati del lavoratore", *Variazioni su Temi di Diritto del Lavoro*, 4, (2016), 684.

The rule therefore acts as a litmus test for the identification of the rights subject to legal and contractual regulation, because it identifies human dignity as the supreme good and, second, the legitimate interests and fundamental rights of those concerned.

Article 88 therefore recognises the legitimate interests of the employer in the collection of information on the execution of the service, but requires coordination with national legislation and collective agreements, which will have the task of specifying the boundary of the legally permissible, that is, to specify, in this author's opinion, the principles of necessity and purpose mentioned above.

In a recent interview of 2 February 2018,[35] the president of the Guarantor Authority for the Protection of Personal Data, Antonello Soro, after expressly recalling the principles of proportionality, transparency and protection of human dignity, pointed out that in our legal system the rules do not allow a delegation of the organisation of work to technologies, and consequently that "there can be no progress or innovation that has no foundation in man".

V Conclusion

In this chapter, the electronic wristband (recently patented by Amazon) as a new working instrument is discussed. In particular, the legality limits of the information collected by this device are investigated in light of the rules established both by the article 4 of the Workers' Statute and by the Privacy Code.

The author attempts to demonstrate that the electronic wristband can be introduced in the new working framework; however, the data collected by the device has to be carefully managed in order to guarantee its licit use. The electronic wristband indeed is able to collect a large amount of extra information, and the difficult task of the researcher is to identify what information could be legally utilised by the employer without compromising the privacy and the dignity of the employee.

The author of this work believes that the electronic wristband can replace the directorial power of the employer, but not their monitoring power and (even more so) their disciplinary power. Consequently, if the device was designed in order to collect additional information with respect to the one necessary for the fulfilment of the contract, then the data collected by the company would not be useable against the worker because it would have been collected for a disproportionate and unnecessary purpose, and would therefore be illicit.

VI Bibliography

Ilario Alvino, "I nuovi limiti al controllo a distanza dell'attività dei lavoratori nell'intersezione tra le regole dello Statuto dei lavoratori e quelle del Codice della privacy", *Labour and Law Issues*, 2, I, (2016), 3.

---

35 You can listen to this interview on the website www.radioradicale.it/scheda/532399/intervista-ad-antonello-soro-sul-braccialetto-elettronico-per-i-lavoratori-brevettato.

Marco Barbieri, "L'utilizzabilità delle informazioni raccolte: il Grande Fratello può attendere (forse)", *Controlli a distanza e tutela dei dati personali del lavoratore*, ed. Patrizia Tullini, (Torino: Giappichelli, 2017), 183.

Norberto Bobbio, *Il futuro della democrazia*, (Torino: Einaudi, 1984).

Maria Teresa Carinci, "Il controllo a distanza sull'adempimento della prestazione di lavoro", in *Controlli a distanza e tutela dei dati personali del lavoratore*, ed. Patrizia Tullini, (Torino: Giappichelli, 2017), 45.

Luigi Andrea Cosattini, "Le modifiche all'art. Stat. Lav. sui controlli a distanza, tanto rumore; per nulla?", *Il Lavoro nella Giurisprudenza*, (2015), 985.

Vezio Crisafulli, "Diritti di libertà e poteri dell'imprenditore", *Rivista Giuridica del Lavoro*, I, (1954), 190.

Emanuele Dagnino, "Tecnologie e controlli a distanza", in *Le nuove regole del lavoro dopo il Jobs Act*, ed. Michele Tiraboschi, (Milano: Giuffrè, 2016), 107.

Riccardo Del Punta, "La nuova disciplina dei controlli a distanza sul lavoro (art. 23, d.lgs. n. 151/2015)", *Rivista Italiana di Diritto del Lavoro*, 2016, I, 77.

Luigi Fiorillo and Adalberto Perulli, *Il Jobs act del lavoro autonomo e del lavoro agile*, (Torino: Giappichelli, 2018).

Michel Foucault, *Sorvegliare e punire. Nascita della prigione*, (Torino: Einaudi, 1975).

Pietro Lambertucci, "Potere di controllo del datore di lavoro e tutela della riservatezza del lavoratore: i controlli 'a distanza' tra attualità della disciplina statutaria, promozione della contrattazione di prossimità e legge delega del 2014 (c.d. Jobs Act)", accessed 2015, http://csdle.lex.unict.it/docs/workingpapers/Potere-di-controllo-del-datore-di-lavoro-e-tutela-della-riservatezza-del-lavoratore-i-controlli-a-di/5405.aspx.

Mariella Magnani, "Il contratto di lavoro subordinato", n. 360, 3–4, accessed 2018, http://csdle.lex.unict.it/docs/workingpapers/Il-contratto-di-lavoro-subordinato/5745.aspx.

Marco Marazza, "Dei poteri (del datore di lavoro), dei controlli (a distanza) e del trattamento dei dati (del lavoratore)", accessed 2016, http://csdle.lex.unict.it/docs/workingpapers/Dei-poteri-del-datore-di-lavoro-dei-controlli-a-distanza-e-del-trattamento-dei-dati-del-lavoratore/5511.aspx.

Arturo Maresca "Controlli tecnologici e tutele del lavoratore nel nuovo art. 4 St. Lav.", in *Controlli a distanza e tutela dei dati personali del lavoratore*, ed. Patrizia Tullini (Torino: Giappichelli, 2017), 1.

Marianna Russo, "Quis custodies custodiet? I "nuovi" limiti all'esercizio del potere di controllo a distanza", in *Labour and Law Issues*, 2, II, (2016), 3.

Vito Pinto, "I controlli 'difensivi' del datore di lavoro sulle attività informatiche e telematiche del lavoratore", in *Controlli a distanza e tutela dei dati personali del lavoratore*, ed. Patrizia Tullini, (Torino, Giappichelli, 2017), 139.

Michele Tiraboschi and Francesco Seghezzi, "Il Piano nazionale Industria 4.0: una lettura lavoristica", *Labour and Law Issues*, 2, II, (2016), 3.

Anna Trojsi, "Controllo a distanza (su impianti e strumenti di lavoro) e protezione dei dati del lavoratore", *Variazioni su Temi di Diritto del Lavoro*, 4, (2016), 667.

Patrizia Tullini, "La digitalizzazione del lavoro, la produzione intelligente e il controllo tecnologico nell'impresa", in *Web e lavoro. Profili evolutivi e di tutela*, ed. Patrizia Tullini, (Torino: Giappichelli, 2017), 3.

Bruno Veneziani, "Art. 4. Impianti audiovisivi", in *Lo Statuto dei Lavoratori. Commentario*, ed. Gino Giugni, (Milano: Giuffrè, 1979), 17.

12 New forms of work and trade unions in the digital age*

María Luz Rodríguez Fernández

I Introduction

Thiébaut Weber, a young trade unionist from the European Trade Union Confederation (ETUC), has made use of the image of the god Janus to illustrate how trade unions should act when faced with the technological revolution.[1] In Roman mythology, Janus is the god of beginnings and endings, and has the gift of telling the future. This is why he is represented as a god with two faces and has given his name to January, when the old year ends, and a new one begins. In the opinion of this author, the image and, above all, the message conveyed through it by Weber are wholly appropriate. Trade unions must face a future characterised by technological advances and their application to the production process and business models, but they should not forget the problems of the past. Not only have these not disappeared from work, but they could well intensify in the age of the digital revolution. Trade unions must therefore combine traditional action with a more cutting-edge approach in meeting those challenges of technological change: looking to the past and looking to the future, like Janus, and doing so in a difficult context, characterised by globalisation and a certain social disenchantment regarding the meaning and purpose of trade unions.

The aim of this paper is to examine how trade unions should organise and embrace both roles as well as to specify those policies and strategies to be followed as a socio-political subject and a key player in labour relations. As we will see later, trade unions will have to bring to the political field demands for the implementation of professional training and recycling programmes that will help workers to adapt to technological requirements as well as the establishment of a minimum income for those who lose their jobs. In the field of labour relations, they will have to bring new contents, such as the right to digital

---

* This paper is a result of the research conducted under the MINECO-funded Project "Digitalisation and Work: the impact of the economy 4.0 on employment, labour relations, and social protection", reference DER2017-82444-R. It was written during my stay at the ILO Research Department, so I would like to thank this institution for its welcome and its interest in my research activity.
1 Thiébaut Weber, "Janus and the trade union challenge of digital technology," *Transfer: European Review of Labour and Research*, 23, 2017, p. 225.

disconnection and data protection, to collective bargaining, but also deal with such phenomena as the rise in freelance work, the increasing dilution of work by digital platforms, the lack of solid professional identities and the bipolarity of the workforce. For this purpose, trade unions must create new spaces as well as solidarity links among workers by using technology and by giving up on some of their traditional attributes.

II New challenges to collective bargaining and employment policies

The first fact that trade unions will have to face in the digital age is probably the working population's fear of losing their jobs due to the advances made in updating machines. The combination of robots, digitalisation and artificial intelligence can, as all signs indicate, cause many job losses. The point now is not to specify how many and which jobs will be lost, although well-known studies provide some relevant figures. The World Economic Forum talks of 5.1 million net jobs that will disappear between 2015 and 2020, given that, even though the drop in jobs will reach 7.1 million, 2 million new jobs will be created during that period.[2] In addition, McKinsey predicts that about 50% of current work activities can potentially become automated, and that more than 30% of the tasks of 6 out of every 10 jobs can become automated.[3] Furthermore, by 2030, the number of working hours that can potentially be automated could reach 30% of the global total. Finally, the OECD provides a more optimistic vision, estimating that a total of only 9% of jobs in all the OECD countries are at high risk of automation, although with two warnings that are important to highlight: the jobs with the highest risk of disappearing are those of workers with lower qualifications and lower income levels.[4]

This provides indications about some of the trends resulting from the advance of technology that must be integrated in trade union action. The first is the risk of job losses for some segments of the working population and the risk, in turn, of the reappearance of the "machine breakers", to use Hobsbawm's terminology.[5] The second is the need for the requalification of large segments of the population so that they do not lose the race against technology. The third is the need to provide income for those who lose their jobs because of the technological revolution. The final, but no less important, is the different

---

2 See World Economic Forum, "The future of jobs. Employment, skills and workforce strategy for the Fourth Industrial Revolution," 2016, p. 13, www3.weforum.org/docs/WEF_Future_of_Jobs.pdf (retrieved 8 March 2019).
3 McKinsey, "What the future of work will mean for jobs, skills, and wages," 2017, www.mckinsey.com/global-themes/future-of-organizations-and-work/what-the-future-of-work-will-mean-for-jobs-skills-and-wages (retrieved 8 March 2019).
4 See Melanie Arnzt, Terry Gregory, and Ulrich Zierahn, "The risk of automation for jobs in OCDE countries" *OECD Social, Employment and Migration Working Papers*, 189, 2016, at pp. 8 and 20.
5 In Eric J. Hobsbawn, "The machine breakers" *Past and Present*, 1, 1952, at pp. 57–70.

impact that technology has on the working population's jobs depending on their qualifications and income, and how this results in a split of the labour market and society into two: the *winners* and the *losers* of the advances of digitalisation, to use the terminology which is currently in vogue. Let us now examine each of these trends.

Despite all the reports that quantify the job losses caused by digitalisation, one may think that anyone can accurately foresee which jobs will disappear. Beyond this fact of job disappearance, it is suggested that rather than focusing on establishing the number of jobs lost, questions should focus on finding where the new jobs will be generated in the technological age. Taking as a starting point the fact that the advance of technology generates and will generate new jobs (a trip to the supermarket confirms that Schumpeter's "creative destruction" is still operating),[6] the key questions to be asked are how many jobs will be created and at what speed, what their quality will be, where they will be geographically located, which qualifications will be required and thus, whether the workers who have lost their jobs due to the advances in technology will be able to occupy the new jobs created by it.[7] Two of the strategies to be designed by trade unions depend on the answers to these questions: the first is the training for employment policy demanded and implemented by trade unions; the second, the unemployment protection policy or in general the social protection policy which trade unions should require from their governments.

1 Digital training policies as a key factor for a fair transition

Actually, the advance of technology has always rendered previous qualifications either obsolescent or obsolete with a requirement for new ones. Furthermore, one of the goals of the introduction of new technologies in production processes is precisely to generate that de-skilling process because, in turn, it reduces the power of qualified workers and lowers production costs.[8] In addition, the demand for more suitable new qualifications for those technological requirements of new jobs generates the opposite phenomenon, that is, it empowers workers with those qualifications and increases production costs. Hence the demand for the expansion of new qualifications and the corresponding demand for workers' professional retraining has an ambiguous effect: it is necessary to continue in the workplace or, to use more up-to-date terminology, improve your employability; but at the same time, it is also necessary to provide companies with more workers, thus reducing the power of qualified workers and consequently lowering

---

6 See Joseph A. Schumpeter, "The process of creative destruction," in *Capitalism, Socialism, and Democracy* (1942) London, Allen & Unwin, at pp. 81–86.
7 See Henning Meyer, "Inequality in the second machine age: the need for a social democratic digital society," *Juncture*, 23, 2016, p. 104.
8 See Nick Srnicek, *Platform Capitalism* (2017) Cambridge, Polity Press, pp. 12–13.

their cost.[9] Despite this ambiguity, I believe that trade unions must demand a public policy for professional training and retraining, thus helping to implement the transition towards new jobs for the majority of the working population, including the public funding required to carry it out.

This is the first of the demands that the ETUC has made to the European Union. It is, however, necessary to pause here and reflect on the trade unions' strategy. In the opinion of this author, one of the weaknesses of trade union action during the 2008 crisis, but also before it, was that it was based almost exclusively on the national territory. If there is one thing that globalisation has made clear, it is the insufficiency of national responses, be they from governments or from social partners, in addressing economic processes that cross national borders. This is even clearer when talking about the digitalisation of the economy, a phenomenon occurring globally, even though with specific traits in each country. Also global is the phenomenon of digital platforms, which can distribute work all over the world. Hence, it is really necessary that trade union action goes beyond nation states' territories to operate in broader economic integration zones, such as the European Union. This means establishing closer relationships between national trade unions and the ETUC, and above all creating firm commitments between them, thus preventing the prevalence of differences between trade union visions and models that have so far and to a large extent hindered European trade union action. In short, to be effective in the face of global challenge, trade unionism must be global and present a global response.

In its *Towards fair digital work* strategy published in June 2016, the ETUC calls for an improvement in workers' initial and on-going training as a key factor for what it terms an "*inclusive* transition towards good and fair digital work".[10] The term "inclusive" must be emphasised because, if workers' training does not reach the dimension that it must have for a majority of workers to access the digital society, one of the most feared effects of the digital advance will take place. There will be a wide gap between the *winners* and the *losers* in the advance of technology in the workplace, generating huge inequality and creating a deep fragmentation in society.[11] To conduct such a training process, involving millions of euros and millions of workers across the European Union, the ETUC (ETUC, 2017) proposes the reconversion and better funding of the *European Fund for Adaptation to Globalisation* through the imposition, if required, of taxes on digital activities.[12] This is a proposal that opens a particularly relevant

---

9 In this sense Ursula Huws, *Labor in the Global Digital Economy. The Cybertariat Comes of Age* (2014) New York, Monthly Review Press, at pp. 33 and 41.
10 Source: ETUC, "Towards fair digital work," 2016, www.etuc.org/documents/etuc-resolution-digitalisation-towards-fair-digital-work#.WlthcxRTO6j (retrieved 8 March 2019).
11 See Daniel Autor, "The polarization of jobs opportunities in the U.S. Labour market," 2010, www.americanprogress.org/wp-content/uploads/issues/2010/04/pdf/job_polarization_execsumm.pdf (retrieved 8 March 2019).
12 Source: ETUC, "Resolution on tackling new digital challenges to the world of labour, in particular crowdwork," 2017, www.etuc.org/documents/tackling-new-digital-challenges-world-labour-particular-crowdwork#.Wlt9fxRTO6g (retrieved 8 March 2019).

debate on the redistribution of the profits and burdens of the digital age. Finally, and this is something that should be highlighted because, in the opinion of this author, it should become a characteristic of trade union policy on digitalisation, the ETUC believes that training for the digital age should also be extended to freelance workers. This means that all workers must have the same right to training, regardless of their legal status as employed or self-employed.

In addition to this proposal for active employment policies, proper to the understanding of trade unions as socio-political organisms, trade unions need to incorporate the strategy of continuous digital training for workers in their own action plans. Moreover, it should be a priority for collective bargaining. Indeed, the advance of the technological revolution and its impact on labour relations will require trade unions to take the plunge also into the workplace (including the digital workplace, mentioned below). As well as those demands for public policies, trade unions should add additional strategies within the production centres, changing the contents and the ways of acting because workers' problems and expectations are also changing. To begin with, trade unions must have a voice in the digital transformation of business – not making it something alien to them to which they react defensively or opposing the advance of digitalisation, but rather becoming actively involved in order to ensure a fair transition for all workers. It is precisely for this reason that training must be a key factor in collective bargaining, given that despite all ambiguities that it implies, job maintenance will depend to a large extent on the continuous adjustment of workers' skills. Thus, trade unions should negotiate and agree digital training plans with companies for all their workers.

2 Right to disconnection and data protection as symbols of new collective bargaining in accordance with technological revolution

Collective bargaining should also be at the forefront as regards new contents directly connected to digitalisation. This is the case of teleworking and the regulation of the right to disconnection, but it also applies to data protection and workers' right to privacy. It is patently obvious that the advance of technology makes it possible for many functions previously located in the workplace to be performed outside that workplace. Furthermore, if some time ago the coordination of all the stages and parts of the production process required the concentration of all the production factors in a single location, technology currently facilitates maximum coordination of all the production factors, even if they are scattered across the world. This is radically transforming the concepts of *workplace* and *working time*, given that the use of technology often makes it possible to work *anytime* and *anywhere*. The positive effects of freedom to work anytime and anywhere are well known. It gives greater autonomy to organising working time and more possibilities of reconciling work and family.[13] However, the

---

13 Source: Eurofound, "New forms of employment," 2015, www.eurofound.europa.eu/sites/default/files/ef_publication/field_ef_document/ef1461en.pdf (retrieved 8 March 2019).

negative effects of working anytime and anywhere are also evident. It blurs the boundaries between private life and professional life[14] and leads to overextended working hours. Working anytime and anywhere can actually become working all the time and everywhere.[15]

Given this, the strategy of trade unions should be to transform collective bargaining into a channel and a barrier for these phenomena: a channel to approach the outsourcing of productive activity through teleworking and a barrier against workers' continual availability. In the opinion of this author, rather than leaving the possibility of teleworking to specific agreements between worker and employer, the possibilities for the expansion of this kind of work would be better served by designing teleworking strategies within collective bargaining. This means specifying by means of collective agreements which workers and/or jobs would be able to perform this kind of work as well as its conditions. In this way, without denying functionality to individual agreements between worker and employer to implement teleworking, collective frameworks could be designed to provide teleworkers with security and certain guarantees and encourage the use of teleworking and a less *presentist* (on-site) culture on the part of companies.

Furthermore, the right to digital disconnection must become a normal part of collective agreements. The French case is well known: in France, the right to digital disconnection started as an innovative part of collective bargaining and became a legal mandate. It is now compulsory to negotiate the forms of digital disconnection in any collective agreements signed in France. The same path has been followed in Spain, where the law ordering collective bargaining regulates the right to digital disconnection. This combination of law and collective agreement as a barrier against workers' continuous availability is, in the opinion of this author, the way forward in putting the right of digital disconnection into operation. This should be implemented for health reasons because overworking causes stress and burnout. It should also be enforced to make professional life and private life compatible, and even for productivity reasons as it is proven that this is impacted negatively by overworking.[16]

Another new factor to be prioritised by collective bargaining in the technological age is the protection of workers' data as well as limitation of the possibilities for continuous technological supervision. One of the most characteristic traits of the digital age is the vast capacity to collect and assess the data provided by technology users, known as *Big Data*. This has many implications, including the debate on ownership of the data (and the profits) generated[17] in a society in which we have all become "prosumers", that is, both data producers and consumers

---

14 See Juliet Webster, and Keith Randler, "Virtual workers and the global labour market" (2016), London, Palgrave McMillan, pp. 13–14.
15 Source: Eurofound, and OIT, "Working anytime anywhere: the effects on the world of work," 2017, www.eurofound.europa.eu/sites/default/files/ef_publication/field_ef_document/ef1658en.pdf (retrieved 8 March 2019).
16 *Ibid.*
17 See Nick Srnicek, *Platform Capitalism, op. cit.* pp. 53–55.

at the same time.[18] But it also has implications for workers. By collecting and analysing the data produced by them when using business technologies, not only information pertaining to work can be found, but also information pertaining to workers' personal lives, which endangers their privacy. There is also a risk to workers' rights to privacy in those cases in which technological tools are used to control job delivery. It enables exhaustive monitoring of their behaviour at work, but their private behaviour can also be supervised and monitored at the same time. The growing relevance that these issues are acquiring in the field of labour relations is evidenced by the public importance that is being given to the rulings of the European Court of Human Rights in this regard, as in Barbulescu *vs* Romania (supervision of private email)[19] and López Ribalta et al. *vs* Spain (use of hidden surveillance cameras to obtain and process private data).[20]

This is why, as a trade union strategy in the field of public policy, the ETUC proposes – and it is a reasonable option, as fundamental rights are at stake – the approval of a directive on privacy in the workplace, based on respect for human dignity, privacy and personal data.[21] But the digital age also requires that trade unions prioritise those contents that are connected to workers' sovereignty over their own data and the fundamental right to privacy. Creating, by means of collective bargaining, protocols for actions that clearly delimit the capacity for control of work activity by companies and its limits has become a crucial task during the technology boom.[22] This is crucial, and not only for the legal validity of some formulas for technological supervision implemented by companies. It is also essential for the creation of a framework of certainty and security in the enjoyment of fundamental rights and freedoms by companies and workers.

3 Provision of a minimum income for loss of employment

In addition to including labour contents proper to the digital economy in collective bargaining, trade unions must face the problem of the loss of labour income, which will probably follow job losses. It seems clear that, even if new technological jobs are created and digital training for the working population is implemented, a double gap may be generated. First, because the period between the loss of jobs resulting from technological advances and the creation of new jobs can be protracted, so that the phenomenon called "technological

---

18 In this sense, see Gérard Valenduc and Patricia Vendramin, "Work in the digital economy: sorting the old from the new," Working Paper ETUI 2016.03, 2016, pp. 11–12.
19 Available from https://hudoc.echr.coe.int/eng#{"itemid":["001-177082"]}.
20 Available from https://hudoc.echr.coe.int/eng#{"documentcollectionid2":["GRANDCHAMBER","CHAMBER"],"itemid":["001-179881"]}.
21 Source: ETUC, "Towards fair digital work," 2016, *op. cit.*
22 See UNI Global Union, "Top 10 principles for workers' data privacy and protection," 2017, www.thefutureworldofwork.org/media/35421/uni_workers_data_protection.pdf (retrieved 8 March 2019).

unemployment" by Keynes[23] will take place. Second, because even if an intensive digital training strategy is developed, it is quite likely that at least a part of the working population will be unable to adapt to the requirements of digital work. This will become even more dramatic if the most pessimistic forecasts on job destruction mentioned above materialise. In any case, the effect that must be highlighted is the same one: as a result of the technological revolution, there will be a significant number of workers who will lose their labour income, a fundamental source of livelihood for the vast majority of them.

Given this fact, trade union strategy should include the justification of a source of income that replaces labour income. This is what the ETUC refers to when it calls for EU authorities to ensure that the transition towards the digital economy is inclusive. This means that technological revolution should not cause an even larger gap between the few *winners* and the many *losers*, which further deepens the increasing inequality in the distribution of wealth.[24] It is not by chance that all the debates and studies on the impact of digitalisation on employment call for the implementation of universal basic income, such as Irani,[25] or the implementation of a negative income tax, such as Brynjolfsson and McAfee.[26] Whether they are pessimistic or optimistic, all specialists expect the digital revolution to cause a net decrease in the number of jobs, and thus an increase in the number of people who may be doomed to poverty. This makes it necessary – for social justice for some and for economic efficiency for others – to establish alternative sources of income for all workers who lose their jobs as a result of technological revolution.

In the opinion of this author, universal income is not the best option, since work is still a crucial factor in people's lives. However, one shares the idea of Ferry[27] when he says that, at this time of technological revolution, it is more important to protect people than their jobs. Therefore, a minimum income system should be established for all those who lose their jobs as a result of technological advances. That is why, as regards the strategy to be followed by trade unions in the digital age, the proposal for a minimum European income, currently included in point 14 of the European Pillar of Social Rights at the request of the ETUC and the European Economic and Social Committee's Employers Group, seems to me to be the right approach.[28]

---

23 See John Maynard Keynes, "Economic possibilities for our grandchildren," in *Essays in Persuasion* (1930), New York, Harcourt Brace.
24 See again ETUC, "*Towards fair digital work,*" 2016, *op. cit.*
25 See Lilly Irani, "*Justice for 'data janitors',*" 2015, www.publicbooks.org/justice-for-data-janitors/ (retrieved 8 March 2019).
26 See Erik Brynjolfssons and Andrew McAffe, *The Second Machine Age. Work, Progress, and Prosperity in a Time of Brilliant Technologies* (2014), New York, W. W. Norton & Company, at pp. 234–249.
27 See Luc Ferry, "*La revolución transhumanista. Como la tecnomedicina y la uberización del mundo van a transformar nuestras vidas*" (2017), Madrid, Alianza Editorial, p. 151.
28 Available from https://ec.europa.eu/commission/sites/beta-political/files/social-summit-european-pillar-social-rights-booklet_en.pdf.

III Platforms and new forms of collective organisation and action

We are entering a space where the impact of the technological revolution has completely transformed the business model and demolished many of the certainties regarding labour relations which we have had until now. Online work platforms, which Degryse[29] calls "21st-century factories", have recently entered the economic arena and their impact on the number of workers is still marginal, given that, according to studies (as there is no official data available), work through platforms is the main source of income for no more than 2.5% of the workforce.[30] However, they have such potential to transform the model of production and labour relations that they are attracting the attention and fears of practically all scholars in the field of labour law.

To begin with, online platforms have established freelance work as the symbol of the new economic model they represent (which, in my view, should not be called *collaborative economy*, since this gives rise to considerable confusion, but rather *platform economy*). This is causing the legal focus as well as the media focus to be concentrated on finding out if people who provide their services through these platforms are actually freelancers or if they have some kind of employment relationship. This is not the right place to deal with this legal discussion with the attention it deserves. But it should be borne in mind that the technology employed by these platforms allows for a highly exhaustive control of the way in which the service providers supply their services. By means of what Schmidt[31] calls *algorithmic management* and *gamification*, the provision of the service is evaluated in such a systematic and continuous way that it is hard to believe that service providers have full autonomy when supplying the service and they are really freelancers. In any case, what is interesting here is to underline that it is having a strong impact on trade unions. Its first effect is connected to the legal classification of these workers; its second effect relates to the need for trade unions to organise these service providers, even if they are actually freelancers.

It must be recognised that it is perfectly logical for the main concern of a classic trade union strategy regarding the rise of work platforms to be the classification of the people working on them as employed or freelancers, given that the application of labour rights depends on this classification as well as the protection of these people through trade union action. The ETUC initiative that, in the field of public policy, requires the creation of a European-level legal

---

29 See Christophe Degryse, "Digitalisation of the economy and its impact on labour markets," Working Paper ETUI 2016.02, 2016, p. 13.
30 Source: Ursula Huw, Neil H. Spencer and Simon Joyce, "Crowd Work in Europe. Preliminary results from survey in the UK, Sweden, Germany, Austria and the Netherlands," 2016, www.feps-europe.eu/assets/39aad271-85ff-457c-8b23-b30d82bb808f/crowd-work-in-europe-draft-report-last-versionpdf.pdf (retrieved 8 March 2019).
31 See Florian A. Schmidt, "Digital labour markets in the platform economy," 2017, http://library.fes.de/pdf-files/wiso/13164.pdf, pp. 11–12 (retrieved 8 March 2019).

framework which, among other factors, includes a presumption of the existence of employment relationships for the providers of services through platforms, unless the presence of genuine self-employment can be proven, must be understood in that sense.[32] The *2016 Frankfurt Declaration*[33] follows the same lines in insisting on the need to correctly classify the providers of services through platforms, so that if they are workers they cannot be refused this status, but they are not deprived – and this is a significant nuance – of the flexibility and freedom provided to workers by platform work.

Furthermore, this *Declaration* is also the first European agreement through which a number of trade unions set their own strategy when faced with the boom of work platforms. It is an agreement drafted by *Fair Crowd Work*, a trade union of digital platform workers, which uses, as the uniqueness of its trade union strategy, a ranking of the various work platforms in order to inform those who would like to work through them. It is also a new trade union sponsored by *IG Metall*, a traditional trade union. Both are traits proper to a new trade union organisation and strategy model, which is emerging due to the rise in work platforms and which started with *Turkopticon*, a forum of *Amazon Mechanical Turk* workers created by Lilly Irani and Six Silverman.[34]

Another defining trait of this new model should be the irrelevance of the legal status of the individual providing the service when it comes to the defence of their interests by a trade union. There is a school of thought which understands that, given the effects being caused by the boom of digital work platforms, the time has come for trade unions to protect the entire working population, both employed and freelancers. The reason for this is that there is a deep inequality between this kind of freelancer and the companies for whom they provide their services. So, if inequality is the basis of the right of workers' trade union freedom, it will also be the basis of the right of trade union freedom and trade union and collective bargaining protection in the case of freelance workers.[35] It is true that freelancers are often a non-unionized group, but this does not mean that trade unions should not make efforts to raise awareness of their collective interests and try to defend them. From another point of view, this could be understood as a restriction on the free competition between economic operators, as a common price for provision of their services would be set by means of the organisation and collective agreements established. That is why, as a sign for this new age of trade union action, both the *Frankfurt Declaration* and some authors call for changes

---

32 Source: ETUC, "Resolution on tackling new digital challenges to the world of labour, in particular crowdwork," *op. cit.*
33 Available from www.igmetall.de/docs_20161214_Frankfurt_Paper_on_Platform_Based_Work_EN_b939ef89f7e5f3a639cd6a1a930feffd8f55cecb.pdf
34 See Lilly Irani and Six Silverman, "Turkopticon: interrupting worker invisibility in Amazon mechanical turk," 2013, http://wtf.tw/text/turkopticon.pdf (retrieved 8 March 2019).
35 See Michele Forlivesi, "La sfida della rappresentanza sindacale dei lavoratori 2.0," *Diritto delle Relazioni Industriali* 3, 2016, p. 669.

in the laws that forbid collective organisation and action for independent contractors.[36]

However, in the opinion of this author, rather than legal problems, trade union action regarding this kind of workers is especially problematic due to their dispersion and complete lack of professional identity. It should be noted that not all digital work platforms are the same, given that some, like *Uber* and *Deliveroo*, locate their services in a specific territory, while others, such as *Amazon Mechanical Turk* and *Upwork*, make it possible to provide their services from and to any location on earth. In the former case, trade union organisation is easier, as providers are located in the same geographic area. In fact, several trade unions of drivers or riders of certain significance already exist in London, Frankfurt, Vienna and Barcelona.[37] However, in the case of digital platforms where services are exchanged, one of the structural characteristics of this type of "digital work markets" is actually their degree of dispersion.[38] Technology makes it possible to outsource activities to the point of paroxysm, not only because a platform enables the distribution of work worldwide, but also because it makes it possible to break work down into hundreds of micro-tasks scattered across the world.[39]

Together with the dispersion of the workforce, the outsourcing process described above produces a process of de-skilling. Let us think about how work develops in one of these platforms. Once a micro-worker has won a bid on the platform for one of the micro-tasks into which what used to be a job has been divided (a platform divides a job into micro-tasks), they perform it, receiving in exchange one of the micro-salaries into which what used to be a salary has been fragmented (a platform shatters wage in micro-salaries).[40] There is no need to point out what this means in terms of job insecurity and poverty, now multiplied by technology. But it also leads – and this is what is most relevant in terms of trade union action – to a lack of labour identity for these workers, who do not know what their profession is (they just perform micro-tasks through an app or a website) or what professional category they can attribute to themselves.[41] Work through digital platforms thus shatters all the identities that had previously served to build the solidarity on which the creation and action of trade actions were, in turn, founded. Territory, business and profession are not factors for

---

36 See De Stefano, Valerio De Stefano, "Non-standard work and limits on freedom of association: a human rights-based approach," *Industrial Law Journal*, 46, 2017, pp. 194–195.
37 Source: ETUC, "Resolution on tackling new digital challenges to the world of labour, in particular crowdwork," *op. cit.*
38 See Vili Lehdonvirta, "Algorithms that divide and unite: delocalization, identity, and collective action in 'microwork'," 2016, http://vili.lehdonvirta.com/files/Lehdonvirta%202016%20Delocalization%20identity%20collective%20action%20in%20microwork.pdf, p. 14 (retrieved 8 March 2019).
39 See Nick Srnicek, *Platform Capitalism, op. cit.*, p. 76.
40 See Juliet Webster, "Microworkers of the gig economy: separate and precarious," *New Labor Forum*, 25 (3), 2016, p. 57.
41 See Vili Lehdonvirta, "Algorithms that divide and unite: delocalization, identity, and collective action in 'microwork'," *op. cit.*, p. 13.

platform workers' cohesion: geographically scattered and/or isolated, unaware of whether the app to which they connect or the anonymous client requesting their services is their employer and not knowing what exactly their profession is, they have no references that will help them to join others in self-organising and acting in the defence of their common interests. Even worse, the platform forces them to compete against each other in an auction to obtain the micro-task offered. This generates a competitive and individualistic behaviour among platform workers that clearly makes it difficult to foster a minimum sense of unity and common interest on which to found collective action.[42]

However, technology may bring together what technology has torn asunder. This is *WorkerTech*, the use of technology to articulate movements for the defence of workers' interests. This is another form of trade unionism, as the use of technology (social media, websites, apps) is the way to connect workers to each other. That is, there are no hierarchies, no organisation, no headquarters, even no affiliation, but rather forums and networks of workers connected to each other by means of a digital platform. In principle, they do not even seek collective action, but rather share experiences and very importantly, knowledge of the platforms for which they work and of the clients who commission micro-tasks through them. *Fair Crowd Work* does just that: on the basis of the experiences described by service providers, it generates a ranking of digital platforms so that other service providers can learn how they operate. This is a way to compensate for the extreme lack of transparency with which digital platforms operate, when sometimes it is not even known for which (lawful or unlawful) purposes the tiny activities commissioned will be used. But it is also a way to generate confidence as well as a certain feeling of belonging and shared identity,[43] without frequently aroused prejudices against trade unions or traditional trade unionism.[44]

In fact, these networks do not even use traditional trade union mechanisms, such as collective bargaining, but rather seek to make the work behaviour of platforms or more generally, the work behaviour of companies known to the general public and the media.[45] These organisations make intensive use of technology and of the possibilities offered by social media to multiply the social impact of their claims, complaints about business behaviours or actions in defence of workers' interests (including strikes). They do not seek – or at least, it is not their starting point – to reach an agreement with the employer, but rather to mobilise customers and the entire population so as to boycott the consumption

---

42 In this sense, Mark Graham and Alex Wood, "Why the digital gig economy needs co-ops and unions," 2017, www.opendemocracy.net/alex-wood/why-digital-gig-economy-needs-co-ops-and-unions (retrieved 8 March 2019).
43 Rochelle LaPlante and Six Silveman, "Building trust in crowd worker forums: worker ownership, governance, and work outcomes," 2016, http://trustincrowdwork.west.uni-koblenz.de/sites/trustincrowdwork.west.uni-koblenz.de/files/laplante_trust.pdf (retrieved 8 March 2019).
44 See Michele Forlivesi, "*La sfida della rappresentanza sindacale dei lavoratori 2.0,*" op. cit., p. 675.
45 See Alex J. Wood, "Networks of injustice and worker mobilisation at Walmart," *Industrial Relations Journal*, 46, 2015, p. 262.

of the company products or services, or else to mobilise the public powers so that they act in some way against the labour problems brought to public light through the use of technology.[46] These organisations do not seek collective bargaining, but rather the involvement of public powers and consumers' activism to force companies to change their work behaviours. In comparison with traditional trade unionism, these networks pose the problem for which they create a mosaic of atomised organisations, disconnected from each other and with a low level of, so to speak, labour ideology. This hinders the creation of a uniform or unitary trade union strategy through them, in the way classic trade unionism has always envisaged.[47] But it is also true that they are not always unrelated to traditional trade unionism; on the contrary, the actions implemented so far in the United States and Germany are in some way orchestrated (and funded) by traditional trade unions, which have opted not to "colonise" these movements with the usual trade union affiliation and action methods. And they have been successful. Thus, it may be that by using technology and giving up its more traditional attributes trade unionism will be empowered in the digital age.

IV Conclusions

We live in a time when technological revolution is changing our societies and our ways of living but also our ways of working and producing. Trade unions should not be oblivious to these changes, and they should adapt their organisation, their strategies and their actions to the demands of this new era. As has been explained above, to face the challenges posed by the technological revolution, trade unions should follow these guidelines: (i) implement their trade union action beyond nation states' borders; (ii) demand that public powers implement strategies for the digital training of workers and establish a minimum income for those who lose their jobs as a result of digital advances; (iii) bring appropriate contents to this technological age, such as the right to digital disconnection and the protection of privacy and workers' data, to collective bargaining; (iv) protect workers, regardless of whether they be employees or freelancers; and (v) employ technology to create new solidarity networks among workers, particularly in the case of digital platforms. In 1999, Richard Hyman[48] said that trade unions themselves were not in crisis, but the way in which trade unionism was acting in defence of the rights and interests of workers certainly was. He also said that trade union hierarchies would have to give way to worker networks, moving towards "virtual trade unions". It appears that the time has now come to do this.

---

46 *Ibid.* p. 270.
47 See Michele Forlivesi, "*La sfida della rappresentanza sindacale dei lavoratori 2.0,*" *op. cit.*, p. 675.
48 See Richard Hyman, "Imagined solidarities: can trade unions resist globalization?" (1999), http://globalsolidarity.antenna.nl/hyman2.html (retrieved 8 March 2019).

V Bibliography

Arnzt, Melanie, Terry Gregory, and Ulrich Zierahn, "The risk of automation for jobs in OCDE countries," *OECD Social, Employment and Migration Working Papers*, 189 (2016), 1–34.

Autor, Daniel, "The polarization of jobs opportunities in the U.S. Labour Market" (2010) www.americanprogress.org/wp-content/uploads/issues/2010/04/pdf/job_polarization_execsumm.pdf.

Brynjolfssons, Erik, and Andrew McAffe, *The Second Machine Age. Work, Progress, and Prosperity in a Time of Brilliant Technologies* (2014), New York, W. W. Norton & Company.

Degryse, Christophe, "Digitalisation of the economy and its impact on labour markets," *Working Paper ETUI 2016.02* (2016), 1–80.

De Stefano, Valerio, "Non-standard work and limits on freedom of association: a human rights-based approach," *Industrial Law Journal*, 46 (2017), 185–207.

ETUC, "Towards fair digital work" (2016) www.etuc.org/documents/etuc-resolution-digitalisation-towards-fair-digital-work#.WlthcxRTO6j.

ETUC, "Resolution on tackling new digital challenges to the world of labour, in particular crowdwork" (2017), www.etuc.org/documents/tackling-new-digital-challenges-world-labour-particular-crowdwork#.Wlt9fxRTO6g.

Eurofound, "New forms of employment" (2015), www.eurofound.europa.eu/sites/default/files/ef_publication/field_ef_document/ef1461en.pdf.

Eurofound, and OIT, "Working anytime anywhere: the effects on the world of work" (2017), https://www.eurofound.europa.eu/sites/default/files/ef_publication/field_ef_document/ef1658en.pdf.

Ferry, Luc, *La revolución transhumanista. Como la tecnomedicina y la uberización del mundo van a transformar nuestras vidas* (2017), Madrid, Alianza Editorial.

Forlivesi, Michele, "La sfida della rapresentanza sindacale dei lavoratori 2.0," Diritto delle Relazioni Industriali, 3 (2016), 664–678.

Graham, Mark and Alex Wood, "Why the digital gig economy needs co-ops and unions" (2017), www.opendemocracy.net/alex-wood/why-digital-gig-economy-needs-co-ops-and-unions.

Hyman, Richard, "Imagined solidarities: can trade unions resist globalization?" (1999), http://globalsolidarity.antenna.nl/hyman2.html.

Hobsbawn, Eric J., "The machine breakers" *Past and Present*, 1 (1952), 57–70.

Huws, Ursula, *Labor in the Global Digital Economy. The Cybertariat Comes of Age* (2014), New York, Monthly Review Press.

Huws, Ursula, Neil H. Spencer, and Simon Joyce, "Crowd work in Europe. Preliminary results from survey in the UK, Sweden, Germany, Austria and the Netherlands" (2016), www.feps-europe.eu/assets/39aad271-85ff-457c-8b23-b30d82bb808f/crowd-work-in-europe-draft-report-last-versionpdf.pdf.

Irani, Lilly, "Justice for 'data janitors'" (2015), www.publicbooks.org/justice-for-data-janitors/.

Irani, Lilly, and Six Silverman, "Turkopticon: interrupting worker invisibility in Amazon mechanical turk" (2013), http://wtf.tw/text/turkopticon.pdf.

Keynes, John Maynard, "Economic possibilities for our grandchildren," In *Essays in Persuasion* (1930), New York, Harcourt Brace.

LaPlante, Rochelle and Six Silveman, "Building trust in crowd worker forums: worker ownership, governance, and work outcomes" (2016), http://trustincrowdwork.west.uni-koblenz.de/sites/trustincrowdwork.west.uni-koblenz.de/files/laplante_trust.pdf.

Lehdonvirta, Vili, "Algorithms that divide and unite: delocalization, identity, and collective action in 'microwork'" (2016), http://vili.lehdonvirta.com/files/Lehdonvirta%20 2016%20Delocalization%20identity%20collective%20action%20in%20microwork.pdf.

McKinsey, "What the future of work will mean for jobs, skills, and wages" (2017), www.mckinsey.com/global-themes/future-of-organizations-and-work/what-the-future-of-work-will-mean-for-jobs-skills-and-wages.

Meyer, Henning, "Inequality in the second machine age: the need for a social democratic digital society" *Juncture*, 23 (2016), 102–106.

Schmidt, Florian A., "Digital labour markets in the platform economy" (2017), http://library.fes.de/pdf-files/wiso/13164.pdf.

Schumpeter, Joseph A., "The process of creative destruction," In *Capitalism, Socialism, and Democracy* (1942), London, Allen & Unwin.

Srnicek, Nick, *Platform Capitalism* (2017), Cambridge, Polity Press.

UNI Global Union, "Top 10 principles for workers' data privacy and protection" (2017), www.thefutureworldofwork.org/media/35421/uni_workers_data_protection.pdf.

Valenduc, Gérard and Patricia Vendramin, "Work in the digital economy: sorting the old from the new", *Working Paper ETUI 2016.03* (2016), 1–51.

Weber, Thiébaut "Janus and the trade unión challenge of digital technology," *Transfer: European Review of Labour and Research*, 23 (2017), 225–227.

Webster, Juliet, "Microworkers of the gig economy: separate and precarious," *New Labor Forum*, 25 (3) (2016), 56–64.

Webster, Juliet, and Keith Randler, *Virtual Workers and the Global Labour Market* (2016), London, Palgrave McMillan.

Wood, Alex J., "Networks of injustice and worker mobilisation at Walmart," *Industrial Relations Journal*, 46 (2015), 259–274.

World Economic Forum, "The future of jobs. Employment, skills and workforce strategy for the Fourth Industrial Revolution" (2016), www3.weforum.org/docs/WEF_Future_of_Jobs.pdf.

13 Emerging skills and occupations in the Fourth Industrial Revolution

How to respond to changing work demands

Aneta Tyc

I Introduction*

As Richard Riley, the US Secretary of Education under President Bill Clinton, pointed out:

> The top 10 jobs (...) in demand in 2010 did not exist in 2004. We are currently preparing students for jobs that don't exist yet, using technologies that haven't been invented, in order to solve problems, we don't even know are problems yet.[1]

The changes triggered by the Fourth Industrial Revolution are considered fundamental challenges to the future of work. Despite the growing debate, attention to emerging occupations and new skills needed in the Industry 4.0 framework and to ways of supporting their development is lacking currently. The purpose of this chapter is to fill this gap by discussing these matters.

But first things first. How did we arrive at the Fourth Industrial Revolution? The First Industrial Revolution, which had its origins in the second half of the eighteenth century, was related to a transformation from manual to mechanised production, especially by using water and steam power. The Second Industrial Revolution, beginning in the later third of the nineteenth century, used electric power to create mass production, involved division of labour and the rise of the oil and steel industries. The Third Industrial Revolution, with the shift from analogue to digital technologies that used electronics and information technology to automate production, was getting underway almost 100 years later, in the 1950s. The Fourth Industrial Revolution has been appearing since the midst of the last century. One of its characteristics is the fusion of technologies that is effacing

---

* The article results from the research conducted at the University of Łódź and funded under the grant for the development of young scientists and doctoral candidates in 2017 (source of funding: Ministry of Science and Higher Education, Poland). Project's number: B171190 0001771.02.

1 Karl Fisch, Scott McLeod, "Shift happens", 2007, video, 6:07, https://shifthappens.wikispaces.com.

the boundaries between the physical, digital and biological spheres.[2] According to Caruso,[3] the Fourth Industrial Revolution (also referred to as Industry 4.0)[4] relies on a new era of technological innovation: multidirectional communication between manufacturing processes and products (internet of things); machine learning; Artificial Intelligence; interconnected collaborative robots; simulation of interconnected machines; integration of the information flow along the value chain, from the supplier to the consumer; 3D printers connected to digital development software; analysis of large databases to optimise products and processes (big data and analytics); and management of large amounts of data on open systems (cloud computing). Moreover, as stated by Schwab, it embraces a wide range of areas, from renewables to quantum computing and from gene sequencing to nanotechnology.[5]

Occupational and skill changes are perceived as having a continuous character and are mostly propelled by technological advancement.[6] "Thanks to technological innovations, the world of work is being enriched with new professions while others are disappearing".[7] However, the transition is reinforced not only by technological progress, but also by other megatrends, for example, globalisation, climate change and demographic shift (ageing population).[8] What should be highlighted is a polarised nature of new jobs and new skills, at least when speaking about developed economies. The polarisation of labour takes the form of a U-shaped curve, where the demand for labour does not rise linearly with the skill level. The polarisation can be described as fostering low-skilled and high-skilled jobs. On the one hand, new employer strategies would produce flexible, highly skilled workers in secure employment, and on the other hand, they would create flexible, low-skilled and highly disposable workers. This generates

---

2 Sean T. Monohan, "Who will lead the fourth industrial revolution?," *Logistics Management* 56, no. 10 (2017): 16; Michael A. Peters, "Technological unemployment: educating for the fourth industrial revolution," *Educational Philosophy and Theory* 49, no. 1 (2017): 3, http://dx.doi.org/10.1080/00131857.2016.1177412; Klaus Schwab, "The fourth industrial revolution: what it means and how to respond," 12 December 2015, accessed 28 April 2018, www.vassp.org.au/webpages/Documents2016/PDevents/The%20Fourth%20Industrial%20Revolution%20by%20Klaus%20Schwab.pdf.
3 Loris Caruso, "Digital innovation and the fourth industrial revolution: epochal social changes?," *AI & Society* (2017), https://doi.org/10.1007/s00146-017-0736-1.
4 Some authors, however, highlight that the two terms do not mean exactly the same thing. See: Luca Mari et al., "Industria 4.0: una nuova rivoluzione?," *Sviluppo & Organizzazione* 277 (August/September 2017): 42–43.
5 Klaus Schwab, "Welcome to the fourth industrial revolution," *Rotman Management* (Fall 2016): 19. See also: Angelo Salento, "*Industria 4.0*, Imprese, Lavoro. Problemi interpretativi e prospettive," *Rivista giuridica del lavoro e della previdenza sociale*, no. 2 (April–June 2017): 175.
6 Miroslav Beblavý et al., "What are the new occupations and the new skills? And how are they measured?," State of the art report, working paper, Leuven, InGRID project, M21.6, (2016): 28. See the cited literature.
7 "Compendium of the Social Doctrine of the Church," accessed 28 April 2018, www.vatican.va/roman_curia/pontifical_councils/justpeace/documents/rc_pc_justpeace_doc_20060526_compendio-dott-soc_en.html.
8 Beblavý et al., "What are," 4 and 7.

confusion not only about the needed assortment of skills, but also about the way training and education policies should go.[9]

Before scrutinising certain forms of supporting development of new skills and occupations in more detail, it is proposed first to define an occupation and a job and concentrate on the new skills themselves.

II Jobs/occupations

A definition of an occupation embraces multiple jobs or job titles that share common characteristics and can be expressed as "a grouping of jobs involving similar tasks, which require a similar skill set". On the contrary, a job "is bound to a specific work context and executed by one person".[10] New occupations burgeon together with the employers' demand for workers who fulfil tasks that have never been fulfilled before. Workers in already existing occupations generally attach these new tasks to their jobs. In this manner, sometimes a specialty can emerge. It can expand to be an occupation in the full sense of the word if the needed task is adequately different and arises as the primary job of enough workers.[11]

It is not easy to identify new occupations and skills. Generally, it can be assumed that new occupations shall mean these, which only recently have materialised and are not yet incorporated into the most current occupational classification system. Examples of classifications of occupations and skills include: International Standard Classification of Education (ISCED), United Nations, International Standard Classification of Occupations (ISCO), United Nations, Dictionary of Occupational Titles (DOT), US Department of Labor, an online version of the Dictionary of Occupational Titles (O*NET), US Department of Labor, Standard Occupational Classification (SOC), US Department of Labor, European Dictionary of Skills and Competences (DISCO), European Commission and European Skills, Competences, Qualifications and Occupations (ESCO), European Commission together with *Centre Européen pour le Développement de la Formation Professionnelle* (CEDEFOP).[12]

A great transformation of the world of work is reflected in the more than 1,500 new job titles that appeared in the occupational classifications from the

---

9 Beblavý et al., "What are," 24; Michael Rose, Penn Roger and Rubery Jill, "Introduction: the SCELI skill findings," in *Skill and Occupational Change*, eds. Roger Penn, Rose Michael, Rubery Jill (Oxford: Oxford University Press, 1994), 3; Hilary Metcalf, "Introduction," in *Future Skill Demand and Supply. Trends, Shortages and Gluts*, ed. Hilary Metcalf (London: Policy Studies Institute, 1995), 1; Carl B. Frey, Michael Osborne, "Technology at work: the future of innovation and employment," *Citi GPS: Global Perspectives & Solutions* (February 2015): 19–21, accessed 28 April 2018, www.oxfordmartin.ox.ac.uk/downloads/reports/Citi_GPS_Technology_Work.pdf; Valeria Cirillo, "Technology, employment and skills," *Economics of Innovation and New Technology* 26, no. 8 (2017): 734, http://dx.doi.org/10.1080/10438599.2017.1258765.
10 Beblavý et al., "What are," 8.
11 Olivia Crosby, "New and emerging occupations," *Occupational Outlook Quarterly* 46, no. 3 (2002): 17.
12 Beblavý et al., "What are," 12 and 14–22.

time when the PC was invented. Digital technology has opened the door to the emergence of entirely new occupations and industries. Thanks to the computer technology, many new occupations (e.g. database administrators and web designers) have recently been created.[13] Among jobs desirable in the digital world are, for example, out-of-the-box thinkers, human interaction designer, artificial intelligence (AI)/machine learning researcher, AI software developer, machine learning applier, data fluency experts, full-stack developers, content engineers, people skills manager and 3D designers[14] or even 4D designers, who could develop self-altering products being able to answer to environmental changes, for example, heat and humidity (this kind of technology could be used in clothing, footwear or for implants designed to conform to the human body)[15] and finally, designers of self-driving cars.[16]

III Skills

"Skill is proficiency at a given task, usually acquired through learning and experience".[17] The stability of expectations is a guarantee of the smooth operation of all types of skills-creation systems. In circumstances where there are whole new sectors, an uncertainty concerning the kind of required preparation appears.[18] New tasks that are introduced determine the identification of new skills and new knowledge.[19] When one considers, for instance, graphic designers, until recently almost all of them designed for print. Web designers became much in demand with the advent of internet and mobile designers with the outset of smart-phones.[20]

According to World Economic Forum,[21] within the skills needed in all jobs across all industries, the skills most required in 2020 will be complex problem-solving skills. There will be an increase in the demand for jobs requiring social skills that involve persuasion, face-to-face or voice-to-voice customer contact and emotional intelligence. The latter (also referred to as emotional

---

13 Frey and Osborne, "Technology," 63.
14 Richa Goel, "Top new skills needed in the world of digitization," 2017, accessed 28 April 2018, www.tutorialspoint.com/articles/top-new-skills-needed-in-the-world-of-digitization.
15 Schwab, "Welcome," 21.
16 See: Jerry Kaplan, *Le persone non servono. Lavoro e ricchezza nell'epoca dell'intelligenza artificiale*, trans. Ilaria V. Tomasello (Roma: LUISS University Press, 2016), 20.
17 Paul Blyton and Jean Jenkins, *Key Concepts in Work* (Los Angeles, London, New Delhi, Singapore: Sage Publications, 2007), 194.
18 Colin Crouch, "Skill formation systems," in *The Oxford Handbook of Work and Organization*, eds. Stephen Ackroyd, Batt Rosemary, Thompson Paul, Tolbert Pamela S. (Oxford: Oxford University Press, 2005), 104.
19 Beblavý et al., "What are," 13.
20 James Bessen, "Employers aren't just whining – the "skills gap" is real," *Harvard Business Review Digital Articles*, 25 August 2014.
21 World Economic Forum, WEF, "The future of jobs. Employment, skills and workforce strategy for the fourth industrial revolution," Global Challenge Insight Report, 2016, 21–22, accessed 28 April 2018, www3.weforum.org/docs/WEF_Future_of_Jobs.pdf.

labour/emotional work) means the capability of regulating one's own and other's emotions[22] so that they are adequate for any given situation. Social guidelines ("a set of shared, albeit often latent, rules") are used in order to help assess the situation correctly, produce the expected feeling and fit together the emotion and the situation. As a consequence, social stability is encouraged.[23] Another among the most needed skills will be process skills (active listening, critical thinking), systems skills (judgement and decision-making, systems analysis) and cognitive abilities (creativity, mathematical reasoning).[24]

Fidler and Gorbis, researchers from the Institute for the Future, indicate ten specific skills that are crucial for the future workforce[25]:

1 Computational thinking (ability to comprehend reasoning based on data; ability to translate large data quantities into abstract concepts)
2 Design mindset (ability to represent and develop tasks and work processes for the wanted effect)
3 Cognitive load management (ability to distinguish and select information with regard to importance; ability to comprehend how to enhance cognitive functioning using a variety of tools and techniques)
4 New media literacy (critical ability to assess and develop content that uses new media forms, e.g. video; ability to use these media for persuasive communication)
5 Transdisciplinary (literacy in and ability to comprehend concepts related to many different disciplines)
6 Sense-making (ability to discover the deeper sense or significance of what is being expressed)
7 Social intelligence (ability to join other people in a direct way; ability to sense and provoke reactions and desired interactions)
8 Novel and adaptive thinking (being good at thinking about and coming up with ideas and solutions beyond those that are scheme based)
9 Cross-cultural competency (ability to perform in diverse cultural arrangements)
10 Virtual collaboration (ability to work productively, drive engagement and display presence as a member of a virtual team)

The O*NET database in the United States proves that the information technology category of occupations has the highest percentage of occupations qualified

---

22 Sharon C. Bolton, "Conceptual confusions: emotion work as skilled work," in *The Skills That Matter*, eds. Chris Warhurst, Grugulis Irena and Keep Ewart (Basingstoke: Palgrave Macmillan, 2004), 19; Francis Green, *Skills and Skilled Work. An Economic and Social Analysis* (Oxford: Oxford University Press, 2013), 22.
23 Bolton, "Conceptual," 23.
24 World Economic Forum, WEF, "The future," 21–23.
25 Devin Fidler, and Marina Gorbis, "Are you fit for the future? 10 new skills that every worker needs," *IESE Insight*, no. 12 (First Quarter 2012): 30–35.

as having a bright outlook through 2022. This means that there is a continued growth for information and communication technologies (ICT) jobs and a need to promote ICT skills among workers.[26] The expansion of the ICT at work augments the demand for:

1 ICT specialist skills to programme, advance applications and manage networks; these skills are needed for the process of development of ICT products and services (e.g. software, web pages, e-commerce, cloud, big data)
2 ICT generic skills to use such technologies for professional aims (e.g. access information online, use software)
3 ICT complementary skills to accomplish new tasks related to the use of ICT at work (e.g. communicate on social networks, brand products on e-commerce platforms or analyse big data)[27]

According to Accenture's report entitled "New Skills Now. Inclusion in the digital economy",[28] the universal skill families and the cognitive capabilities needed for inclusion in the digital economy are:

1 Learn to Earn (foundational skills to get work and be ready for the workforce)
2 Build Tech Know-How (skills and know-how to use, manipulate and create technologies and data)
3 Apply We'Q (skills to interact, establish relationships and display self-awareness necessary to work effectively with other people in person and online)
4 Create and Solve (skills to approach problem solving creatively, using logic, novel thinking and empathy)
5 Cultivate a Growth Mindset (skills to stay relevant, ceaselessly learn and be capable of adapting to change)
6 Specialise for Work (proper skills to respond to local market and industry needs)

IV Methods of supporting the development of emerging skills and occupations

Is law an appropriate measure to promote the development of emerging skills and occupations? Is enhancement of skills a question of law? It might seem that it

---

26 OECD, "Skills and jobs in the Internet economy," OECD Digital Economy Papers, no. 242 (Paris: OECD Publishing, 2014): 4, http://dx.doi.org/10.1787/5jxvbrjm9bns-en.
27 OECD, "New skills for the digital economy: measuring the demand and supply of ICT skills at work. 2016 ministerial meeting on the digital economy technical report," OECD Digital Economy Papers, no. 258 (Paris: OECD Publishing, 2016): 4–5, http://dx.doi.org.002d1d8f67d9. han3.lib.uni.lodz.pl/10.1787/5jlwnkm2fc9x-en.
28 Accenture, "New Skills Now. Inclusion in the digital economy," (2017): 13, accessed 28 April 2018, www.accenture.com/t20171012T025413Z__w__/in-en/_acnmedia/PDF-62/Accenture-New-Skills-Now-Report.pdf.

is not at all. However, as rightly stated by Servais,[29] legal measures are necessary in order to deploy the suitable policy. The author then argues that:

> It is through legal texts that the principles underpinning the system are established, choices made or comprises reached between sometimes conflicting objectives. It is through them that concepts are translated into action, i.e. into training programmes and conditions for the granting of benefits, into means of stimulating workers to retrain, into administrative and financial structures, into consultations with employers' and workers' organizations. (...).

In searching for a legal foundation of vocational training, we should refer to international law. In the article 6 of the United Nations International Covenant on Economic, Social and Cultural Rights (1966), vocational guidance and training programmes are seen as a step to be taken by a State Party to the Covenant to achieve the full realisation of the right to work. By contrast, in the article 13 they are linked to the right of everyone to education.

The International Labour Organisation (ILO) Constitution names the organisation of vocational and technical education as a measure of improvement of labour conditions. According to the Declaration concerning the aims and purposes of the ILO (Declaration of Philadelphia): "The Conference recognizes the solemn obligation of the International Labour Organization to further among the nations of the world programmes which will achieve: (...) (c) the provision (...) of facilities for training (...)". In 1975, the ILO adopted the Convention concerning Vocational Guidance and Vocational Training in the Development of Human Resources (No. 142) and in 2004, the Recommendation concerning Human Resources Development: Education, Training and Lifelong Learning (No. 195). ILO's Convention concerning Paid Educational Leave (No. 140) of 1974 discerns the need for adult education.[30]

UNESCO adopted the Revised Recommendation concerning Technical and Vocational Education (1974), the Convention on Technical and Vocational Education (1989) and the Recommendation concerning the Status of Higher-Education Teaching Personnel (1997).

Leaving aside the legal issues and focusing on the policymaking, some of the proposals made in the area of supporting the development of emerging skills and occupations are: upskilling and reskilling jobseekers (using periods of unemployment), establishment of bipartite training funds,[31] standards-based educational reforms which, as an example of a successful programme undertaken by a Boston

---

29 Jean-Michel Servais, *International Labour Law* (Alphen aan den Rijn: Wolters Kluwer, 2014), 160.
30 See more: Servais, *International*, 156–157.
31 World Employment Confederation, WEC, "The future of work. White Paper from the employment industry," 2016, 18, accessed 28 April 2018, www.weceurope.org/fileadmin/templates/ciett/docs/WEC___The_Future_of_Work_-_What_role_for_the_employment_industry.pdf.

public elementary school shows, are neither simple nor cheap, and involve both a great deal of direct student-teacher interaction and guided interaction among students.[32] Besides, initiatives such as supporting mobility, targeting female talent and cross-industry and public-private collaboration are under discussion in order to improve the future workforce planning.[33] Moreover, supporting lifelong learning should be mentioned.[34] It is important to promote Massive Open Online Courses (MOOCs) and Open Educational Resources (OER), which enable a greater number of people to obtain access to good quality resources over more flexible hours.[35] The great advantage of MOOCs is linked to the fact that students can access the best teachers and content, notwithstanding their location. Additionally, virtually no cost is associated with starting a new course while looking for employment.[36] As highlighted by Peters,[37] by providing accessible, flexible and affordable courses, the MOOCs promise to open up school-level and higher education. Open education and a range of platforms being used create opportunities for innovation and exploration new learning models and practices. Policymakers, on the one hand, need to embrace openness and make education accessible and affordable, but also, on the other hand, not forget to make it profitable for institutions in an open higher education level. By modifying the learning process and giving students a choice of skills and competencies to acquire without necessarily completing a standardised academic programme, MOOCs have a potential to provide modularised approaches to education. This is likely to meet with approval of employers looking to retrain their workforce.[38] However, online courses should not be treated as a full substitute for on-campus teaching. Physical interactions between students and students and teachers are

---

32 Frank Levy and Richard J. Murnane, *The New Division of Labor: How Computers Are Creating the Next Job Market* (New York: Russell Sage Foundation, and Princeton and Oxford: Princeton University Press, 2004).
33 World Economic Forum, WEF, "The future," 30 and 32.
34 World Employment Confederation, WEC, "The Future," 18. See more: Guus Heerma van Voss, "Life-long-learning as an individual social right," in *Social Responsibility in Labour Relations. European and Comparative Perspectives*, eds. Frans Pennings, Konijn Yvonne, and Veldman Albertine (Austin-Boston-Chicago-New York-The Netherlands: Wolters Kluwer, 2008), 119 et seq.
35 OECD, "Skills for a Digital World: 2016 Ministerial Meeting on the Digital Economy Background Report," OECD Digital Economy Papers, no. 250 (Paris: OECD Publishing, 2016): 4, http://dx.doi.org.002d1d8f67d9.han3.lib.uni.lodz.pl/10.1787/5jlwz83z3wnw-en.
36 Frey and Osborne, "Technology," 90.
37 Peters, "Technological," 5.
38 See also: Erik Brynjolfsson, Andrew McAfee (2014), *La nuova rivoluzione delle macchine. Lavoro e prosperità nell'era della tecnologia trionfante*, trans. Giancarlo Carlotti (Milano: Giangiacomo Feltrinelli Editore Milano, 2014), 212–213 and 222. Moreover, ICT are beneficial when it comes to self-learning, because learning retention by "doing" is 80% and by reading or hearing only 5%–10%. This could be an important tool for closing the skills gap itself. See: European Commission, "Employment in the Information Society," in *Rise of the Knowledge Worker*, ed. James W. Cortada (Boston-Oxford-Johannesburg-Melbourne-New Delhi-Singapore: Butterworth-Heinemann, 1998), 196.

likely to become even more important, because, as it has been stated before, social, creative and problem-solving skills will be relevant in the future.[39]

According to Fidler and Gorbis,[40] it may become a necessity for human resources professionals to rethink the existing methods for identifying, selecting and developing talent. The possible direction of change can be based on collaborating with providers of executive education or universities in order to deal with lifelong learning and skills improvement. Within the fields to be reconsidered, the authors mention:

1. Broadening the learning constituency across all age groups
2. Putting extra stress on developing skills (e.g. critical thinking, insight and analysis capabilities)
3. Devoting attention to experiential learning which provide significance to soft skills[41] (e.g. the ability to read social cues, respond adaptively, collaborate and work in groups)
4. Concentrating more on interdisciplinary training, which allows people to gain skills and knowledge across a broader range of disciplines
5. Focusing more on new media literacy and incorporating it into training programmes

Moreover, after the relevant skills were obtained by the employees, companies should enhance their ability to ensure that those skills are constantly renewed with the aim of achieving and sustaining business objectives.

The OECD has elaborated a comprehensive Skills Strategy entitled "Skills for a Digital World", with the aim of helping countries to find out the strengths and weaknesses of their national skills systems and compare them internationally. The goal of the OECD Skills Strategy is also to enhance policies aimed at transformation of better skills into better jobs, social inclusion and economic growth. The document presents the three-step approach to address the opportunities and challenges for skill development in the digital economy. The first step is to detail the sort of skills needed in the digital economy. The definition of an agreed framework for digital literacy, the development of new surveys and further cross-country analysis of existing datasets can be useful for the achievement of this objective. The second step is to analyse the way these changes may affect curriculum reform, teacher training and professional development. The third step is to make use of the ICT to extend the access to education and training and

---

39 Frey and Osborne, "Technology," 90–91. See more: Riccardo Staglianò, *Al posto tuo. Così web e robot ci stanno rubando il lavoro* (Torino: Giulio Einaudi editore s.p.a., 2016), 145–158; Martin Ford, *Il futuro senza lavoro. Accelerazione tecnologica e macchine intelligenti. Come prepararsi alla rivoluzione economica in arrivo*, trans. Matteo Vegetti (Milano: il Saggiatore, 2017), 142–145.
40 Fidler and Gorbis, "Are you," 35.
41 About digital soft skills for management see: Francesco Venier, "La forza lavoro digitale e il futuro dell'organizzazione," *Sviluppo & Organizzazione* 277 (August/September 2017): 56–57.

to enhance their quality. This should be done, for example, through new learning tools at school, adequate recognition of skills acquired through informal learning and online courses, what has been discussed above.[42]

In relation to the problem of new skills, we should also recognise the efforts made by the European Commission, which in 2008 published a communication entitled "New Skills for New Jobs: Anticipating and matching labour market and skills needs".[43] In 2010, the Expert Group on New Skills for New Jobs issued a report entitled "New Skills for New Jobs: Action Now",[44] which was prepared for the European Commission, and in 2016 the debate was underpinned by the communication entitled "A New Skills Agenda for Europe. Working Together to Strengthen Human Capital, Employability and Competitiveness".[45]

V Conclusions

The purpose of this chapter was to explore emerging occupations and new skills needed in the Industry 4.0 framework, and to identify forms of supporting their development. Along with new businesses and new markets come new job categories. In this context, an indicative phrase, pronounced by the Rector of Harvard in the well-known movie "The Social Network" (2010, directed by David Fincher), sounds particularly true: "Harvard undergraduates believe that inventing a job is better than finding a job".[46] In fact, many of the most popular jobs in Industry 4.0 did not exist 10 years ago. Cloud computing specialists, app developers, data scientists, rideshare drivers, drone operators and driverless car engineers are examples of high-demand jobs created, thanks to technological advancement.[47] The analysis of the extant literature reveals that, of the skills needed in all jobs across all industries, the ones most required in 2020 will be complex problem-solving skills. There will be an increase in the demand for jobs requiring social skills, process skills, systems skills and cognitive abilities. There is little doubt that the expansion of the ICTs at work augments the demand

---

42 OECD, "Skills for," 4–5.
43 European Commission, "Communication from the Commission to the European Parliament, the Council, the European Economic and Social Committee and the Committee of the Regions: New Skills for New Jobs: Anticipating and matching labour market and skills needs" (Brussels, 2008), COM (2008) 868/3.
44 Expert Group on New Skills for New Jobs, "New Skills for New Jobs: action now. A report by the Expert Group on New Skills for New Jobs prepared for the European Commission," 2010.
45 European Commission, "Communication from the Commission to the European Parliament, the Council, the European Economic and Social Committee and the Committee of the Regions. A new skills agenda for Europe. Working together to strengthen human capital, employability and competitiveness" (Brussels 2016), COM(2016) 381 final, http://eur-lex.europa.eu/legal-content/EN/TXT/HTML/?uri=CELEX:52016DC0381&from=EN.
46 Claudio Panella, *A proposito di lavoro. Da Labor a Industria 4.0* (Bordeaux, 2017), 25–26.
47 Paul Baldassari and Jonathan D. Roux, "Industry 4.0: preparing for the future of work," *People & Strategy* 40, no. 3 (2017): 21.

for ICT specialist skills to programme, advance applications and manage networks; ICT generic skills to use such technologies for professional aims; and ICT complementary skills. Findings suggest that law should be treated as one of the methods of supporting the development of emerging skills and occupations. It is surely correct to support other methods: for example, upskilling and reskilling jobseekers, establishing bipartite training funds, standards-based educational reforms, supporting mobility, targeting female talent, cross-industry and public-private collaboration, and lifelong learning.

VI Bibliography

Accenture. "New skills now. Inclusion in the digital economy." 2017. Accessed April 28, 2018. www.accenture.com/t20171012T025413Z__w__/in-en/_acnmedia/PDF-62/Accenture-New-Skills-Now-Report.pdf.

Baldassari, Paul and Jonathan D. Roux. "Industry 4.0: preparing for the future of work." *People & Strategy* 40, no. 3 (2017): 20–23.

Beblavý Miroslav, Akgüc Mehtap, Fabo Brian and Lenaerts Karolien. "What are the new occupations and the new skills? And how are they measured?" State of the art report, Working paper, Leuven, InGRID project, M21.6 (2016).

Bessen, James. "Employers aren't just whining – the "skills gap" is real." *Harvard Business Review Digital Articles*, August 25, 2014.

Blyton, Paul, and Jean Jenkins. *Key Concepts in Work*. Los Angeles, London, New Delhi, Singapore: Sage Publications, 2007.

Bolton, Sharon C. "Conceptual confusions: emotion work as skilled work." In *The Skills That Matter*, edited by Chris Warhurst, Grugulis Irena and Keep Ewart, 19–37. Basingstoke: Palgrave Macmillan, 2004.

Brynjolfsson, Erik and Andrew McAfee. *La nuova rivoluzione delle macchine. Lavoro e prosperità nell`era della tecnologia trionfante*. Translated by Giancarlo Carlotti. Milano: Giangiacomo Feltrinelli Editore Milano, 2014.

Caruso, Loris. "Digital innovation and the fourth industrial revolution: epochal social changes?" *AI & Society* (2017) https://doi.org/10.1007/s00146-017-0736-1.

Cirillo, Valeria. "Technology, employment and skills." *Economics of Innovation and New Technology* 26, no. 8 (2017): 734–754, http://dx.doi.org/10.1080/10438599.2017.1258765.

"Compendium of the Social Doctrine of the Church." Accessed April 28, 2018, www.vatican.va/roman_curia/pontifical_councils/justpeace/documents/rc_pc_justpeace_doc_20060526_compendio-dott-soc_en.html.

Crosby, Olivia. "New and emerging occupations." *Occupational Outlook Quarterly* 46, no. 3 (2002): 17–25.

Crouch, Colin. "Skill formation systems." In *the Oxford Handbook of Work and Organization*, edited by Stephen Ackroyd, Batt Rosemary, Thompson Paul, Tolbert Pamela S., 95–114. Oxford: Oxford University Press, 2005.

Expert Group on New Skills for New Jobs. "New skills for new jobs: action now. A report by the Expert Group on New Skills for New Jobs prepared for the European Commission." 2010.

European Commission. "Employment in the information society." In *Rise of the Knowledge Worker*, edited by James W. Cortada, 189–198. Boston-Oxford-Johannesburg-Melbourne-New Delhi-Singapore: Butterworth-Heinemann, 1998.

European Commission. "Communication from the Commission to the European Parliament, the Council, the European Economic and Social Committee and the Committee of the Regions: new skills for new jobs: anticipating and matching labour market and skills needs." Brussels, 2008. COM(2008) 868/3.

European Commission. "Communication from the Commission to the European Parliament, the Council, the European Economic and Social Committee and the Committee of the Regions. A new skills agenda for Europe. Working together to strengthen human capital, employability and competitiveness." Brussels 2016. COM(2016) 381 final, http://eur-lex.europa.eu/legal-content/EN/TXT/HTML/?uri=CELEX:52016DC0381&from=EN.

Fidler, Devin, and Marina Gorbis. "Are you fit for the future? 10 New skills that every worker needs." *IESE Insight*, no. 12 (First Quarter 2012): 29–35.

Fisch Karl, Scott McLeod, "Shift happens." 2007, video, 6:07, https://shifthappens.wikispaces.com.

Goel, Richa. "Top new skills needed in the world of digitization." 2017. Accessed April 28, 2018. www.tutorialspoint.com/articles/top-new-skills-needed-in-the-world-of-digitization.

Ford, Martin. *Il futuro senza lavoro. Accelerazione tecnologica e macchine intelligenti. Come prepararsi alla rivoluzione economica in arrivo.* Translated by Matteo Vegetti. Milano: il Saggiatore, 2017.

Frey, Carl B. and Michael Osborne, "Technology at work: The future of innovation and employment." *Citi GPS: Global Perspectives & Solutions* (February 2015), accessed April 28, 2018, www.oxfordmartin.ox.ac.uk/downloads/reports/Citi_GPS_Technology_Work.pdf.

Green, Francis. *Skills and Skilled Work. An Economic and Social Analysis.* Oxford: Oxford University Press, 2013.

Kaplan, Jerry. *Le persone non servono. Lavoro e ricchezza nell'epoca dell'intelligenza artificiale.* Translated by Ilaria V. Tomasello. Roma: LUISS University Press, 2016.

Levy, Frank, and Richard J. Murnane. *The New Division of Labor: How Computers Are Creating the Next Job Market.* New York: Russell Sage Foundation, and Princeton and Oxford: Princeton University Press, 2004.

Mari Luca, Astuti Samuele, Ravarini Aurelio, Ruffini Renato, "Industria 4.0: una nuova rivoluzione?" *Sviluppo & Organizzazione* 277 (August/September 2017): 40–52.

Metcalf, Hilary. "Introduction." In *Future Skill Demand and Supply. Trends, Shortages and Gluts*, edited by Hilary Metcalf, 1–5. London: Policy Studies Institute, 1995.

Monohan, Sean T. "Who will lead the fourth industrial revolution?" *Logistics Management* 56, no. 10 (2017): 16–17.

OECD, "Skills and jobs in the Internet economy." OECD Digital Economy Papers, no. 242. Paris: OECD Publishing, 2014. http://dx.doi.org/10.1787/5jxvbrjm9bns-en.

OECD. "New skills for the digital economy: measuring the demand and supply of ICT skills at work. 2016 ministerial meeting on the digital economy technical report." OECD Digital Economy Papers, no. 258. Paris: OECD Publishing, 2016. http://dx.doi.org.002d1d8f67d9.han3.lib.uni.lodz.pl/10.1787/5jlwnkm2fc9x-en.

OECD, "Skills for a digital world: 2016 ministerial meeting on the digital economy background report." OECD Digital Economy Papers, no. 250. Paris: OECD Publishing, 2016. http://dx.doi.org.002d1d8f67d9.han3.lib.uni.lodz.pl/10.1787/5jlwz83z3wnw-en.

Panella, Claudio. *A proposito di lavoro. Da Labor a Industria 4.0.* Bordeaux, 2017.

Peters, Michael A. "Technological unemployment: educating for the fourth industrial revolution." *Educational Philosophy and Theory* 49, no. 1 (2017): 1–6. http://dx.doi.org/10.1080/00131857.2016.1177412.

Rose, Michael, Penn Roger and Rubery Jill, "Introduction: the SCELI skill findings." In *Skill and Occupational Change*, edited by Roger Penn, Rose Michael, Rubery Jill, 1–37. Oxford: Oxford University Press, 1994.

Salento, Angelo, "Industria 4.0, Imprese, Lavoro. Problemi interpretativi e prospettive." *Rivista giuridica del lavoro e della previdenza sociale*, no. 2 (April-June 2017): 175–194.

Schwab, Klaus. "The fourth industrial revolution: what it means and how to respond", December 12, 2015, accessed April 28, 2018, www.vassp.org.au/webpages/Documents2016/PDevents/The%20Fourth%20Industrial%20Revolution%20by%20Klaus%20Schwab.pdf.

Schwab, Klaus. "Welcome to the fourth industrial revolution." *Rotman Management* (Fall 2016): 19–24.

Servais, Jean-Michel. *International Labour Law*. Alphen aan den Rijn: Wolters Kluwer, 2014.

Staglianò, Riccardo. *Al posto tuo. Cosí web e robot ci stanno rubando il lavoro*. Torino: Giulio Einaudi editore s.p.a., 2016.

Van Voss, Guus Heerma. "Life-long-learning as an individual social right." In *Social Responsibility in Labour Relations. European and Comparative Perspectives*, edited by Frans Pennings, Konijn Yvonne, and Veldman Albertine, 119–130. Austin-Boston-Chicago-New York-The Netherlands: Wolters Kluwer, 2008.

Venier, Francesco. "La forza lavoro digitale e il futuro dell'organizzazione." *Sviluppo & Organizzazione* 277 (August/September 2017): 54–64.

World Economic Forum, WEF. "The future of jobs. Employment, skills and workforce strategy for the fourth industrial revolution." Global Challenge Insight Report, 2016. Accessed April 28, 2018. www3.weforum.org/docs/WEF_Future_of_Jobs.pdf.

World Employment Confederation, WEC. "The future of work. White paper from the employment industry." 2016. Accessed April 28, 2018, www.weceurope.org/fileadmin/templates/ciett/docs/WEC___The_Future_of_Work_-_What_role_for_the_employment_industry.pdf.

14 The resilience

The main skill for the Industrial Revolution 4.0

Christian Thomson Vivas García[1]

I Introduction

The idea of a future without inconveniences for workers is not an affirmation that the whole race will be competitive in the Industrial Revolution 4.0. Totally true, the career to be competitive in the Industrial Revolution 4.0 has already started. Countries like Germany, for example, discovered how to cope with the technological impact, what changes should be addressed by social structures to face the irruption of technology and how education was their main ally.

In any of the positions, they are alerting, about the measures that must be employed to face that reality, they do not announce the extinction of work as it is known today and others not only maintaining these figures but also incorporating the creation of new jobs. In both cases, are studies that are carried out to draw attention to those who must take measures to face that reality, they do not announce their extinction of the planet.

These measures have a double path course of an organisational and a political nature. At the organisational level, companies must seek to achieve innovation to continue existing, which means that their human component must also be prepared to understand innovation and make it their own. However, states, workers, companies and international organisations must, within the social dialogue, identify the ordinances that regulate the new forms of contracting within labour law and make them effective; with this, making decent work possible.

From these circumstances, and based on the available reports, an approach is made to understand what is thought or believed to be the future of work, taking as a sample studies about the automation of work in the future and the skills required for new jobs, contrasting realities of current work with future needs and questioning the need for continuity of work *versus* the imposing future and the presence of the worker as a constant element in the transformation of that world. Thus it emerges that in the apparent struggle between man and machine (apparent because man and machine have worked well together and have contributed

---

1 Lawyer, Specialist in Labor Law and Specialist in the Exercise of Fiscal Action. Director of Atenea Consulting Group. Member of CIELO Laboral, litigant and legal advisor, and in human resources. Email: vivas.christian@gmail.com. Twitter: @analisislaboral.

to our present), man will have some advantages over new devices and algorithms, based on his human characteristics, such as thinking and reasoning, highlighting the capacities of adaptation, socialisation and rationality in the face of life situations, tools that have gone unnoticed in the field of work and have not been exploited by the organisation.

One of the most important of these capabilities is adaptation, that is, making maximum use of worker capacity for resilience in the face of challenges of future work. This will be the human characteristic which will enable them to sustain their employment, and learn and apprehend innovations. That will be the main tool before Industrial Revolution 4.0.

Finally, emphasis is placed on education and training processes, taking into account labour pedagogy, already used in the area of the business organisation but which nonetheless pursued productivity and competitiveness, a circumstantial issue that does not provide tools needed by all workers of a company to face the necessary technological innovation.

This work paper is a reflective material about experiences that were applied in other times and that proved to be effective in the face of the technological impact towards employment, only now, it should not catch all those who integrate social security systems without proper preparation, in defence of what the ultimate objective of labour legislation represents.

II Protect employment in the new labour market

The continuous and constant innovation in digital technology of the Industrial Revolution 4.0 is transforming the world of work, particularly employment, as well as the way in which it must be provided or in what conditions it must be done, strengthening inequalities, extending the polarisation of employment, increasing labour migration and generating a digital divide which is strengthened in depth – in short, affecting work from its sociological perspective.

The technology does not give rise to adjustments, it is imposed at any level, every time it faces and confronts the labour market, it is a kind of intraspecific competition (biologically speaking), it gains ground and space and only capable individuals move forward. This human fact seeks to make life easier for the individual, producing goods and services of a different quality, improving the industry and the factory. The Technology changed the way people communicate, unifying languages and spreading tastes. As a consequence of this change, the way of producing was also modified, so the individual had to adapt and work with it.

In analyses conducted in the United States and the United Kingdom by Bakhshi, Downing et al.[2] give reasons for optimism about the change in employment by the year 2030, at which time many occupations should have a

---

2 Bakhshi, Hasan, Downing, Jonathan, Osborne, Michael and Schneider, Philippe (2017). *The Future of Skills: Employment in 2030*. Pearson and Nesta, London.

high perspective of employability without being condemned by technological innovation, considering also that it will be the combination of the various skills of the workforce that will allow new opportunities to be achieved. The real interest, according to the authors, is to give an early warning to the measures to be adopted not only by workers and employers but also by the States and the International Labour Organisation (ILO) in relation to employment policies as well as the training elements where investment in new skills should be directed.

The labour market, as we know it today, has been transformed in such a way that the professions, trades and tasks that are documented and described in the companies and organisations' voluminous books of job profiles have lost validity as compared to the overwhelming technology. There is no doubt that technology and its development in any field mutate the state of things, one of them being the way work is provided.

One can only ask in the face of this phenomenon whether the jobs will disappear, and with them their workers, or whether the workers will use their experiences to adjust to the demands of new jobs in the design of the labour relations of the future of work.

In order to satisfy this demand, the need to create and sustain decent employment will depend, to a large extent, on the positive actions taken by employers for the workers' adjustment. Significant experiences have been documented by Clegg (2018), published in the *Financial Times*, about companies like American Telephone and Telegraph (AT&T), Spanish Society of Tourism Cars (Sociedad Española de Automóviles de Turismo SEAT) and International Business Machines Corporation (IBM), which could be a start to a focus on leveraging all human talent and turning a company into a school of innovation, drawing on the experience of pedagogy in this area, the most senior workers and the acumen of the new ones as key to increasing their levels of employability, and creating and organising low-cost policies that will benefit those who are part of the working relationship.

The alternative scenario, although it is positive, does not hide the concrete realities and the anguish that it would cause; however, previous technological revolution and its impact on the labour market left a wealth of experience that could shed light on Industrial Revolution 4.0 and those that will follow. Also, it is no less true that the decisions of the future cannot be addressed with the cognitive habits of the past, so new smarter ways of assessing the opportunities and dangers that arise from technological advances are needed.

In this regard, the Oxford Martin Programme on Technology and Employment, in the study carried out by Frey and Osborne, examined the impacts of future computerisation in the US labour market, estimating that around 47% of total employment is at risk, stating further that workers must acquire creative and social skills; this study implies the extinction of work since it is a guide to generate employment policies.

Using the same arguments and technical parameters, the non-governmental organisation *Bruegel.org* made calculations based on the results and techniques of the work carried out by Frey and Osborne,[3] interpreted by Bowles (2014), as for the probability of the automation of work within the European Union, it resulted in the work force that will be affected by technological advances in the coming decades, ranging between from 46.69% to a little more than 60%, of the States that make up the European Union.

But it is not only employment that will be affected – the sources of work will be as well; in that sense, a report made by Wade, Shan et al. emphasises that, in the next 5 years, 40% of companies will be displaced or disappear if they fail to transform themselves digitally. The authors also add that all sectors are in a sort of "digital vortex" which "represents the inevitable movement of industries towards a digital center in which commercial models and value chains are digitised to the maximum".[4] To not adjust to the digital age is to risk the disappearance of employment.

There is no doubt that the efforts of the worker of the future must be efficient and pragmatic in the industrial revolution. Employers have a great burden, which extends beyond the logic of the production to maintaining employment of their workers against the inevitable irruption of technology, thus increasing the sense of belonging that result in benefits for both.

It is important to emphasise the fact that, since the Third Great Industrial Revolution, the economic principle stated by Lionel Stoleru in his article "Le chômage de prospérité" ("Unemployment of Prosperity"), published in *Le Monde* in 1986 and quoted and analysed by Gorz,[5] has been closer to what is believed in this new reality:

> A wave of technological progress makes a whole series of jobs useless and massively suppresses jobs without, on the other hand, creating as many others. [It] will allow us to produce more and better with less human effort: cost-price economies, the economies of working time will improve the purchasing power and create on the other hand in the economy (although it is only in the activities dedicated to leisure) new fields of activity.

For Gorz, this idea that tries to explain the advantages of technological progress is intended not to provide work or a better job but to economise it. Stoleru was emphatic with his economy of working time, the creation of new activities and the flourishing of labour market phenomena; examples

---

3 Frey, Carl, Benedikt and Osborne, Michael. A. (2013). *The Future of Employment: How Susceptible Are Jobs to Computerization?* Oxford Martin School, University of Oxford, Oxford. At: //www.oxfordmartin.ox.ac.uk/downloads/academic/The_Future_of_Employment.pdf, accessed 15 December 2017.
4 Wade, Michael, Shan, Jialu and Noronha, Andy (2017). *Life in the Digital Vortex. The State of Digital Disruption* in 2017. IMD International Institute for Management Development. Lausanne, p. 3.
5 Gorz, Andre (1991). *Metamorphosis of Work. Search for Meaning. Critique of Economic Reason.* Editorial System, Madrid, p. 12.

such as the polarisation of employment and the loss of average jobs, either because they will have lower pay or simply move to other locations; Technological progress also implies that its access will not be so easy or immediate for the rest of the world, creating a greater gap between countries with high development and less development, or even within the same territory of each country.

But it is not just employment, in statistical terms, that will be polarised; the work and its social structures will be affected, and families will be fractured by the search for greater income and economic sustainability when time as a family disappears and is replaced by crippling hours of work without days off to recover from fatigue, which will cause health problems that oscillate between common diseases to those requiring professionals, creating chaos in social security pension systems. In addition to the fact that labour migration totally disconnects permanence with families and their integration.

It is a recurring statement in the aforementioned studies that, on the occasion of the changes caused by technology and the quick transmission of data, skilled workers will become totally inadequate in a short period of time; the only way to combat this technological obsolescence will be to increase the proportion of skilled workers to stimulate or encourage companies to introduce new technologies that help them to increase productivity. This is equivalent to saying that any worker who does not adjust to technology must leave their job, in a sort of technological dismissal, legitimising it – inappropriately – with just cause, transferring the company's obligations (training) towards their workers.

However, even when technology will transform and adjust employment in other activities regulated in the world of work, other type of activity lead to a trade regulation, and still others disappear; the harsh reality, though, cannot be a constant statement that encourages the termination of employment. Decent work is based on generating policies that allow for the subsistence of employment, mechanisms of job stability and dignified and safe working conditions that generate the sustainability of social security systems in each country when Industrial Revolution 4.0 makes its presence felt and breaks down the economy, converting it into an innovation with a high ethical sense for work.

As has been stated in various studies on the future of work, the worker should develop new skills, both creative and social; to assist in this, the companies in charge of training in human resources have designed training and training courses to stimulate those skills. However, even when these companies play a role in vocational training, they do not always conform to what the company requires and the worker needs to face the intrusion into their work environment and not out of it.

According to this order of ideas, to ensure that those new skills emerge in a worker, you must make use of resilience as a tool that will promote the skills needed to cope with the technological revolution, taking advantage of the knowledge of the worker and his experience in the organisation.

III The resilience, tool necessary for decent employment in Industrial Revolution 4.0

Throughout life, an individual reacts to a number of adverse situations or painful stimuli, being able, most of the time, to overcome them, provided, of course, that they do not threaten his/her essence; he makes use of the human skills that differentiate and individualise him, discovering them day by day and applying them in every situation that arises, that is, he makes use of his resilience.

The field of psychology, given its complexity, does not have an exact answer or single text; authors such as Luthar, Cicchetti and Becker[6] claim, which is a dynamic process that encompasses positive adaptation within the context of a significant adversity,[7] an assertion directed at the field of mishap. Similarly, Dr Michael Ungar, Director of the Resilience Research Center, makes a defining definition of well-being integrated into a socio-ecological framework:

> In the context of exposure to significant adversities, resilience is both the ability of people to navigate towards the psychological, social, cultural and physical resources that sustain their well-being, and their individual and collective ability to negotiate these resources to be provided with culturally significant ways.[8]

It stands out that resilience – from a psychological point of view – in situations of great contrariety (e.g. among victims of natural disasters) is a process that requires constant support to workers because they not only will be supplied with resources that strengthen their well-being (be these psychological, social, cultural or physical) but will also need a close collective, such as their and other families; the community where he develops; and the support of the State, as long as it is applicable. The individual, from this perspective, would achieve total integration as a social being.

The previous definition of socio-ecological content, as defined by its author, is integrated into the world of work perfectly and used to pursue to achieve a better job in the future. This is because, in the new Industrial Revolution 4.0, the irruption of technology causes evident anguish among workers, even among those who are most qualified. The negative stories – diffused or spread – that precede the previous revolution, cooperate in that feeling of uncertainty and little help to understand the progress in benefit of work.

---

6 Luthar, S. S., Cicchetti, D. and Becker, B. (2000). The construct of resilience: A critical evaluation and guidelines for future work. *Child Development*, 71: 543–562.

7 As cited in Becoña, Elisardo (2006). Resilience: Definition, characteristics and usefulness of the concept. *Journal of Psychopathology and Clinical Psychology. RPPC*, 11(3): 127.

8 Ungar, Michael (2008). Resilience across cultures. *British Journal of Social Work*, 38: 218–235, at https://academic.oup.com/bjsw/article/38/2/218/1684596, accessed 4 March 2018, p. 225.

Another statement that aims to rescue the positive traits of the individual and collective support, as stated by Trujillo (2006), is that resilience is a characteristic that may occur as a result of positive interaction between the personal and the environmental component of an individual but also as a way to be able to respond to situations of conflict.

In order for resilience to be potentialised, it is important for its capacity be cultivated both individually and organisationally. The changes that companies will experience will occur more and more quickly, and this is why resilience will become essential for employees and organisations. Being able to respond positively to evolving challenges will help people succeed in any work environment.[9]

It is necessary to take into account the fact that resilience must be used with prudence; it is an opportunity to navigate and sustain in the Industrial Revolution 4.0. It is not a kind of universal cure against the ills of the world of the future. It is not something that was recently invented or discovered. The maximum and best use is obtained by integrating it and combining it with the knowledge acquired, in addition to what is known to be already functioning.[10]

Drs Salvatore Maddi and Deborah Khoshaba, who developed the research model of resistance to stress management, performance and leadership (The HardiTraining ®), affirm that the key to resilience lies in the strength gained from difficult situations. They also add that "resilient people resolve conflicts, transform disruptive changes in new directions, learn from this process and become more successful and satisfied in the process".[11] The authors insist that all that is required is commitment at work; control in the face of positive or negative situations; and an attitude of defiance towards what is to come, which in general produces optimism for the future.

If we understand that resilience contributes to the development of employability, this must be supported by your employer; taking advantage of the experience of the workers; and making contacts with the elements of the professions and the trades of the future: for example, teamwork, social intelligence, positive transculturation, collaboration of logical analysis of situations, virtual collaboration and constant training – these are key to sustaining jobs. McKinsey Global Institute[12] calls this a new "Marshall Plan" for the workforce.

---

9 Davies, Anna, Fidler, Devin and Gorbis, Marina (2011). *Future Work Skills 2020*. Institute for Future for the University of Phoenix Research Institute. http://www.iftf.org/futureworkskills/, accessed 20 September 2017.
10 Béné, Newsham et al. (2013).
11 Maddi, S, Khoshaba, Deborah (2005). *Resilience at Work: How to Succeed No Matter What Life Throws at You*. Amacom, New York, p. 3.
12 McKinsey Global Institute's (2017). Jobs lost, jobs gained: workforce transitions in a time. On the website: www.mckinsey.com/~/media/McKinsey/Global%20Themes/Future%20of%20Organizations/What%20the%20future%20of%20work%20will%20mean%20for%20jobs%20skills%20and%20wages / MGI-Jobs-Lost-Jobs-Gained-Report-December-6-2017.ashx, accessed 4 March 2018.

In a compilation of skills that should be present in the workforce of the future, the Institute for the Future (IFTF), through Fidler,[13] has grouped in 4 main lines, the necessary skills that will be required for work in the future, hoping to be fully integrated into the training and evaluation processes of the workforce; Its purpose is to serve as a tool to face emerging challenges. These skills are:

1. Personal skills: Behaviour in the face of work and its commitment as well as responsibility and professionalism. These transversal skills are accompanied by treating others with respect, willingness to work and looking for new challenges and adaptability.
2. People's skills: These refer to the social behaviour of the individual – agility in cultural interaction, working effectively with others, keeping open lines of communication to work with other people of diverse origins and ages, and achieving greater scope in fluency and information management.
3. Applied knowledge: This is the ability to logically analyse information in order to foster communication, critical thinking and analysis. In fact, many of the emerging skills that we have discussed here have particularly strong roots in this type of analytical thinking.
4. Workplace skills: These skills, such as planning and organisation, problem-solving, decision-making and knowledge in the use of tools (in their broad sense) and technologies, are the skills that employers need in future employees.

Every time a job or occupation is attained by the technological breakthrough, the worker immediately undergoes a transformation; at this stage, he will expose to the maximum your best tool – resilience – since his job is at risk. In the context of the above skills, it can be inferred that resilience represents only one factor that will serve as a vehicle for the other skills and attitudes of the worker.

The worker in such circumstances has great advantages: he knows the company, he has experience in what he does and he has skills that cannot be replicated by a machine, all of them acquired throughout his career; he only needs the employer to help him in adapting, demonstrating the trust the employer places in the worker.

In this phase, employers must be the most important subjects of work transformation. Their commitment should be directed to protecting sources of employment and modernising their productive activity, to combining the skills of the worker with the expectations of future work and initiating processes of worker training in the company, adjusted to the expectations of innovation.

By relating resilience as a personal skill, together with the skills of people and the execution of applied knowledge and skills in the workplace, we find a responsible worker, committed and willing to face any challenge, even if their activity is changed inside the company.

---

13 Fidler, Devin (2016). *Future Skills. Update and Literature Review.* Institute for the Future, at www.iftf.org/futureskills/, accessed 20 September 2017.

If decent work depends, in essence, on the existence of jobs, and "these jobs are occupied by workers", the effort in promoting the skills of the worker with teaching mechanisms within the company is necessary. Adapting the work pedagogy to the Industrial Revolution 4.0 will empower the skills of each worker in each task, taking advantage of their level of adaptability, which will sustain employment by investing in education.

IV A different vision in the training for work before digital innovation

In moments in which knowledge and the various factors that accompany it produce far-reaching changes in economic structure and labour markets, pedagogy sciences are required to define strategies for education and training, adjusted to the reality of a future that has now irrupted precipitously.

Until now, the training processes within some companies have sought to inculcate the workers into the productive society that exists today; it is necessary to be competitive, to be amalgamated to the productive process that will turn it into a tireless production machine at the service of a benefactor (company); is to be a part of the production gear that works for the growth interests of the company, with a scheme based on Fordism and Taylorism.

These training practices in some the companies have forgot the development of fundamental elements in the education process that, in turn, seek to raise the competence and skills of the worker in the face of technological breakthroughs and diversify their experience in order to share it with their colleagues, not only for the obvious economic purposes but also to give support to employment.

At the same time, it will help to distance the concept of the worker as a piece of gear from another that designs the training system based on their learned knowledge as well as those apprehended during their second training process. This is able to raise their employability level in the face of the challenge of the future of work, taking advantage of their abilities.

The way in which the training of the worker should be approached pedagogically in the future should come, for example, from the perspective and objectives of the labour pedagogy, as Fernández-Salinero (1999) states, cited by herself and De la Riva[14]:

> The Labor Pedagogy requires the intervention of both elements [work and training] in search of three basic objectives: enable progressively to perform tasks of greater preparation and responsibility (socio-labour objective); update the technical competencies of workers, required by the continuous organisational and technological progress (professional objective), and

---

14 Fernández-Salinero Carolina and de la Riva Picatoste, Beatriz (2016). Labor Pedagogy as a professional specialty in the 21st century, *Revista Española de Pedagogía*, LXXIV(265), on the website: https://revistadepedagogia.org/lxxiv/no-265/la-pedagogia-laboral-como-especialidad-profesional-en-el-siglo-xxi/101400005743/, accessed 4 March 2018.

achieve an improvement of transversal competencies, making work a source of learning and personal satisfaction (individual objective).[15]

But, in addition, it is essential to consider training as a proactive (anticipatory) pedagogical issue, conceiving it as a strategic tool for business development, or reactive (responsive), more specific and aimed at people and specific situations within the organisation.[16]

These basic objectives focus on the process of training the individual in terms of competencies at a personal, professional and social level within their work environment. preparing them for eventualities and improving their transversal competences by making the connection of resilience with other worker skills.

Arnold,[17] in a study carried out at the height of the third industrial revolution, presented before the Economic Commission for Latin America (ECLAC), says that vocational training must become a constant development of professional competences for life. This author directs the reader's attention to the formation of "professional competence" because it will be oriented to the subject, to its global pretension of the person, since she pursues that the apprentice, organises his work by himself, openly learns the necessary values that diversify their professional performance; unlike the formation of the "professional qualification", which is limited to certain circumstances and needs of the occasion, in a certain period and under a specific certification scheme.

The previous assertion comes from a comparative study of the situation of the labour market in Germany at a crucial stage in its history, which also makes it relevant to the present scenarios as regards the future of work, where history returns to the present to say, "do not forget that it was done, and it worked".

Hence, these experiences in training processes must be systematised and, *mutatis mutandis*, projected into the new teaching approach that new students must have and, of course, those of workers who need to adapt to the new time. In this aspect, Homs i Ferret states that "training systems must be able to provide individuals with the necessary skills to successfully circulate in a very turbulent job market", where the subjects must adapt to what best possible changes come in to the company as their educational level is not enough to guarantee their future. Therefore, they should enhance their skills as a person and with other people as well as their knowledge, and take these to the workplace. Also, these systems "have to contribute to driving innovation and creativity in a context of high technological and scientific sophistication".[18]

---

15 Fernández-Salinero (1997).
16 Fernández-Salinero Carolina and de la Riva Picatoste, Beatriz (2016). *op. cit.*, p. 560.
17 Arnold, Rolf (1998). Technological and organizational changes in vocational training. In www.cepal.org/es/publicaciones/31117-cambios-tecnologicos-organizativos-la-formacion-profesional, accessed 7 March 2018.
18 Homs i Ferret, Francesc (2008). Vocational training in Spain. Towards the knowledge society. *Social Studies Collection*, (25): 191. Caixa Social, available at: https://obrasociallacaixa.org/

Senge[19] points out that the advanced processes of education at work will provide the tools required to meet the needs of both the worker and the company, generating "smart organisations", which will become relevant in the future and will be those that discover how to take advantage of the enthusiasm and the learning capacity of people at all levels of the organisation. If a tool is replaced, the employer requires its worker to know it and be able to solve and update the application, not away from it but on site, with the appropriate pedagogical techniques.

Today, work and education must be a perfect binomial, which prepares the worker for any circumstance; This process of continuous and ongoing education and training must be carried out in the company (the new school); It is the ideal place for knowledge to be present in the face of new technologies: the critical thinking of the worker is part of his great human skill that must be profited. The company will be a new school, where the knowledge of the individual and that acquired by new technologies will be combined.

Today, it is necessary to remember Master Freire (1969) with this phrase: "Once again men, challenged by the dramatic nature of the present time, propose themselves as a problem. They discover how little they know about themselves, about their place in the cosmos, and they worry about knowing more".

V Conclusions

As a fundamental premise, the new professional competencies of the worker merit education and training techniques; turning the company into a school in the face of innovation would be key to increasing companies' employability levels, and creating and organising low-cost policies that will work for the benefit of those who make up the work relationship.

It is necessary for resilience to be potentialised, but this capacity must be cultivated both at an individual and at an organisational level. The changes experienced by companies will occur at an increasingly fast rate, so resilience will become essential for employees and organisations, and give a sense of continuity to eventual changes. Therefore, resilience represents only a factor that will serve as a vehicle for the other skills and attitudes of the worker; it is not the cure of the world's ills. For this reason, the employer should encourage it as one of the most important subjects of the transformation of work. To combine the skills of the worker with the expectations of future work, initiate processes of education on the competencies of the worker in the company, adjusted to the expectations of the innovation.

---

documents/10280/240906/vol25_es.pdf/f5b85ed7-1849-46bf-b23b-078ac1e9b18f, accessed 26 January 2018.
19 Senge, Peter (2005). *The Fifth Discipline. The Art and Practice of the Organization Open to Learning*. Editorial, Granica, Argentina.

The labour pedagogy will be able, as it has already done, to generate methods and ways in which the teaching processes can adjust to the Industrial Revolution 4.0. It must be maximised!.

VI Bibliography

Arnold, Rolf (1998) Technological and organizational changes in vocational training, in www.cepal.org/es/publicaciones/31117-cambios-tecnologicos-organizativos-la-formacion-profesional, accessed March 7, 2018.

Bakhshi, Hasan, Downing, Jonathan, Osborne, Michael and Schneider, Philippe (2017) *The Future of Skills: Employment in 2030*. Pearson and Nesta, London.

Becoña, Elisardo (2006) Resilience: Definition, characteristics and usefulness of the concept. *Journal of Psychopathology and Clinical Psychology. RPPC*, 11(3) December.

Luthar, S.S., Cicchetti, D. and Becker, B. (2000) The construct of resilience: A critical evaluation and guidelines for future work. *Child Development*, 71: 543–562.

Béné, Christophe, Newsham, Andy and Davies, Mark (2013) Making the most of resilience, Institute of Development Studies (IDS), In Focus Policy Briefing 32. England. Taken from the website: www.ids.ac.uk/publication/making-the-most-of-resilience, accessed February 2018.

Bowles, Jeremy (2014) Chart of the week: 54% of EU jobs at risk of computerization. Bruegel.org, website http://bruegel.org/2014/07/chart-of-the-week-54-of-eu-jobs-at-risk-of-computerisation/, accessed March 4, 2018

Clegg, Alicia (2018) Older staff, new skills: employers adapt the workforce, in *Financial Time*. "Older staff, new skills: employers retrofit the workforce" (www.ft.com/content/0e0855ce-fab9-11e7-9bfc-052cbba03425?utm_content=67141880&utm_medium=social&utm_source=twitter, accessed March 4, 2018.

Davies, Anna, Fidler, Devin and Gorbis, Marina (2011) Future work skills 2020. Institute for Future for the University of Phoenix Research Institute. www.iftf.org/futureworkskills/, accessed September 20, 2017.

Carolina, Fernández-Salinero and De la Riva Picatoste, Beatriz (2016) Labor Pedagogy as a professional specialty in the 21st century, *Revista Española de Pedagogía*, LXXIV(265), on the website: https://revistadepedagogia.org/lxxiv/no-265/la-pedagogia-laboral-como-especialidad-profesional-en-el-siglo-xxi/101400005743/, accessed March 4, 2018.

Fidler, Devin (2016) Future skills. Update and literature review. Institute for the Future, at www.iftf.org/futureskills/, accessed September 20, 2017.

Freire, Paulo (2005) *Pedagogy of the Oppressed*, 2nd ed. Siglo XXI Editores, Mexico.

Frey, Carl Benedikt and Osborne, Michael A. (2013). *The Future of Employment: How Susceptible Are Jobs to Computerization?* Oxford Martin School, University of Oxford, Oxford. At: www.oxfordmartin.ox.ac.uk/downloads/academic/The_Future_of_Employment.pdf, accessed December 15, 2017.

Gorz, Andre (1991) *Metamorphosis of Work. Search for Meaning. Critique of Economic Reason*. Editorial System, Madrid.

Homs i Ferret, Francesc (2008) *Vocational training in Spain. Towards the knowledge society*. Social Studies Collection. No. 25. Caixa Social, available at: https://obrasociallacaixa.org/documents/10280/240906/vol25_es.pdf/f5b85ed7-1849-46bf-b23b-078ac1e9b18f, accessed January 26, 2018.

Maddi, S. and Khoshaba, Deborah (2005) *Resilience at Work: How to Succeed No Matter What Life Throws at You*. Amacom, New York.

McKinsey Global Institute's (2017) *Jobs Lost, Jobs Gained: Workforce Transitions in a Time*. On the website: www.mckinsey.com/~/media/McKinsey/Global%20Themes/Future%20of%20Organizations/What%20the%20future%20of%20work%20will%20mean%20for%20jobs% 20skills% 20and% 20wages / MGI-Jobs-Lost-Jobs-Gained-Report-December-6-2017.ashx, accessed March 4, 2018.

Senge, Peter (2005) *The Fifth Discipline. The Art and Practice of the Organization Open to Learning*, Editorial, Granica, Argentina.

Trujillo, María (2018) Resilience in social psychology. In www.psicologia-online.com/la-resiliencia-en-la-psicologia-social-2618.html, consulted on January 11, 2018.

Ungar, Michael (2008) *Resilience across cultures*. British Journal of Social Work, 38, 218–235, at https://academic.oup.com/bjsw/article/38/2/218/1684596, accessed March 4, 2018.

Wade, Michael, Shan, Jialu and Noronha, Andy (2017) *Life in the Digital Vortex. The State of Digital Disruption in 2017*. IMD International Institute for Management Development, Lausanne.

Index

Note: **Bold** page numbers refer to tables; *italic* page numbers refer to figures and page numbers followed by "n" denote endnotes.

Act respecting transportation services by taxi (ARTST) 24, 27, 27n29
agile work 5; *see also* Spanish telework and Italian agile work
Agreement-in-Principle 28, 28n35, 35
algorithmic management and gamification 169
Aloisi, A. 14
Amazon electronic wristband 154–155, 154n20, 155n23, 155n24
Amazon Mechanical Turk 170, 171
Annex of the Inter-Confederal Agreement for Collective Bargaining (AINC) 104–105, 104n20
Antimonopoly Act 45, 45n16
article 4, Law n. 300/1970 149, 150–153
article 13 of Workers' Statute (ET) 104
article 88 159
Artificial Intelligence (AI) 80, 116, 116n2, 118
asset-heavy and asset-light model 52, 52n19
Association haïtienne des travailleurs du taxi (Haitian taxi drivers' association, AHTT) 25, 25n25
authorization 29, 33–35
automation 6, 137–140, 137n37
autonomous work/self-employed 5, 73
Autor, D. 142

bargaining powers of parties 74–75
Benítez, S. 108
Bentham, J. 147
Benz, D. 79
Big data: artificial intelligence 80; characteristics 80; China Cybersecurity law 84; consent 83; control and privacy 81–82; data portability 82–83, 83n29; Draft Organic Law on Data Protection 84; General Data Protection Regulation (GDPR) 82–83; Information technology – Personal Information Security Specification (GB/T 35273-2017) 84; ownership 82; personal data 80–81; "Profiling" 83, 83n30; refusal of applications/e-recruiting 83–84; work domains 81
Big Data 166–167
bilateral relationships 39, 39n1
blockchain technology 5, 90–92
Booth, H. 136
"botsourcing" 120, 123, 124
Buckingham, W. 137

Caruso, L. 177
Central Arbitration Committee (CAC) 75, 75n12
changing work demands 7–8
Cherry, M. 14
Chile digital economy: e-commerce 62, 63; education and internet use 63; entrepreneurship 63–65; "*Estudio Índice País Digital*" 63, 63n9; Facebook marketplace 63, 63n11; free digital services 62–63; "Fundación Sol" 64, 64n16; GDP 62–63; gig economy 64; health insurance 66; informality (*see* informality); Information Technology (IT) infrastructure 62; internet connectivity 62; pension insurance 66; self-employed 65, 66; social protection 66; turnover 63

204 *Index*

Chinese government: DIDI company 48; Guideline on Promoting the Development Sharing Economy 48, 48n2; labour relationship 49–52; National Information Center of the Sharing Economy and Sharing Economic Work Committee of the National Internet Society report 48–49; structural unemployment 48, 48n1; supply-side structural reform 48; Trail White Paper 49, 49n5; worker status 49; *see also* labour relationship in China
civil liability action 35
Clinton, B. 176
CoBots 119, 120
Coiquaud, U. 3
collaborative economy 169
collaborative robots 11
Collective Agreement 177 on "Work at Home" 103
collectivisation for whole workforce 2–3
Commission des transports du Québec (Quebec Transportation Commission, CTQ) 24, 28
"commoditisation" of work 72
communication technologies 11
consumer protection 25
contract implementation 58
"control criteria" 74–75
control procedures 89
"cooperative turn" 17–18
court action against Uber Quebec 35
Cox, J.D. 134
creative destruction 133–136, 135n16
Crisafulli, V. 153
criteria of objectivity and necessity 150
crowdsource model 4; contract of service 53; contract performance 55–56; "cooperation agreement" 53–54; demanding information 53; economic dependence 55, 56; employee status 53; "FlashEx" platform case 54–55, 54n25; "Good Chef" platform case 54, 54n24; personal subordination 56; temporary employment demand 53; working time and work load 53

data protection 166–167
degree of workforce dispersion 171–172
Degryse, C. 169
"Denying the Legal Entity of the Direct Employer" 42–43
de-skilling process 163–164, 171–172

Després Report 24–25
De Stefano, V. 76
Diebold, J. 137
digital breach and social cost 121
digital citizenship 118–119, 119n8
"digital ecosystem" 96–97
digitalisation 11–12
digital training policies 163–165, 168
Directive of the European Parliament and the Council of 2017 105, 105n25

economic dependency 41–42, 55, 56, 59
economic subordination 50
electronic wristband 6–7, 148, 148n4; *see also* Amazon electronic wristband
employer: contractual relationship 16; crowd work structure 15–16; definition 16; digital working structures 16–17; functions 16; objective criteria 16; responsible for obligations 15–16
employment-like working style 3; China 40; contract type 43–44; "Denying the Legal Entity of the Direct Employer" 42–43; economic dependency 41–42; employer concept 42; employers' responsibility 42–43; Labour Contract Act 42; labour outcome 39; Labour Standards Act 41; labour supply and demand 40–41; Labour Union Act 42; multi-layered contracting 40; new forms of work 39, 39n4; "presence of usage dependency" 41, 41n7; primary and secondary jobs 44, 44n15; registered type and regular type dispatch 40–41; "Study Group on Employment-like Working Style" report 40, 40n5; subcontracting 40; "Theory of the Implied Employment Contract" 43, 43n14; third party receive labour 39; traditional labour regulations 39; tripartite relationships 39, 39n3; worker and its extension 41–42; worker nature approval 42; working hours and remuneration 44–45
Employment Tribunal Decision 74, 74n9
employment *vs.* self-employment: employee classification 13–14; employee like persons 14–15; employment relationship 13, 14; hybrid third category 14–15; level of protection 15; online crowd workers 13, 13n8; rating system 13, 13n6; rules on minimum wage 14–15; status identification 12–13,

12n5; time, work and hours 14–15; UBER drivers 12–13
entrepreneurship 63–65
European Framework Agreement on Teleworking (AMET) 100, 103–105
European Fund for Adaptation to Globalisation 164
European Pillar of Social Rights 76, 168
European Trade Union Confederation (ETUC) 161, 164, 167
external platforms: online crowd work 12; work on demand via app 12

Fair Crowd Work 170
fair digital work 164, 165
Fernández, R. 7
Ferry, L. 168
Fidler, D. 180, 184
Finkin, M. 6
"FlashEx" platform case 54–55, 54n25
flexible employment 59, 59n32
Fordist model 17, 89
formal employment 68
Fourth Industrial Revolution 7; Accenture's report 181; arrival 176; article 6 of the United Nations International Covenant on Economic, Social and Cultural Rights (1966) 182; characteristics 176–177; European Commission 185; future workforce skills 180; information and communication technologies (ICT) 181; International Labour Organization (ILO, Declaration of Philadelphia) 182; jobs/occupations 178–179; legal measures 181–182; lifelong learning and skills improvement 184; Massive Open Online Courses (MOOCs) 183, 183n38; "New Skills for New Jobs" 185; occupational and skill changes 177–178; OECD Skills Strategy 184–185; Open Educational Resources (OER) 183; polarisation of labour 177; policymaking 182–183; skills 179–181; technological innovation 177; UNESCO's Revised Recommendation 182; vocational and technical education 182–183
Frankfurt Declaration, 2016 170
freelance workers 170
"Fundación Sol" 64, 64n16

Gaeta, L. 100
García, V. 8

General Data Protection Regulation (GDPR) 82–84
gig economy 64, 67; *see also* Chile digital economy
Good Chef platform 54, 54n24
Gorbis, M. 180, 184
Gordon, R. 141, 142
government justification 29–30
Grau Ruiz, M.A. 6
gray market 21
de Grazia, S. 145
Great Depression 137, 137n30
Guideline on Promoting the Development Sharing Economy 48, 48n2

Harding, S. 23
Heilbroner, R. 138
hiring, workers 89
Hobsbawm, E. 133
Home Work Act 46

ICT-based mobile work 1
"IG-Metal" 18–19
illegal transportation 26–27
Inclusive Robots 119, 120
independent contractor/service provider 73, 73n7
Industrial Revolution 4.0 189; *see also* resilience
Industry 4.0 1, 7, 8, 11, 11n2, 147, 176; *see also* Fourth Industrial Revolution
informality: choice and necessity 65–66; cost–benefit evaluation perspective 68; definition 64–65; earnings/status 66; economic sectors 65, 65; formal employment 68; "Fundación Sol" 64, 64n16; health insurance fund 66; labour codes 67; labour market 64–65, 64n16; micro-enterprises 67; neoliberal perspective 66–67; occupational category 65; pension system 66; poverty level/work precariousness 66; public corruption 67, 67n28; resistance movement 67; self-employed 65–66; social protection 66
informal work 4
Information and Communication Technologies (ICT) 77, 78, 100, 181
in-service intermediary 28
Institute for the Future (IFTF) 196
internal platforms 12
internet platform 3

"Internet reservation taxi management service administrative provisional method" 43–44
Irani, L. 170

Jacoby, S. 136
Japanese laws and regulations: Home Work Act 46; self-employed telework 46–47, 46n17; Subcontract Act 45, 45n16; *see also* employment-like working style jobs 178–179
Jobs Act 151, 153
joint employer responsibility 60, 60n34

Killingsworth, C. 138

Labour Contract Act 42, 60
Labour Dispute Settlement Authority 4
labour identity 171–172
labour law protection 2; code of conduct for platforms 18–19; collective bargaining 17; collective representation 17–19; "cooperative turn" 17–18; crowd workers isolation 19; digitalisation 11–12; employer 15–17; employment *vs.* self-employment 12–15; "IG-Metal" 18–19; legislator 17; outsourcing and networking strategies 17; platform operators 18–19; technological innovation cycles 17; trade unions 17–18
labour market 1
labour outcome 39
labour platforms: collectivisation for whole workforce 2–3; labour law protection 2; online and physical services 1, 2; professional and non-professionals services 1
labour relationship 4
labour relationship in China: asset-heavy and asset-light model 52, 52n19; contract implementation 58; crowdsource model 53–56; economic dependency 59; Employment Relationship Recommendation (No. 198) 58, 58n31; employment relationship *vs.* 49; flexible employment 59, 59n32; identification 58–60; internet technology 52; joint employer responsibility 60, 60n34; non-labour relationship 52; Order (2016) No. 60 51; organisation subordination 59; outsource model 56–58; personal subordination 59; regional characteristics 58; sham labour outsources 60; sharing economy rules identification 51–52, 51n16, 52n18; subordination 50–51, 50n11; subordination initiators 59; Temporary Regulation on the Labour Dispatch, article 27 60
Labour Standards Act 41
Labour Union Act 42
Law 81/2017 104, 104n17, 105
layering 22
legal relationship 5
Legislative Decree n. 196/2003 156, 158
limits of usability of technologies 156–159, 157n27, 157n28, 158n33
Liu YaYa 56
Li Xiangguo 55

Mahoney, J. 22
Mann, C. 63
"Marshall Plan" 195
Martone, M. 110
Massive Open Online Courses (MOOCs) 183, 183n38
Measures for the protection of non-entrepreneurial self-employment and measures to encourage flexible articulation in the time and place of subordinate work 104n17
Meirosu, D. 4
Mendez, M. 107
Menken, H.L. 140
Meo, D. 6
micro-enterprises 67
minimum income system 167–168
Morissette, L. 3
multilateral relationships 39, 39n2
multi-layered contracting 40
Murcia, A. 5

National Commission on Technology, Automation, and Economic Progress 139, 139n49
National Information Center of the Sharing Economy and Sharing Economic Work Committee of the National Internet Society report 48–49
negative income tax 139, 168
non-labour relationship 52
non-standard forms of employment (NSFE) 71

occupation 178–179
online car-hailing service 51–52, 51n16
online crowd workers 13, 13n8
Open Educational Resources (OER) 183
organisation subordination 50, 59
outsource model 4; information intermediary platform 56; Labour Contract Law of China, article 94 57; labour service contract 56n27; Liu YaYa case 56–57, 56n26; platform enterprise as employer 57–58; Shi Lei case 57, 57n29; subcontractor as employer 56–57; Tang Tongyang case 56n28, 57

personal data breach 83n30
personal subordination 50, 56, 59
pilot project 21
platforms 169–173
platform work: autonomous work/self-employed 73; bargaining powers of parties 74–75; Central Arbitration Committee (CAC) 75, 75n12; client-platform relationship 72, 72n5; "commoditisation" of work 72; contract of employment 75–76; "control criteria" 74–75; Employment Tribunal Decision 74, 74n9; enforceability of rights 76–77; European Pillar of Social Rights 76; independent contractor/service provider 73, 73n7; informalisation and precarisation of work 72; "non-standard forms of employment" (NSFE) 71; regulation 76–77; reputation management 77; requirements and obligations by platforms 73–74, 73n7, 73n8; services delivered digitally and physically 71–72; standard employment relationship 71, 71n1; taxation 77; third category of worker 76; Uberisation of the economy 71; workers' status and rights 72, 74
polarisation of employment 190, 193
Poletti, G. 155
Prassl, J. 16
"principle of caution" 119, 119n9
Privacy Guarantor 157, 158
"professional competence" 198
"Profiling" 83, 83n30
putting-out system 132

QQE Framework (Quality, Quantity and Economic controls) 23, 26, 33

redistribution of profits 164–165
refusal of applications/e-recruiting 83–84
Regroupement des travailleurs autonomes Métallos (United Steelworkers' independent workers' association, RTAM) 25
remunerated transportation services 26, 27
reputation management 77
resilience 8; adaptation 190; current work with future needs 189; dangers from technological advances 191–192; decent work 193; "digital vortex" 192; economic principle 192; employability 195; employers 196; employment in new labour market 190–193; experiences in training processes 198; future computerisation 191; hardened situations 195; human characteristics 190; Institute for the Future (IFTF) 196; "Marshall Plan" 195; new skills development 193; optimism about employment change 190–191; personal and environmental component interaction 195; polarisation of employment 190, 193; "professional competence" 198; prudence 195; psychological point of view 194–195; skilled workers 193; skills and attitudes of worker 196; skills for future workforce 196; "smart organisations" 199; training for work 197–199; vocational training 198; well-being into socio-ecological framework 194; work and education 199; work and social structures 193; workers' adjustment 191–192; work pedagogy 197
rights and obligations of telework 109–111, 109n40, 110n43
"right to disconnection" 110, 112, 112n47, 166
right to rest and vacations 109, 111
Riley, R. 176
Risak, M. 16
Robotics 6; Artificial Intelligence (AI) 116, 116n2, 118; "botsourcing" 120, 123, 124; characterisation and classification of robots 119, 119n12, 127; CoBots and Inclusive Robots 119, 120; competent authority 125; conditional basic income 127; digital breach and social cost 121; digital citizenship 118–119, 119n8; Directive 2000/78 123; "emerging technologies" 117; employment

208 Index

precariousness 120; 'entities' 118n5; financial legal order 124–125; forms of employment 122–123; human-machine relationship 117; interactive robot 125; International Monetary Fund (IMF) 126; job destruction and structural unemployment 126, 126n30; labour law and financial implications 116, 128; "Labour Law evasion" 122; labour market 120, 127–128; mandatory regulation 118; as moral agents 117; negative tax on income 127; net redistributive impact 126; "principle of caution" 119, 119n9; regulations 118, 128; remuneration and required personnel 125; rights and responsibilities among human beings 125, 128–129; roboethics 117, 117n3; "safety net" for workers 123; social dimension 116–117; social inequalities 121; Social Security network 125, 126; taxation 125; "technological neutrality" 119; techno-pessimism and techno-optimism 120, 120n15; transitional period problems 120–121; transitional tax 127, 127n36; universal basic income (UBI) 126–127, 126n32, 129; worker concept 122–123; working conditions 123–124
Roosevelt, F.D. 136
Royal Legislative Decree 2/2015 89

Salomens, A. 142
Sánchez, V. 5
Sánchez-Urán, M.Y. 6
Schmidt, F.A. 169
Schumpeter, J. 135
Schwab, K. 177
Sehnbruch, K. 66
self-employed 15, 46–47, 46n17; see also employment vs. self-employment
Serrani, L.E. 101
Servais, J.-M. 182
services delivered digitally and physically 71–72
Shakespeare, W. 147
sharing economy 4
Shi Lei 57
Silverman, S. 170
smart labour contract 5; accessibility to contractual content 93, 95; art. 1278 of the Civil Code 92–93; article 8.5 WS 94, 95; automatable transaction 91–92; automated response 92; bargaining power 94; blockchain technology 90–91; code wording 96; computer and common language discrepancies 96; computer protocol 90; concept 90–91; "condition" 90; consent 96; content 96–98; contract essential conditions 94–95; contractual automation 90–91; contractual modalities 92–93; "digital ecosystem" 96–97; drafting 92–95; efficiency and security 91; electronic contracting 90; employment contract 94, 94n17; formalisation of employment contract 95; interpretative purposes 97; labour law 92; Law 7/1998 93; legal culture 97–98; legal framework shortcomes 95; legal uncertainty and judicial discretion 98; object and cause 96; programmed order 97; protection of contracting party 93–94; requirement for written form 93; rights and guarantees of workers 92; semantic barrier 96; signing the contract 90; standardised contracting 91; synallagmatic contract 92; see also blockchain technology
"smart organisations" 199
smart robots 1, 11
social protection 66
Soro, A. 159
Spanish telework and Italian agile work: 1973 law 103; "agreement" 110–111; Annex of the Inter-Confederal Agreement for Collective Bargaining (AINC) 104–105, 104n20; article 13 of Workers' Statute (ET) 104; characteristics 106; concept 103–104; criticisms 111; definition 106; Directive of the European Parliament and the Council of 2017 105, 105n25; European Framework Agreement on Teleworking (AMET) 104–105; formal requirements 108; imperative rules 111; Inter-Confederal Agreement 103; Law 81/2017 104, 104n17, 105; legal concept 106–108, 106n27, 107n28, 107n34, 108n38, 111; non-compliance 111–112; preponderance 107–108; purpose 105–106, 105n23, 106n26; regulation by autonomous communities 104, 104n19; rights and obligations 109–111, 109n40, 110n43; "right to disconnection" 110, 112, 112n47; right to rest and vacations

111; telependurismo 108; "Work at a distance" 106–108, 107n33
standard employment relationship 71, 71n1
"structural unemployment" 137–140
Subcontract Act 45, 45n16
subordination 4; identification criterion 50–51, 51n11; indicators 51; kinds of 50; Ministry of Human Resources and Social Security (MOHRSS) Notice 50–51, 51n11; Trial Guidelines on Labour Disputes, article 6 51
synallagmatic contract 92

Tang Tongyang case 57
taxation 77
taxes on digital activities 164–165
"tech firm" 26, 26n28
technological innovation: advantages 77; automation and robotisation 70; Big data 80–84; challenges 70; digitalisation 77–80 (*see also* time and space dimensions); Information and Communication Technologies (ICT) 77, 78; negative impact 78; "non-standard forms of employment" (NSFE) 71 (*see also* platform work); regulations and policies 70; standard employment relationship 71, 71n1; Uberisation of the economy 71; workers' status and rights 72, 74
technological Revolution 7
technological servitude 89
"technological unemployment" 136–137, 167–168
technologies and powers: Amazon electronic wristband 154–155, 154n20, 155n23, 155n24; article 4, Law n. 300/1970 149, 150–153; article 88 159; criteria of objectivity and necessity 150; electronic wristband patent 148, 148n4; employee work supervision 147–148; employer's powers 156–159; human and artificial intelligence 148; human privacy 153, 153n17; Industry 4.0 147; installation and use of equipment 152, 152n13; Italian regulatory framework and European law 148; Jobs Act 151, 153; Legislative Decree n. 196/2003 156, 158; limits of usability 156–159, 157n27, 157n28, 158n33; man and machine ("M2M") relationship 148; monitoring power of employer 150–151; obligation 148; "organizational and production requirements" 151, 151n11; paragraph 2 153, 153n16; pervasiveness 150; Privacy Guarantor 157, 158; remote monitoring 151–152, 152n13; remote work characteristics and regulation 149, 149n5; rules of parties in contract 149; worker performance control 150
technology and jobs: agony 141–145, *143*; automation 137–140, 137n37, 138n48; canning process 134; cappers 134–135, *135*; claim of novelty 132; coal miners 134; collective bargaining 144, 144n69; containerised shipping 134; creative destruction 133–136, 135n16; displacement of labour 132–133, 133n3; ecstasy 145–146; enterprise and labour 133; glass bottle makers 133; Great Depression 137, 137n30; hard rock mining 133–134; hostlers 135–136; inequality 141, 141n58, 144–145, 145n70; invention and perfection of technology 133–134; job matching 144, 144n68; labour cost reduction 134; labour-management cooperation 140; middle-level manufacturing jobs 141–143, *143*; National Academies' report 141, 141n59; National Commission on Technology, Automation, and Economic Progress 139, 139n49; "negative income tax" 139; "orderly progressive character" 133; processed food industry 134–135, *135*; productivity 136–137; putting-out system 132; recommendations 139; stratigraphy of anxiety 136–140; "structural unemployment" 137–140; "technological unemployment" 136–137; World Bank Report 143, 143n67
techno-pessimism and techno-optimism 120, 120n15
telework 1, 4–5; Collective Agreement 177 on "Work at Home" 103; data protection 11; definition 100; digitalisation 100–101; European Framework Agreement on Teleworking (AMET) 100, 103–105; "false self-employed" 102; framework agreement 80; information and communication technologies (ICT) 100; labour legislation 100; overtime work 78–79; problems 11, 11n1; Recommendation

210 Index

n.184 103; regulations 102; reversibility 102; space and time 100; Spanish employees 101, 101n7; surge of 101–102; systematic breach of legislation 102–103; types 78; uncertainties 100; voluntariness of 102; "work at home" 101, 101n6; working time 11; working time regulations 79–80; *see also* Spanish telework and Italian agile work
Temporary Regulation on the Labour Dispatch, article 27 60
temporary two-tier regime 30, 33–34
Thelen, K. 22
"Theory of the Implied Employment Contract" 43, 43n14
Thibault, J. 101
third category of worker 76
time and space dimensions: overtime work 78; "right to disconnect" 79; telework 78–80; work and leisure 78, 78n18; working time regulations 79–80; work-life balance 78
Tiraboschi, M. 101
trade unions 7, 17–19; "21st-century factories" 169; algorithmic management and gamification 169; *Amazon Mechanical Turk* 170, 171; *Big Data* 166–167; data protection 166–167; degree of workforce dispersion 171–172; de-skilling process 163–164, 171–172; digital training policies 163–165, 168; digital transformation of business 165; *European Fund for Adaptation to Globalisation* 164; European-level legal framework 169–170; European Pillar of Social Rights 168; *Fair Crowd Work* 170; fair digital work 164, 165; *2016 Frankfurt Declaration* 169–170, 170n33; freelance workers 170; future 161; indications about trends 162–163; job losses 162; labour identity 171–172; labour relations 161–162; minimum income for loss of employment 167–168; national territory 164; negative income tax 168; online platforms 169–170; platforms and new forms of collective organisation and action 169–173; redistribution of profits 164–165; right to disconnection 166; social justice 168; taxes on digital activities 164–165; technological change 161; "technological unemployment" 167–168; training for employment policy 163; unemployment/social protection policy 163; universal basic income 168; wealth inequality 168; work behaviour of platforms 172–173; workers' rights to privacy 167; *WorkerTech* 172; working anytime and anywhere effects 165–166
traditional Japanese labour law theory: contract type 43–44; primary and secondary jobs and employer's responsibility 44, 44n15; working hours and remuneration 44–45
Trail White Paper 49, 49n5
training for employment policy 163–165, 168
training for work 197–199
Transport Act, 1973 24
Travieso, M. 4
tripartite relationships 39, 39n3
Tugwell, R. 136, 145
Tyc, A. 7

Uberisation of the economy 71
Uber Quebec 3; *Act respecting transportation services by taxi* (ARTST) 24, 27, 27n29; AGQ and Government 35; Agreement-in-Principle 28, 28n35, 35; authorization 29, 33–35; civil liability action 35; collective organisation 26; *Commission des transports du Québec* (Quebec Transportation Commission, CTQ) 24, 28; consumer protection 25; content of pilot project 30–32, **31**, **32**; context and framework principles of pilot project 29–30, 29n41; court action 35; damages 35; Déprés Report 24–25; effects of pilot project 33–35; fares comparison **31**, 31–32, 31n46; government justification 29–30; illegal transportation 26–27; information analysis on services 33; in-service intermediary 28; institutionalisation 25; layering 26; legalisation 27–28; legal literature 22; need for regulation 25–26; neo-institutional literature 22; pilot project 21; provisions 28; QQE Framework (Quality, Quantity and Economic controls) 23, 26, 33; quality and availability of services 25–26, 33; regulatory framework 27, 27n30, 34; regulatory law 22–23; remunerated transportation services 26, 27; Revenu Québec 26; sales taxes 26; security requirements 32; as service intermediary 28–29; "sharing" economy

26, 26n28; supply management and number of permits 25–26, 31; "tech firm" 26, 26n28; temporary two-tier regime 30, 33–34; traditional actors 34; training requirements 32, **32**; *Transport Act*, 1973 24

unemployment/social protection policy 163

universal basic income (UBI) 126–127, 126n32, 129, 168

universal skill families and cognitive capabilities 181

vocational training 198

Weber, T. 161

Weiss, M. 2

well-being 194

Wirtz, W.W. 140

"work at home" 101, 101n6; *see also* telework

worker and its extension 41–42

worker nature 42

workers' adjustment 191–192

Workers' Statute Act 89, 93, 94

WorkerTech 172

workforce planning 8

work pedagogy 197

Xiaohui Ban 4

Zhong, Q. 3